Christmas 2022

THE DIAGHILEV BALLET IN LONDON

Enjoy ♡

By the same author

ANTHOLOGY
    A Miscellany for Dancers

BIBLIOGRAPHY
    A Bibliography of Dancing

COSTUME AND SETTING
    Design for the Ballet
    Five Centuries of Ballet Design

DICTIONARY
    A French-English Dictionary of Terms used in Classical Ballet

HISTORY
    A Short History of Ballet
    A History of Ballet in Russia (1613–1881)

STUDIES
    Enrico Cecchetti
    Serge Diaghilev
    Fanny Elssler
    Michel Fokine and his Ballets
    Three French Dancers of the 18th Century
    Three French Dancers of the 19th Century
    Alicia Markova
    The Monte Carlo Russian Ballet
    Vaslav Nijinsky
    Anna Pavlova
    The Romantic Ballet in Lithographs of the Time
    The Vic-Wells Ballet

STORIES OF THE BALLETS
    The Complete Book of Ballets

TECHNIQUE
    A Primer of Classical Ballet for Children
    A Second Primer of Classical Ballet for Children
    A Manual of the Theory and Practice of Classical Theatrical Dancing
    The Theory and Practice of Allegro in Classical Ballet

TRANSLATIONS
    Vaslav Nijinsky by F. de Miomandre
    Orchesography by Thoinot Arbeau
    Letters on Dancing and Ballets by J. G. Noverre
    The Dancing-Master by P. Rameau
    Marie Taglioni by André Levinson
    The Romantic Ballet as seen by Théophile Gautier
    Ballet: Traditional to Modern by Serge Lifar

The Diaghilev Ballet
in London

A Personal Record

By
CYRIL W. BEAUMONT

THE NOVERRE PRESS

First published in 1940

This edition published in 2017 by
The Noverre Press
Southwold House
Isington Road
Binsted
Hampshire
GU34 4PH

Copyright © 2017 by The Noverre Press

ISBN 978-1-906830-78-6

TO

MY WIFE

Who first introduced me to Ballet

AND TO

PERIN DALAL AIMEE WADIA
AND FALY WADIA

With whom I have so often discussed
my memories of Diaghilev.

INTRODUCTION

THIS book differs from all my other works relating to Ballet in that it is the most intimate and the most personal.

With the exception of their first two visits in 1911, I saw every season of Diaghilev's "Ballets Russes" in London until their final appearance in 1929. Before 1914 I saw the performances as a member of the general public, but, from 1918 onwards, I was admitted to the high privilege of viewing the ballets both before and behind the curtain; and, as the years passed by, I made the acquaintance of the director himself, and enjoyed the friendship of his lieutenant, Serge Grigoriev, his technical adviser, Maestro Enrico Cecchetti, and his business manager, Randolfo Barocchi. I also met all the choreographers, most of the principals, many of the soloists, and many members of the *corps de ballet*, not to mention certain of the composers and painters who wrote the music or designed the settings for the ballets. I watched the evolution of certain ballets in the course of production, and I saw the actual performances from all kinds of angles.

I have sought to record the company's activities in London over all those years. As a general principle I have not attempted to give detailed descriptions of the

INTRODUCTION

productions, since I have already done this at length in my *Complete Book of Ballets*. I have, however, given some account of ballets which I considered too special or too ephemeral for inclusion in the volume mentioned.

I have also been at some pains to give an impression of the principal dancers of the Diaghilev Ballet in the roles they made famous. When one attempts to discover how the great dancers of other centuries looked, moved, and danced, it is rare indeed to find any passages in contemporary memoirs which afford such information. With a view, therefore, to the provision of authentic material for the future historian of ballet in this century, to revive old memories for those who formed part of the audiences of the period in question, and, more important still, to convey to our present dancers and ballet-goers something of the great days that are past, I have set down my impressions while they are still clear.

Naturally enough, my recollections of certain dancers and certain ballets are sharper in some instances than in others, and perhaps this even has a certain virtue in that the things which have made the deepest impression upon me are probably those facts most worthy of being placed on record. But that is not all. I have also attempted pen portraits of important personalities, of the dancers at class, at rehearsal, and making-up in their dressing-rooms; to depict what a ballet looks like when viewed from behind the scenes; and to describe the various characteristic phases attendant on the production of a ballet. I have re-

INTRODUCTION

corded little intimate incidents that occurred on particular occasions, things said in my hearing, and my own personal experiences.

This varied material differs, of course, in its degree of importance, yet, just as a number of separate and vari-coloured pieces of stone may be combined to form a mosaic, so I venture to submit that these multifarious details, added together, and considered as a whole, do present a picture in the round of what the Diaghilev Ballet was like.

It is salutary, too, to reflect on the achievements of that superb organization, for, relentlessly driven by its tireless director to overcome all manner of obstacles and prejudices, and to explore so many untrodden fields of artistic endeavour—some fruitful, some barren —it exerted, and still exerts, an enormous influence on the arts of dancing, music, and painting. Indeed, it would be difficult to state in which branch its influence has been the most pronounced.

Those who did not see the performances of the Diaghilev Ballet will never be able to appreciate the standard of artistic and technical achievement to which it attained. For this reason we may excuse those who have only seen the ballets presented in London during the last decade for having formed the opinion that nothing could be superior.

I, who have seen, as it were, the "best of both worlds", can and do declare that there is a wide gulf between the productions of the Diaghilev Ballet and those of the companies of the immediate present. I have none the less found much to admire in certain of

INTRODUCTION

the productions of Col. de Basil's "Ballets Russes", and of M. René Blum's "Ballets de Monte Carlo", although it must not be forgotten that much of the success of those companies has been due to the collaboration of former members of the Diaghilev Ballet, both as regards choreographers and dancers. I have also been greatly impressed by the splendid progress made by our own English companies, particularly the Vic-Wells Ballet directed by Ninette de Valois, which has so triumphantly emerged from the most modest of beginnings. But, promising as these varied efforts are, the standard established by Diaghilev remains unequalled. Nothing, however, is impossible, as events in other spheres of activity during the past fateful months have shown only too clearly. So one or more of these companies may eventually come to rival the parent company, the Diaghilev Ballet, which inspired their birth—*but that day has still to come.*

C. W. B.

75 CHARING CROSS ROAD
August 1940

CONTENTS

	PAGE
PRELUDE	3

CHAPTER I. 1912 - - - - - - 9

My first visit to Diaghilev's "Ballets Russes"—*Thamar*—Thamar Karsavina—Adolph Bolm—*Les Sylphides*—Karsavina's dancing in the classical tradition—Vaslav Nijinsky: his appearance, technique, and artistry—*L'Oiseau de Feu*—Bakst's costume for Karsavina—*Le Carnaval*—Bolm as Pierrot—Karsavina as Columbine—Nijinsky as Harlequin—Cecchetti as Pantalon—*Le Spectre de la Rose*—How Nijinsky acknowledged applause—*Polovtsian Dances from "Prince Igor"*—*Le Lac des Cygnes*—Nijinsky as Prince Siegfried—*Le Pavillon d'Armide*—*Schéhérazade*—Nijinsky as the Gold Negro—Cecchetti as the Chief Eunuch—*Narcisse*—The relation between audience and artist.

CHAPTER II. 1913 - - - - - 41

I become a subscriber to the "Ballets Russes"—*Petrouchka*—Triumph of Nijinsky as Petrouchka—Karsavina as the Dancer—Cecchetti as the Old Showman—*L'Après-Midi d'un Faune*—Bakst's costume for Nijinsky—Nijinsky as the Faun—Gustave de Beer—Acquaintance with Bolm—*"L'Oiseau et le Prince"*—*Le Dieu Bleu*—*Cléopâtre*—Sophie Fedorova as Ta-Hor—My visit to the *Comœdia Illustré*, Paris—Maurice de Brunoff—La Belle Edition—Barbier's *Vingt Dessins sur Vaslav Nijinsky*—Paul Iribe—Widespread influence of Bakst on decorative design —*Jeux*—Its novel choreography—Exhibitions and publications relating to the "Ballets Russes"—*La Tragédie de Salomé*—Nijinsky in private life—*Le Sacre du Printemps*—Marie Piltz as the Chosen Maiden.

CONTENTS

CHAPTER III. 1914 - - - - - 77
Nijinsky's secession from the "Ballets Russes"—His ill-fated season at the Palace Theatre—An instance of temperament—Exhibition of portraits of Nijinsky—Return of the "Ballets Russes"—Changes in *Thamar*—*Daphnis et Chloé*—Protest from Maurice Ravel—Diaghilev's Reply—*Papillons*—I plan a book on Karsavina—Visit to the *ballerina*—Breakfast à *la Vie de Bohème*—*Le Coq d'Or*—Bolm as Dodon—Karsavina as the Queen of Shemakhân—*Le Rossignol*—*Midas*—*La Légende de Joseph*—Successful début of Leonide Massine.

CHAPTER IV. 1918-1919 - - - - 102
Zenon—Diaghilev returns to London—The "Ballets Russes" at the Coliseum—Changes in personnel—British dancers added to the *corps de ballet*—*The Good Humoured Ladies*—Lydia Lopokova—*Cléopâtre* revived with new setting—Tchernicheva as Cleopatra—revival of *Le Carnaval*—New mood of the ballet—Idzikowsky's Harlequin compared with that of Nijinsky—Randolfo Barocchi—Acquaintance with Lopokova—Her dressing-room—Lopokova at home—Another example of temperament, with a humorous ending—Revival of *Schéhérazade*—Massine as the Gold Negro—*Sadko*—*The Midnight Sun*—I plan the series *Impressions of the Russian Ballet*—*Children's Tales*—Its unusual setting—Revival of *Thamar*.

CHAPTER V. 1919 - - - - - 128
Revival of *L'Oiseau de Feu* with Lopokova—Arcadian days and nights—The Alhambra greenroom—Preparations for *La Boutique Fantasque*—André Derain—Henry Defosse—Ernest Ansermet—Return of Karsavina—Triumphant *première* of the *Boutique*—The costumes for the Poodles—Vera Clark as the Brown Poodle—Lopokova and Massine as the Can-Can Dancers—Lopokova leaves the "Ballets Russes"—Vera Nemchinova takes over Lopokova's role in the *Boutique*—More *Impressions*—Lopokova sits to Glyn Philpot and to Vivian Forbes—Prepara-

CONTENTS

tions for *The Three Cornered Hat*—Picasso's setting and costumes—Triumph of Massine in the *"Farruca"*—Friendship with Stanislas Idzikowsky—Idzikowsky develops an interest in printing and its sequel—*Parade*.

CHAPTER VI. - - - - - - 151

Behind the scenes at the Ballet—Before the performance—The dancers take up their positions—Last-minute touches—What can be seen by the watcher in the wings—How the dancer makes her entrance and her exit—The fragrance of the stage—The magic of stage-lighting—How the audience appears to the dancer—A curtain call—Striking the scene—The importance of the conductor.

CHAPTER VII. 1920 - - - - - 159

Pulcinella—Massine's expressive rendering of the title-role—A minor sensation—*Le Astuzie Femminili*—I arrange for Karsavina and Idzikowsky to be photographed and the lamentable sequel—Vera Clark becomes Vera Savina—Massine and Savina fall in love—Diaghilev's offer to Savina conditional on her renouncing Massine—Diaghilev's displeasure at her refusal—Savina and Massine resign from the company—My ambition to write a work on the technique of the classical ballet—Acquaintance with Maestro Cecchetti—Idzikowsky initiates me in the Cecchetti Method—The book begun—Enforced interruption resulting from Idzikowsky's departure on tour—I apply to Cecchetti for help, his interest in the proposed book and promise of assistance.

CHAPTER VIII. - - - - - - 173

Cecchetti's appearance—His studio—His method of book-keeping—Relation between master and pupil—Maestro as teacher—His robust and satirical humour—Cecchetti at home—I continue the book under Cecchetti—Cecchetti as mime—I commission Randolph Schwabe to illustrate the book—Cecchetti poses under difficult conditions—The *Manual* completed.

CONTENTS

PAGE

CHAPTER IX. 1921 - - - - - 183
Leon Woizikowsky—Return of Lopokova—*Cuadro Flamenco*—Maria Dalbaicin—How the Spanish dancers received the applause of the audience—The Spanish dancers behind the scenes—Dalbaicin as the Miller's Wife—*Chout*—Michel Larionov—Sokolova as the Miller's Wife—Preparations for production of *The Sleeping Princess*—A costume rehearsal—A lighting rehearsal—How Diaghilev edited *The Sleeping Princess* — His reckless extravagance — Bakst's designs—The *première* before and behind the curtain—Failure of the stage machinery—Petipa's *variations*—Olga Spessiva—Vera Trefilova—Excursions into *bijouterie*—Maestro's jubilee—*The Sleeping Princess* plays to dwindling houses—The ballet withdrawn—Diaghilev's embitterment.

CHAPTER X. 1922–1925 - - - - 215
Disintegration of the "Ballets Russes"—The dancers form themselves into miniature companies—Acquaintance with Michel Fokine—*Hassan*—Fokine's appearance—Fokine at rehearsal—Members of the Russian State Ballet appear at the Empire—Reconstitution of the "Ballets Russes" and the company's return to the Coliseum—*Le Train Bleu*—Triumph of Anton Dolin—*The Faithful Shepherdess*—Acquaintance with Serge Lifar—Boris Kochno—*Aurora's Wedding*.

CHAPTER XI. - - - - - 231
Serge Diaghilev—His appearance, character, and personality—His four devils—His love of Venice—His superstitions—Serge Grigoriev—His appearance—His manifold responsibilities—His famous pocket-book—Grigoriev as mime.

CHAPTER XII. 1925 - - - - - 244
Nicholas Legat joins the company—The Russian Ballet drop-curtain—*The House Party*—Triumph of Vera Nemchinova—*Les Fâcheux*—*Les Matelots*—Its setting—Lifar makes a hit—*Zephyr and Flora*—*Première* of *Barabau*.

CONTENTS

PAGE

CHAPTER XIII. 1926 - - - - - 255
Loss of Nemchinova—*Les Noces*—The two double grand pianos—*Romeo and Juliet*—*Pastorale*—Festival Erik Satie—Diaghilev's ambition to produce a ballet on an English theme — Enlists help of Sacheverell Sitwell—Sitwell introduces Diaghilev to the Juvenile Drama—Sitwell completes script of *The Triumph of Neptune*—Revival of *L'Oiseau de Feu* with new settings and costumes by Goncharova—Visit to May's—*Première* of *The Triumph of Neptune*—Beauty of the flying-ballet—Balanchine as Snowball—Sokolova and the foil-stone tunic—Triumph of Danilova and Lifar in the Hornpipe—Sitwell contributes an unexpected ending—A new dance added and how it originated.

CHAPTER XIV. 1927 - - - - - 272
The Cat—Diverting incidents attendant on the erection of the talc setting—The stage-cloth that was oiled—Revival of *Les Fâcheux* with new choreography by Massine—*Le Pas d'Acier*—*Mercury*.

CHAPTER XV. 1928 - - - - - 282
Apollo Musagetes—*Las Meninas*—*Ode*—Its unusual setting—The mystic and intellectual appeal of its dances—I plan a book of drawings of Lifar—Some sittings—*The Gods go a-Begging*.

CHAPTER XVI. 1929 - - - - - 292
The Prodigal Son—Triumph of Lifar in the title-role—Diaghilev inclines towards the acrobatic—*Renard*—Illness of Diaghilev—Death of Diaghilev—The end of the "Ballets Russes".

APPENDIX - - - - - - - 301

INDEX - - - - - - - 345

THE DIAGHILEV BALLET IN LONDON

PRELUDE

~ 1911 ~

BEFORE 1911, the year of my twentieth birthday, I doubt if I would have crossed the road, as the saying is, to see a dancer or a ballet. This was not because I had never seen a ballet, for my father was fond of every kind of theatrical entertainment and often took me with him to see a play, varied with occasional visits to the Alhambra or the Empire, where Ballet was the principal attraction. Yet the Ballet never thrilled me or aroused my enthusiasm in the way that the Drama did. And at the Empire my gaze would stray from the dancers to the promenade, where the comedy and tragedy of life itself gripped my attention far more than the actual stage performance.

This was not the case with the Drama, which affected me quite differently. From early years I had possessed a succession of toy theatres, some purchased ready-made, some fashioned by myself, and I was never so happy as when producing my own version of a Shakespeare play, or presenting one of Pollock's pieces, to a family audience. And if, after providing for the incessant claims and ambitions of my model stage, there remained any balance of pocket-money, it invariably found its way to the box-office of one theatre or another. But it was always the Drama and never the Ballet that I myself paid to see.

My own career had long been determined. I was to be a research chemist, and all my studies were directed to that end. But, in 1910, my whole course was changed by a sudden whim of Fortune, and I became a bookseller in the Charing Cross Road.

The previous year, in 1909, the first Russian dancer to visit London for many years appeared at the Coliseum. Her name was Thamar Karsavina, and she made a considerable impression. In April, 1910, Anna Pavlova and Michael Mordkin made their début at the Palace Theatre and in one night became the rage of London. Before the month was out, Lydia Kyasht and Adolph Bolm were drawing big audiences to the Empire. On May 13th, Olga Preobrajenskaya, with a company of twenty, including Ludmilla Schollar and George Kiaksht,[1] appeared at the Hippodrome in a condensed version of *Le Lac des Cygnes*. On May 16th, Karsavina, with a troupe of thirteen, including Mlle. Baldina and Alexis Koslov, returned to the Coliseum in a ballet styled *Giselle or la Sylphide*, presumably *Giselle ou les Wilis*.

These were the advance guards of the mass invasion that was to follow. But already the Russians had conquered. The word Ballet had acquired a quite new significance; the old standards had vanished and with them the traditions of a quarter century and more.

[1]Brother of Lydia Kyasht, whose real name, "Kiaksht", was altered to the simpler form of "Kyasht".

PAVLOVA'S DANCING A REVELATION

Faithful to the Drama, I remained indifferent to the seductions of the Russian Dancers, but the impression they produced on those who went to see them had all the force of a revelation.[1] The dramatic critics and musical critics one and all recognized that the dancing of the newcomers, particularly that of Anna Pavlova and Michael Mordkin, was of a beauty and perfection hitherto unknown to them. They were almost mystified by the discovery that ballet dancing could attain such heights of aesthetic beauty and they were no less puzzled that the dancing of Mordkin—a male dancer—should be so pleasing and so finished.

Again, the critics were greatly impressed by the precision and gusto with which the company danced. Such dancing was far removed from the customary stereotyped movements of the *corps de ballet* generally to be seen at London theatres, which, from sheer force of habit, they had come to regard as the ultimate standard. Henceforth, all was changed, the dancing of the *corps de ballet* could no longer be "a mere display of clothes or the lack of them", it had to be of a high technical standard, expressive in itself, and governed by genuinely artistic ideals.

In April, 1911, Pavlova and Mordkin returned to London at the Palace Theatre. The lady who afterwards became my wife suggested that we should go and see those dancers, who had aroused such extraordinary ad-

---

[1] The extraordinary effect of Pavlova's dancing, which evoked a quite different attitude towards Ballet in this country, is admirably recorded in the contemporary article *If Pavlova had never Danced*. [*See* Appendix A.]

DIAGHILEV BALLET IN LONDON

miration. I was reluctant and observed that, if entertainment were the object, a play was infinitely to be preferred. But the lady was insistent, and she possessed an advantage over me in that she had vivid memories of Karsavina's début at the Coliseum. And so, still protesting, I surrendered, and saw my first Russian dancer.

I shall not attempt to describe what I witnessed, I can only say what I felt. Until then I had no conception that dancing could rise to such heights. The dancers and the music were one, and they seemed able to express every emotion they pleased. With each new dance you were swept from gaiety to spiritual ecstasy, from sadness to a wild savage delirium that made you long to leap on the stage and join in the dancing. There were times when I could hardly keep still, so passionately stirred was I by the surge and rhythm of their movements. For hours afterwards the images of Pavlova and Mordkin dominated my thoughts.

Before many days had passed I was back at the Palace. Those visits became more and more frequent. I still loved the Drama, but my affections were divided, and Pavlova and Mordkin held first place.

In June there was a fresh sensation. The Imperial Russian Ballet—so the company was styled—headed by Karsavina and Nijinsky, and directed by Serge de Diaghilev, had arrived in London and were to open on the 21st at Covent Garden. The troupe had a repertory of seven ballets: *Le Pavillon d'Armide*, *Le Carnaval*, *Polovtsian Dances from "Prince Igor"*, *Le Spectre de la Rose*, *Les Sylphides*, *Cléopâtre*, and *Schéhérazade*. I was minded

EFFECT OF A SOUVENIR PROGRAMME

to go, but I felt that nothing could surpass Pavlova and Mordkin, and I stayed away.[1]

The Diaghilev Ballet returned to Covent Garden on October 16th for a three weeks' season with three additions to the repertory: *Giselle*; a *pas de deux* "*L'Oiseau d'Or*", better known as "*L'Oiseau Bleu*"; and a condensed version of *Le Lac des Cygnes*.

But for some reason, which I cannot now recall, I also missed this second opportunity.

The following year (1912), on June 5th, Pavlova returned to the Palace, with a new partner, Laurent Novikov. How pleased I was to renew acquaintance with her dancing! This time she brought not only dances, but a ballet, called *Amarilla*. However, this was only interesting as a vehicle for the art of Pavlova, it was of little importance in itself. The reader will observe that I was already becoming critical.

On June 12th, the Diaghilev Ballet returned to Covent Garden. They had come straight from their season in Paris. A few days before their arrival, a friend of mine, who had seen them in Paris, showed me the Souvenir Programme which had been issued for the occasion. He knew of my admiration for Pavlova and strongly urged me to see the Diaghilev Ballet, which he declared to be superb. I turned over the pages of the ivory and gold programme, with all its coloured reproductions of Bakst's lovely designs

---

[1] Those readers who may like to have some idea of the reactions of the London Press to the first appearance of the Diaghilev Ballet are referred to the far-sighted article in *The Times* of June 24th—*See* Appendix B.

for *L'Après-Midi d'un Faune* and *Le Dieu Bleu*, and I was amazed and captivated. I was all eagerness to go to Covent Garden.

On June 18th, I saw my first performance of the Diaghilev Ballet.

So began an acquaintance which has procured me some of the happiest hours of my life—never-to-be-forgotten hours whose aesthetic joys still remain unmatched.

CHAPTER I

~ 1912 ~

MY first visit to Diaghilev's "Ballets Russes" made me acquainted with three ballets: *Thamar*, *Les Sylphides*, and *L'Oiseau de Feu*, which last had its London *première* on that evening.

Thamar was a fine dramatic conception and the opening notes of Balakirev's score set the mood for the ballet. The air seemed suddenly heavy and the darkened theatre charged with foreboding. A half-wistful, half-tragic melody rose above a throbbing undercurrent of sound, a suggestion of a swiftly moving river coursing and churning over a rocky mountainside.

Then the curtain rose slowly to reveal Bakst's setting—a great room with walls coloured mauve and purple, and slanting ceiling painted green. The lighting was subdued, save for the dull glow of a dying fire. The scene was dominated by a huge divan set against the far wall, and upon the divan reposed Karsavina in the role of Thamar, Queen of Georgia. Stretched at full length, she occasionally stirred uneasily in her sleep. A waiting-woman sat near her couch, other retainers stood in the shadows, their attitudes strained and watchful.

DIAGHILEV BALLET IN LONDON

I can still recall the mood established by that scene. It was just as though some terrible menace had been halted, leaving behind a perceptible tenseness which suggested that the threat was about to be renewed. There was only that silent group of watchers; all was still save for the restless stirring of the sleeping woman. But the curiosity aroused was intense. What was about to happen?

That scene has always remained in my mind as an object lesson of the immense value of restraint, for, used with taste and skill, there are few qualities so telling in a ballet.

Those who have seen only the post-War[1] performances of *Thamar* will have little idea of its first tragic beauty. Like so many revivals of Diaghilev ballets, it has shed its original atmosphere. Nowadays, there seems to be a vulgar clamour for more and more light, and so the setting is shown in a crude glare unknown to the Diaghilev Ballet of pre-War[1] years. That glare banishes every suggestion of the drama and mystery so essential to certain ballets.

Karsavina was a splendid Thamar, a dangerous, feline creature, as she stretched languorously on her couch, her pale brooding features made sinister by the dark eyebrows which crossed her forehead in a single line. Her appearance as Thamar, undoubtedly her greatest tragic role, has been admirably recorded in the well-known portrait by the late Glyn Philpot.

There were many dramatic moments in the ballet, some of which are still imprinted on my memory. The

[1] The war to which I refer is the first World War, 1914-1918.

first was when the stranger Prince—played by Adolph Bolm—was ushered into the room. You must imagine him as a dominating personality with a big head, swarthy face, high and prominent cheek-bones, large mouth, determined nose, and dark piercing eyes. He had a strange head, half warrior, half musician, the embodiment of action and intelligence.

I can still see his entrance on a *crescendo* in the music, when he was led forward by two of the Queen's men sent to invite the passing traveller in. Bolm's fine figure was enhanced by his conical cap of astrakhan, the thick scarf wound round his neck, and the great black cloak draped about him. With what queenly dignity and smiling, but calculating, glance did the Queen advance to greet him. Then, as they drew close, her expressive hands, half eagerly, half caressingly, darted to his throat, to loosen his scarf and reveal his features, while the Prince blinked in the unaccustomed light and peered curiously at his hostess and her surroundings.

There was another moment when the Queen, wishing to stimulate her flagging senses, ordered her guards to dance. This was a thrilling *ensemble*, very different from the milk-and-watery affair seen in recent years. It was a wild Caucasian dance, a blur of nodding caps, tossing sleeves, and flashing boots, in which the men danced holding a dagger in the right hand, now whirling it down and up in a circular movement, now hurling it into the floor and leaping over it, to drag the dagger forth while still quivering, only to hurl it down once more. Those daggers hit the floor, point first, with a thud which could be heard in the gallery. At one point in the dance, there emerged two men armed with swords, who slashed viciously at the dancers' feet to make them leap the higher.

Then there was Bolm's dance before the Queen in endeavour to win her favour. This was another Caucasian measure, danced almost on the tips of his soft riding boots, with an unusual rigidity of leg which gave a curiously exotic quality to his movements. At times, this would be broken with a leap into the air, the head—elongated with the pointed cap—tilted to one side, one arm flung down and one raised vertically upwards above the head, while the body was arched like a strung bow. You must think of this dance as being executed with the utmost precision, the leaps becoming higher and higher, the arm movements each more forceful than the last. As the dance came to an end, the excited Queen kissed her suitor on the lips and then twisted from his grasp. He dashed in pursuit. It was not difficult to imagine the sequel.

Presently the Prince returned, staggering and gasping from the violence of the passionate conflict. So vivid and forceful was Bolm's miming that you almost shared in the emotional crisis. Then the Queen returned, menacing and wild-eyed, to manœuvre him near a secret panel in the wall. She slipped an arm about his neck, drew back his head, and, leaning over him and smiling into his eyes, suddenly stabbed him to the heart. I can still see Bolm's answering smile change swiftly to mingled horror and surprise, and the bitter reproach in his eyes as he fought to keep his

BENOIS' SETTING FOR LES SYLPHIDES

failing senses. The panel behind him slid open, he tottered, reeled, and fell headlong through the gap.

It is possible that my description conveys an impression of melodrama. Should that be the case, I hasten to disavow it. The parts played by great tragedians have often been melodramatic in situation and in language, sometimes "poor fustian stuff", but the true artist, using that material as a vehicle for his art, will invest the scene with a dignity and emotional appeal which will sway the most sophisticated spectator.

Thamar, as presented in recent years, may smack of the Juvenile Drama, but, in the hands of Karsavina and Bolm, and with a company whose inherent savagery had not yet been dulled by prolonged absence from Russia, it was a work which never failed to thrill me with its vivid presentation of an intensely dramatic situation set in a barbaric age.

Les Sylphides was an excursion into the world of spiritual ecstasy. It was the Romantic Ballet *in excelsis*. The Benois setting of this period was a poetical conception, fragrant with the traditions of Romanticism; the wings were formed of tall tree-trunks, the backcloth depicted the wall of a ruined monastery and the vague outline of a tomb silhouetted against a moonlit sky. The subdued lighting, a soft yellowish green, evoked a chaste and tender mood. Against this background moved twenty-two dancers in white ballet dresses and one male dancer in white tights and shirt, black shoes and jerkin. The scene was set to give the fullest dancing space; there was none of that cramped effect so typical of latter-day performances.

The ballet-dresses were of muslin, with pointed bodices boned to fit the figure. When the dancers were seen in the soft subdued light, they became animated wisps of cloud or mist. There were none of those sack-like bosoms and vulgar satin bodices with their horrid gleam, such as are so often to be encountered nowadays. The faces of the dancers were sad and pale, as befitted phantoms; there were no cocktail-party complexions to destroy the elegiac mood. You thought of the moving figures not as dancers, but as silver moths, skimming close to the ground or winging their way through the cold night air.

Karsavina in *Les Sylphides* was poles apart from the Karsavina of *Thamar*. The vampire Queen had become a tender wraith with beautiful regular features and the dark-brown liquid eyes of a gazelle. Is it not Gautier who speaks somewhere of eyes like two pieces of jet floating in a pearly sea? It is an image which might justly be adapted to describe Karsavina's eyes with their eloquent appeal. Her dancing in the classical tradition, excellent technically, was distinguished by its poetry. All her movements were soft, rounded, and infinitely graceful. There was nothing forced, nothing affected. There was no playing to the gallery, no flicks of the hand to attract attention. She scorned such tricks of stage-craft.

Her dancing radiated pure poetry; it was neither sensuous nor coldly chaste. Her features were serene, only rarely did she permit herself the glimmer of a smile. Her hands and arms were soft, well-shaped, and expressive. Her timing was admirable, she knew to a

MY FIRST SIGHT OF NIJINSKY

second how long to hold a pose, and could bring out a *tempo rubato* to perfection. Her *arabesques* revealed the true beauty of that geometrical pose, for she was the personification of Blasis's theory of an oblique line crossing a vertical line at one third its height.

Nijinsky astonished me. Until that evening I had regarded Mordkin, a splendidly virile dancer with a figure that would have delighted Pheidias, as the supreme male dancer. Henceforth, Nijinsky was and still remains my ideal, and nothing I have seen during twenty-eight years of ballet-going has changed my opinion.

Nijinsky, alas, has passed into legend, but his name has become synonymous with achievement. When a dancer begins to show a little promise, zealous press-agents begin to describe their protegé as "the modern Nijinsky" or "the successor to Nijinsky". Yet, as a general rule, these people never saw Nijinsky dance, and are therefore quite unqualified to make such comparisons. Worse still, the public, too often gulled by such statements, gape at the dancer before them, under the quite erroneous impression that he is the counterpart of that dancer who once conquered the world with his dancing. Too often is it forgotten that Nijinsky was not only a rare technician, but also an artist of exceptional distinction. I have seen very few male dancers whose merits entitled them even to tie the string of Nijinsky's ballet-shoes.

Nijinsky was slight, well formed, and under medium height. His features were inclined to be Mongolian, with their high cheek-bones and the curiously slanting eyes, so characteristic of his appearance. He had unusually muscular thighs and his calves were over-developed, even bulbous. But his every movement was so graceful that he seemed ideal, almost god-like.

In *Les Sylphides* he wore a fair wig just as he had done when the ballet was first presented, the fair wig which has now become a tradition. While dancing *terre à terre* he seemed never to touch the ground, but always to travel just above it. His *élévation*, his ability to leap into the air, was prodigious. There was no flurry, no seeming preparation; he vaulted upwards, or bounded forwards, with the effortless ease of a bird taking flight. This apparent "freedom of the air" cannot easily be imagined by those who never saw Nijinsky dance, for no contemporary dancer of my knowledge possesses this facility in anything approaching the same degree. To this unique *élévation* he united dazzling "beats"; a faultless poise, feeling for timing, and sense of line; while his *pirouettes*, *tours en l'air* and *jetés en tournant* were unmatched for their brilliancy and control.

His *pas seul* in *Les Sylphides* was outstanding. The reader may well ask, "In what way?" In essence, its especial quality was its suggestion of melody. When you watch a great violinist playing, it is not the violin alone that is a sounding-board for the precious tones called forth by the bow gliding over the taut strings, the violinist's very body seems to respond to his music. Nijinsky's dancing in this ballet was imbued with the same quality. He danced not only with his limbs, but with his whole body, and the sequence of movements composing the dance flowed one into the other, now swift, now slow, now retarded, now increasing in speed, with a suggestion of spontaneity that had all the quality of melody. So I recall memories such as the billowing of his white silk sleeve as he curved and extended his arm; then that lovely movement when, on extending his leg in a *développé*, his hand swept gracefully from thigh to shin in a movement so graceful and so delicate as to suggest a caress; and then again the end of a *pirouette*, when he came smoothly and with increasing slowness to rest, like a spun wheel which had exhausted its momentum.

I always think of Karsavina and Nijinsky as the perfect partners. Admirably matched in height and thoroughly acquainted with each other's moods and qualities—for they had been pupils together at the Imperial School of Ballet—they danced as one—the poet with his muse. But these were not mortals. It was the poet's shade visiting, in company with the spirit of his dead mistress, the moonlit grove which had once inspired his imperishable odes.

The third ballet was *L'Oiseau de Feu*, and, as I look back, it seems curious that on my first visit to the Diaghilev Ballet I should have seen Karsavina in three types of role—character in *Thamar*, academic in *Les Sylphides*, and *demi-caractère* in *L'Oiseau de Feu*.

Regarded purely as music, I prefer *L'Oiseau de Feu* and *Petrouchka* to all Stravinsky's other works. *L'Oiseau de Feu* has always seemed to me a supreme example of how music, although having no meaning in itself, can, particularly with a programme hint of its intention, evoke a mood appropriate to the ballet concerned. I never tire of hearing the overture with its brilliant and highly coloured orchestration, its suggestion of gloom and mystery and enchantment, the low rumblings and mutterings and hint of underground delving varied with the suggestion of a bird whirring its wings in circular flight.

Then the mental image was completed by the sight of the stage itself, a scene of impenetrable gloom except for a luminous space in the centre where stood a small tree laden with golden apples. The whirring of wings grew louder and a figure radiating orange light flashed across the dark background. A moment later, Karsavina, glowing with orange radiance, darted upon the stage, flitted about the tree, and vanished among the shadows.

The costume which Bakst had designed for her was a charming conception, a woman's head and shoulders emerging from a bird-like body. She wore a greenish bodice, the top edge trimmed with feathers, the lower ending in a mass of swansdown fitting close to the hips. Over her pink tights she wore trousers of fine orange gauze which, as they caught the light, made her legs seem to emanate an orange glow. Her hair was dressed in two long plaits which fell over her breast, while her head was covered with a cap decorated with curved feathers.

One of the most interesting moments in the ballet occurred almost at the beginning, when the stage lightened slightly to reveal a wall to the right of the tree. No sooner had the bird vanished than the head and shoulders of a man rose above the wall. He drew himself up to the parapet, then dropped lightly into the mysterious garden.

Bolm's costume was simple and effective. He was attired in a short pink-and-white jacket, with dull pink breeches tucked into soft riding boots. He wore a fair mediaeval wig and a low-crowned hat, sewn with pearls, and adorned on either side with a small winglike ornament, from which depended a looped string of pearls which hung just below his chin.

No one has equalled Bolm in this episode. He walked slowly and deliberately, his crossbow held in the crook of one arm, leaning backwards and forwards in sculpturesque attitudes as, shading his eyes with his other hand, he sought for the gleaming bird, or stared in amazement at his fantastic surroundings. When the whirring of wings was heard once more, he glided into the shadow. Presently, the bird returned to play amid the leaves of the golden tree. The Prince drew nearer and nearer and suddenly grasped the bird.

I can still see that serene countenance change to fear when the bird felt her wings imprisoned. How beautifully Karsavina expressed with the tremor of her fettered arms and the anxious look in her eyes the emotions of a captured bird passionately longing for freedom. The hunter, half afraid, half delighted, by his gleaming prize, encircled the bird with his arms. Her struggles unavailing, she relaxed as though exhausted and gazed up at him with pleading eyes, promising to help him in the hour of need if only he would set her free. For token she offered him a golden feather torn from her breast. The generous hunter accepted the token and released the bird. What a grateful glance she bestowed upon her captor, as she quickly flitted into the friendly shadows.

This has always seemed to me one of the most moving episodes in the ballet. The situation arises naturally and convincingly, and it was mimed and danced by Karsavina and Bolm with a nobility and tenderness which made the incident a choreographic poem.

There were some other moments of beauty, for instance, when the twelve princesses and their leader, the Tsarevna (Mlle. Piltz), entered the garden, plucked the golden apples from the enchanted tree, and, throwing them to one another, danced a charming Khorovod.

But, from the moment the gates closed upon the princesses, the ballet became stagy. The demons and Kostcheï (even though played by Cecchetti), the dance with which the Bird of Fire forced the demons and their leader to dance until they fall exhausted, were all too obvious. It was good theatre, but the ballet was no longer a choreographic poem.

On June 20th there was a matinée at which I saw *Le Carnaval*, Fokine's ballet based on Schumann's well-known pianoforte piece of the same name. The principal characters were: *Columbine*, Thamar Karsavina; *Chiarina*, Piltz; *Estrella*, Baranovich; *Papillon*, Nijinska; *Pierrot*, Adolph Bolm; *Arlequin*, Vaslav Nijinsky; *Pantalon*, Enrico Cecchetti; *Eusebius*, Sergeyev; *Florestan*, Semenov.

LE CARNAVAL

At this time, the setting—by Bakst—consisted of a curtain surround, emerald green in colour, and decorated with a broad dado of gold tulips. The curtain, although apparently continuous, was composed of sections, through which joins the dancers made their exits and their entrances.

I was charmed with this ballet, which went with a swing from beginning to end. It might so easily have been a "chocolate-box" ballet, which it is inclined to become when not interpreted by first-rate artists.

Carnaval, as everyone knows, consists of a series of amorous episodes, which take place during a masked ball; the whole being linked together to form a ballet. It is not the fête itself that you see, but the little intrigues that occur in the lounge leading to the ballroom.

Carnaval, as produced at this period, was a bittersweet ballet. It was something more than a little flirting and badinage; each episode had a sting. You saw such incidents as the coquette trifling with true affection, youth mocking age, the butterfly who lived for her pleasure alone ... and the piece was dominated not by Columbine or Harlequin, but by Pierrot.

Bolm was Pierrot, and I can pay him no greater compliment than to say that I think Deburau would have approved his portrait. Bolm was attired in traditional pierrot's costume with the long pendant sleeves, his trousers were lightly powdered with pale green spots and decorated with a green pompom, and he wore socks of a bright emerald green. His face was made up white with dark shadows beneath the eyes.

His hair was compressed into a black skull-cap such as Deburau wore, but, contrary to him, his neck was framed in a wide, but thin, black ruff.

Something of his character could be deduced from his first entrance, when his head slowly emerged through a fold in the centre of the back curtain, to peer anxiously from side to side, as if fearful of being seen. Having assured himself that the room was empty, he slowly extended one leg through the curtain fold and finally stepped into full view. Flapping his long sleeves with a dismal air, he wandered aimlessly about, opening and shutting his mouth as if hungering for a kiss, the picture of utter dejection. He symbolised the shy, needy lover, disdained and mocked by the object of his affections because he had neither wealth nor good looks to offer.

Truth to tell, he was not only shy and simple, but even a little fey. Witness the episode of the butterfly. When Papillon flitted about the room, Pierrot, now wearing his tall conical hat, and crouched behind a settee, watched her with feverish interest. Here, at any rate, was a prize within his grasp. Keeping in the shadow, he took off his hat, and, holding it hollowed, ready to strike, crept nearer and nearer to his quarry. He almost trembled with excitement. Suddenly, he flung his hat down, and Papillon as quickly darted away. But he was far too sure of his success to notice that. Kneeling before the hat, he clasped his hands together, pressed them to his breast, in an ecstasy of delight. He bent forward and, with a proud smile on his face, listened now on this side, now on that, to the imagined fluttering of the insect imprisoned within. He rocked back on his haunches, desirous of prolonging the sweet moment of triumph. Bending down once more, with infinite care he pinched together the brim and held the hat before him. The moment had arrived! He delicately opened the cap, expecting to see the butterfly emerge. But there was nothing. He turned the cap this way and that, shook it, but to no avail. How bitter his disappointment at this new blow to his hopes! And so, all through the ballet, Pierrot was a tragic figure thrust outside the world of beauty and gaiety which he longed to enter.

Papillon, so selfish and so restless, flitting here and whirling there, always dashing madly from one place to another, personified the social butterfly, for which reason it has always seemed to me that the role of Papillon is best interpreted by a dancer who is technically brilliant but lacks feeling, or suggests that she is devoid of that quality.

Karsavina's Columbine has remained for me the best interpretation of that role. She made Columbine a beautiful young woman, well aware of her beauty, and determined to exploit it to the utmost. Karsavina's Columbine was as dainty as a Dresden china figure, but she had very human failings. She was a heartless coquette who inspired admiration and then snubbed the fool who thought his affection would be returned. She let Pantalon make advances to her, even accorded him a rendezvous, and then, just when the old beau was in the seventh heaven of anticipation, enlisted the aid of Harlequin and made him the butt for their mockery. Youth can be very cruel to age. She admired Harlequin, who admired her no less. But did they really love each other? Was it not rather a mutual tribute to each other's knowledge of the game which each played so well?

I cannot hope to bring before you the full glory of Nijinsky as Harlequin. You must imagine his lithe figure clothed in white tights chequered in red and green, white shirt, and black tie. He wore a black skull cap and half mask. Think of him as one lively as Mercury and as maliciously mischievous as Tyl. Think of him one moment poised in an attitude of mockery, the next bounding and rebounding in the air with the ease of a bouncing rubber ball, or twirling round with the facility and precision of a spun wheel. All his movements were precisely timed; the gracefully extended hand with the beckoning finger; the impish mockery of his one big step to Columbine's dainty two, as they entered with their arms about each other's waists (*Renaissance*); then his thrilling solo (*Paganini*) with the *pirouette à la grande seconde*, ending in his unflurried sitting on the ground with crossed legs. His *pirouettes*, as I have already stressed, were quite extraordinary. He twirled like a spun wheel and in the most difficult positions; he could stop at will, he could turn at the same speed, or at varying speeds. He did not so much as dance to the music, he appeared to issue from it. His dancing was music made visible.

Pantalon, portrayed by Cecchetti, was another creation, a masterly presentation of an old beau. Bakst's costume—brown coat, mustard-coloured

CECCHETTI AS PANTALON

trousers, green gloves, stove-pipe hat, and curly hair and waxed moustache of a suspiciously bright yellow hue—clothed the character to which Cecchetti gave warm life. He presented a middle-aged masher of the courtly type, who thought himself a rare devil with the ladies. How excited he was in anticipation of the arrival of his latest conquest. How he fussed over his appearance, setting his tie, pulling down his coat, placing his hat at a rakish angle, and continually springing to his feet to gaze at his watch. Time could not pass too quickly for him. But there was nothing forced, nothing exaggerated; the foibles of amorous old age were hit off with a suavity and ripe good humour which induced a succession of smiles. It was one of those full-bodied creations that seemed to swell and swell until it filled the stage. With Cecchetti's departure, Pantalon has become just a quaint character, sometimes endowed with a grim aspect surely out of keeping with the character, or else reduced to a figure of low comedy, one remove from a pantomime "broker's man"!

My next visit to the Ballet took place on July 1st, when I saw two productions new to me—*Le Spectre de la Rose* and the *Polovtsian Dances from "Prince Igor"*.

Le Spectre de la Rose was another ballet in the spirit of Romanticism. The theme, by the French poet, J. L. Vaudoyer, had been adapted from Gautier's poem about the young girl just returned from a ball, who dreams of the rose given to her by her lover. The ballet was set to Berlioz's orchestration of Weber's well-known *L'Invitation à la Danse*; the scenery and costumes were by Bakst; and the choreography by Fokine. There were only two characters: *the Young Girl*, Thamar Karsavina, and *the Spirit of the Rose*, Vaslav Nijinsky.

The setting was charming and showed the bedroom of a young girl of the Victorian era. The walls were covered with a bluish-grey paper, flecked with white blossoms; the window-frames, skirting, and dado were all white. The french windows—in the background—reached from dado to skirting. Two of the windows were open, that on the right revealing a glimpse of the garden, which showed a rose-bush overhung with a deep blue sky. The room was bathed in a sentimental moonlight which cast yellowish-green shadows on the floor.

It is not easy to pick out great moments in the *Spectre*, for the ballet remains the most perfect choreographic conception that I have ever seen. It was the evocation of a young girl's innocent dream, and you saw the ballet in a kind of trance. It seemed too beautiful, too flawless, too intangible, to be real; and when it was over you had a feeling as though the warm theatre had caused you to doze and you had suddenly awakened from an entrancing dream. It was only when your ears were surprised by the applause, that you were brought back to earth and realised that what you had seen was not a vision, but a reality fashioned by art and expressed by great artists.

The opening passage lives in my memory. I can still see Karsavina as the Young Girl, wearing her demure bonnet and cloak, as she walked slowly from the garden into the room, to draw off her cloak, revealing her simple white crinoline, and then settle down in her friendly armchair. She looked affectionately at her lover's gift, a red rose, and pressed it to her lips as though recalling those delicious moments when she had danced with him, those moments in reality so recent, but which now seemed so far away. As she pondered, her eye-lids drooped and she fell asleep. The rose slipped through her limp fingers and stained the floor.

Suddenly the tempo changed to an infectious whirl of rhythm, and Nijinsky, in rose-coloured tights and a cap and tunic of rose petals, flashed through the window high in the air, then floated down with the lightness and slow descent of a falling leaf, to descend by the sleeping girl. He spun slowly round, and then, passing his hands over the maiden's head, with an exquisite gesture drew her from her chair as though by a magnetic force, and guided her, still sleeping, to dance to the ever-quickening rhythm of the waltz. . . . At the end, he returned the maiden to her chair, glided across the floor to the opposite side of the room, and, rising into the air, disappeared through the open window and into the night whence he had come.

I saw the *Spectre* many times and on one occasion the applause was so tremendous that Diaghilev ordered the whole ballet to be repeated, which, for him, was almost unprecedented.

In this ballet Nijinsky did not convey the impression of visible music as in *Les Sylphides* and *Le Carnaval*. There was an ethereal and intangible quality about his dancing peculiar to the role. He suggested a cluster of leaves wafted by a light breeze, an impression heightened by the costume he wore. The pale features and bare arms and neck, emerging from the crimson petals, suggested a spirit inhabiting a rose. The make-up was unusual in that there was a crimson blush each side of the temples which gave the strange slanting eyes a most fascinating appearance.

According to a story current at this time, it was said that Nijinsky, before dancing this role, sought to evoke an appropriate mood by sprinkling himself with attar of roses. I cannot say whether the anecdote is true, I merely mention it as a trifle not without interest.

I should like to record how Nijinsky took applause, for he was unusual in this as in all things. He went quickly forward towards the footlights and, placing his right hand on his left shoulder, swept the arm down from left to right in a graceful gesture, at the same time inclining his head. His bearing was modest and dignified, his features were composed. It was a curious experience to contrast the quietly bowing figure on the stage with the frenzied applause and excited gestures of the enraptured audience.

It seems to me deplorable that directors of ballet companies should have thought fit to revive the *Spectre*, presumably because of its traditional fame, for, without Karsavina and Nijinsky, the ballet can never be itself. Moreover, quite often the setting is horrible, the costumes bad, the choreography defective, the lighting devoid of all period atmosphere, while many

POLOVTSIAN DANCES FROM PRINCE IGOR

of the dancers seem quite unable to invest their movements with that imperative romantic quality which is the touchstone of the piece.

The *Polovtsian Dances from "Prince Igor"* was at the other end of the scale. Where the *Spectre* wafted you to the region of the sublime, *"Igor"* was of the earth, and set you on fire with its stirring ferocity. There is no ballet, in my opinion, which so recaptures the thrill of warlike exercises. The reddish brown, earth-coloured costumes, the dull red skull-caps barbarically sewn with pearls, the weather-beaten faces smeared with the soot of the smoking campfires, were exactly in keeping with Borodine's wild savage music, whose surging rhythm, flowing in irresistible mounting waves of sound, impelled the dancers to extraordinary efforts.

Bolm was the Chief and I have yet to discover his equal, although I have seen some excellent interpretations of the role, notably that of Leon Woizikowsky. But Bolm, with his fine figure, warrior-like features, and burning eyes, was the personification of a tribal chieftain; and he danced with a gusto and an elemental ferocity that were thrilling to watch. Inspired by his example, the warriors thudded their feet, leapt, and twirled like men excited to a mad frenzy. Yet, with all this savagery, the steps and movements were exactly in harmony with the music.

I once asked Bolm how he worked the dancers up to such a delirium. He said:

"Oh a few heads get banged together, and some get unlucky knocks from the whirling bows."

He smiled as if at some secret thought. I noticed

that there was seldom a performance under his leadership when some of the dancers did not break their weapons.

This ballet, which so often brought the evening's performance to a close, made such an impression upon me, that, as I strolled home along Long Acre, with the rhythm still singing in my ears, I felt compelled to attempt to leap into the air as I had seen the dancers do, if only to expel the rhythm which I seemed to have stored up in my body as electricity is accumulated in a Leyden jar.

I next saw *Le Lac des Cygnes*. This was not the complete ballet, but a condensed version of it in 2 acts and 3 scenes. These were the lakeside scene, the ballroom scene, and a short return to the first scene, at which the Prince fell unconscious as the Swan Queen was forced to return to the power of the Evil Geni.

The first scene was designed by C. Korovine, the second scene and the costumes were by A. Golovine. Petipa's choreography was retained, with the interpolation of a Valse and a Solo for the Prince, composed by Fokine.

The principal characters were as follows: *Swan Queen*, Thamar Karsavina; *Prince*, Vaslav Nijinsky; *Evil Geni*, Serge Grigoriev; *Princess Mother*, Mlle. Kulchytska; *Prince's Fiancée*, Mlle. Astafieva; *Prince's Friend*, M. Semenov; *Grand Master of Ceremonies*, Enrico Cecchetti; *Master of Ceremonies*, M. Fedorov.

I must confess that I have hardly any memories of this particular production, except for two mental images of Nijinsky.

NIJINSKY IN LE LAC DES CYGNES

I recall vaguely the setting of the first scene, a forest grove bordered by a distant lake gleaming faintly in the moonlight. The scene was admirably lighted to suggest a vague mistiness, you could almost feel the dank air rising from the waters of the lake.

The Prince, attended by his friend, entered the glade. Nijinsky wore doublet and hose; on his head was a cap decorated with a long feather. The costume was entirely black except for the hose, which were relieved with vertical pink stripes. Nijinsky's slanting eyes and pale make-up, made paler still in contrast with his dark clothes, gave him a mystic air, the appearance of a man haunted by a vision which he yearns to see again. As he walked near the lake, peering up at the tree-tops or gazing towards the placid water, he made you aware of the presence of mist by the contraction and dilation of his nostrils, and by an almost imperceptible groping movement of his hands, as though he were brushing the mist aside.

In the second scene I remember his sitting at a table watching the dancers dancing in his honour. But his eyes stared beyond the dancers as though he saw some haunting vision, that cherished form of the phantom Swan Princess, visible to him alone.

Before the season ended, I saw three more ballets: *Le Pavillon d'Armide*, *Schéhérazade*, and *Narcisse*, which last had its London *première* on July 9th.

I was only able to see a portion of *Le Pavillon d'Armide*, the performance of the ballet, at this time, being limited to the second act. Here, as in the case of *Le Lac des Cygnes*, my recollections are few. The score, by Tcherepnine, contained some charming melodies, perhaps a little reminiscent of Tchaikovsky's manner, but no less attractive for that. From the musical point of view alone the ballet is well worth reviving.

I can visualize the garden setting with its green hedges trimmed to the formal shapes dear to the followers of Le Nôtre. I recall the beauty of Karsavina as Armide, attired in a balletised version of 18th century costume, a white skirt, with paniers and bodice, and turban, all of pale blue and silver.

But I can remember best of all Nijinsky as Armide's slave. His costume was inspired by that of a ballet-dancer of the 18th century—a coat with puffed sleeves, the skirts hooped in a small *tonnelet*, breeches, stockings and shoes; the colouring, cream and gold. His appearance has been recorded in a drawing made of him by John S. Sargent.

There was one thrilling *variation* in which he crossed from one side of the stage to the other, travelling parallel to the audience, by a series of vertical bounds, *entrechats*, and *tours en l'air*. His *élévation* was extraordinary. He rose into the air, came to the ground, and reascended, rising, falling, and rising again in continued succession, with the effortless ease of a bouncing india-rubber ball, and he rose so high that, seen from certain parts of the house, it almost appeared as though he would disappear into the "flies".

I should like to stress the point that Nijinsky's dancing in this role was something very much more than a rare ability to leap high into the air. That leap was achieved with a grace, a poise, a modesty of

BAKST'S SETTING FOR SCHÉHÉRAZADE

demeanour, and a sense of style which made that series of incredible bounds something not only to marvel at, but something which compelled the greatest admiration.

Schéhérazade, with its voluptuous setting by Bakst, almost took my breath away. I cannot convey the thrill I received at the first sight of that splendid setting, that great expanse of emerald green curtain, flecked with red and gold, caught up to reveal the viridian walls of Shahriar's harem, with those three doors of a shimmering metallic blue, and that immense carpet of a burning crimson. From the green and gold ceiling hung two huge lamps of Arabic design, fretted and many-tasselled, which emitted a dull blue light.

When I recall what I saw then and what has been recently put forward as Bakst's setting, to say nothing of the commonplace lighting, I am consumed with impotent wrath and long to stand up in the theatre and cry, "Ladies and gentlemen, I protest against this setting being attributed to Bakst, when it is only something suggested by it, a very different thing."

It is fashionable for some of our young students of stage decoration to talk of Bakst as though he were a minor painter who achieved an easy success by flinging pots of colour at a dull audience of Edwardians. Unfortunately, our young enthusiasts have never seen a Bakst setting as it was originally conceived and presented, with its own costumes and its proper lighting.

Those who did not live in those wonderful years before the First Great War can have little idea of the immense influence exerted by Bakst, whose name was then on everyone's lips, and whose bold and novel use of colour and design afforded new inspiration and new life to stage decoration which in the main was fast becoming frankly realistic or merely pretty-pretty. There are few painters who have exerted so stimulating and revolutionary an influence on the decorative art of their time as did Bakst, and without whose inspiration many of our own designers might never have come to flower.

The principal characters in *Schéhérazade* were as follows: *Zobeida*, Thamar Karsavina; *Zobeida's Favourite Slave*, Vaslav Nijinsky; *Shahriar, King of India and China*, Adolph Bolm; *Shah Zeman, his Brother*, Serge Grigoriev; *Chief Eunuch*, Enrico Cecchetti.

When the ballet opened, Shahriar was discovered seated cross-legged on a great mound of cushions, with Zobeida on his left, and his brother on his right. This elevation of the characters into full view of the audience had the effect of a close-up in a film, and the silent group, motionless save for an impatient or a loving gesture, or a fleeting facial expression, such as Shahriar's suspicious frown or questioning sidelong glance at Zobeida, as his brother's sneering lips poured insidious distrust into his ear, acquired an intensity of meaning quite lost when the characters are seated on a low cushion, almost on the ground, as in later revivals.

Schéhérazade, like *Cléopâtre* and *Thamar*, is a ballet on the theme of passion, and, like those two ballets, requires skilful handling so that drama remains drama, and does not degenerate into melodrama.

There are three dominant characters: Zobeida, her

Slave, and the Grand Eunuch. Zobeida is one of the very few roles in which Karsavina failed to satisfy me; she always gave me the impression, doubtless quite mistaken, that the role never appealed to her. The movements and gestures indicated by the choreographer were reproduced to perfection, but they lacked the conviction which is only attained when a movement or gesture is not merely the imitation of something demonstrated, but also the product of an appropriate emotion, evoked by the use of the imagination.

Nijinsky as the Negro wore a gold handkerchief tied on his head; baggy gold trousers, tight at the waist and ankles, but of a shimmering fullness elsewhere; and a gold band over his chest. He was made up not black, but a curious shade of dark blue, not unlike the bloom on black grapes.

I well remember his amazing entrance. When the Chief Eunuch, in obedience to Zobeida's menacing threats, had reluctantly opened the last blue door, Nijinsky shot out of his room like an arrow from a bow in a mighty parabola which enabled him to cross in one bound a good two-thirds of the width of the stage. I never saw this entrance from behind the scenes, so I do not know whether he took a running leap or not, but the actual effect was as though he leaped from a crouching position, the kind of leap a tiger might make.

There was another great moment for him at the end of the ballet when Shahriar, who had only feigned to depart on a hunting expedition, suddenly returned and was confronted by the scene of orgy. In a merciless rage he ordered slaves and women to be put to the sword. The Gold Negro was the last of the victims, and it was a thrilling experience to see him now darting this way and that, now doubling on his pursuers in a desperate, frenzied anxiety to escape the avenging scimitars. But a blade flashed and he fell headlong, to spin on the back of his neck with his legs thrust rigid in the air. Then the body fell, rolled over, and was still. This simulated death scene invariably aroused a storm of well merited applause, for, apart from the rare skill obviously essential to its performance, it looked dangerous in the extreme. I have wondered in view of his later illness whether that tremendous strain on his spine could possibly have affected his brain.

The Chief Eunuch's role, with the passing of Cecchetti, has dwindled to a shadow of its former importance. What was in his hands a memorable dramatic figure has become a low comedy character, whose only place is in the Morocco of a pantomime version of Dick Whittington, or the East as understood in musical comedy.

I can still see old Cecchetti in all the finery of his red and gold costume, leaning back to counterbalance his simulated pot belly, as he waddled to and fro in slippered feet, the nodding head of senility accentuated by his tall fez with its trembling feathered tassel. How subtly he conveyed his fatuous pride in his office, his intense cupidity, and his constant anxiety to serve his own interests without incurring the wrath of his master, whose punishment he well knew to be swift and final.

He had few scruples at releasing the copper and the

NARCISSE

silver clad negroes, but when it came to letting loose the single gold negro, fear showed in every line of his quavering, pendulous cheeks. When Zobeida declined to accept his refusal and forced him by mingled bribery and threats to open the last door, there was something both pathetic and sinister in the spectacle of the Eunuch's realisation that he was enmeshed in toils of his own contriving.

Narcisse was a pleasing mythological ballet based on the legend of Narcissus, the music by Tcherepnine, the scenery and costumes by Bakst, and the choreography by Fokine. The principal characters were: *Echo*, Thamar Karsavina; *Narcissus*, Vaslav Nijinsky; and *Bacchante*, B. Nijinska.

I recall the opening scene, a green forest glade of tall willows and beeches, joined by a rocky bridge, and in the distance the red glow of the rising sun. In the semi-darkness a strange band of wood-sprites with olive green bodies and large pointed ears emerged from the shadows, some hopping crouched half-upright, some gliding on all-fours.

Karsavina was dressed in a violet pleated peplum, decorated with silver leaves, her long hair loose and hanging down her back. I remember one inimitable gesture, which alone made the ballet worth while; the burying of her face in the crook of her arm, a moving demonstration of her grief when Narcissus disdained her love.

Nijinsky wore a fair Grecian wig, a white chlamys with one shoulder bare, and, I think, green or gold sandals with the legs cross-gartered. I can recall nothing of his dancing which, I believe, was mainly *terre à terre*, but I do remember his final pose when, crouched by the edge of the pool, he gazed spell-bound at his own image, bending down with infinite grace closer and closer to the water, until he disappeared beneath its surface, while in his stead rose a single narcissus flower.

The one blemish on Diaghilev's artistic reputation is that he should ever have sanctioned that blatantly false bloom, perched on the end of a stick which wobbled so clumsily as it was pushed into view from below.

Then there was Nijinska as the Bacchante, wearing, if I remember aright, a wig of flowing red hair and a classic robe coloured red and blue. She danced sometimes holding a beaker of wine in one hand and a wine-cup in the other, and sometimes holding a red and blue scarf which she held extended between her raised hands, or allowed to curl gracefully into the air. Years afterwards, while watching from the wings, I saw Sokolova perform the same dance. When she came off, she asked me to hold the scarf for her. I was astonished to find that the material I had thought to be light as chiffon, was, on the contrary, quite thick and heavy.

The season ended on August 1st, the programme consisting of *Le Carnaval, Thamar, Les Sylphides, Le Spectre de la Rose,* and the *Polovtsian Dances from "Prince Igor"*—the management was more generous in those days. I congratulated myself on having been able to see, during my first season of Russian ballet, practically all the ballets in the company's repertory, and I saw each ballet not once, but many times.

PRE-WAR AUDIENCES AND THE BALLETS RUSSES

I little thought then that Ballet was to encroach more and more on my thoughts and on my various interests, gradually to absorb, in one way or another, the greater part of my time. Yet, when I look back and reflect on the innumerable hours of delight that Ballet has bestowed upon me, I have no hesitation in saying that, if I could live those years again, I would not change their course.

I should like to record that the attitude of audiences towards Ballet then was different from what it is now. The not unmixed blessings of propaganda together with the education of the general public to the realisation that Ballet is something more than a kicking-up of one's legs—in fact, one of the most beautiful of the arts of the theatre—have worked many changes. Much good has been done, and also some harm. What Ballet needs is ballet-goers, not ballet-fans. The pre-War audiences knew little about Ballet, but they were quick to recognise art, great art, and they went to the performances of Diaghilev's "Ballets Russes" in a spirit of reverence, as worshippers to a shrine where something rarely beautiful was to be revealed; and the performances acquired a particular fragrance from that manner of approach.

The public of those days had, too, little or no knowledge of the dancers, save their stage personalities, and they judged them solely on their merits, and when these were clearly considerable, those artists were regarded almost as immortals, as gods come to earth. How many persons then could boast that they were on friendly terms with this or that dancer, and had the *entrée* to his or her dressing-room? I cannot help thinking that the present tendency on the part of some managements to connive at or frankly promote personal acquaintance between their leading dancers and members of the general public is aesthetically wrong, and opposed both to the interests of the art and the prestige of the individual artist. Did not Irving say, "Mystery is one of the actor's greatest assets." And did not Pavlova herself declare, "The artist should show himself to the public only on the stage, never in private life."

How different then when to catch a passing glimpse of Karsavina or Nijinsky walking down a street was considered a piece of rare good fortune, a precious moment to be re-lived and re-enjoyed over and over again. And when the curtain rang down on those early performances there was a tempest of applause which burst on the ears with the force of a deluge, when members of the audience rose from their seats and clapped and shouted until they could clap no more, not from any motives of partisanship, but simply to demonstrate their gratitude for the hour or two of beauty afforded them. In later years there were occasionally demonstrations of that intensity, but they were never so consistent, almost night after night, as in the years 1912 to 1914—that Golden Age of Ballet before the First World War.

CHAPTER II

~ 1913 ~

THE year 1913 was marked by two seasons of Diaghilev's "Ballets Russes", the first being given at Covent Garden in connection with Thomas (later Sir Thomas) Beecham's season of opera.[1] The ballet company was much the same as in the previous year, with the addition of Sophie Fedorova and Lydia Nelidova to the soloists, while the male dancers were strengthened by Alexander Kotchetovsky, an excellent character dancer.

I now rose to the rank of subscriber and booked a series of five-shilling amphitheatre stalls, endeavouring, as everyone does, to take in the *premières* of all the new productions. It may be of interest to give the prices of seats at this time. Grand Tier Boxes, £5 5s., First Tier Boxes, £2 2s., Second Tier Boxes, £1 1s., Orchestra Stalls, 15s. and 10s. 6d., Balcony Stalls, 7s. 6d., Amphitheatre Stalls, 5s. and 3s., Gallery (unreserved), 2s.

---

[1]Sometimes, as in 1912, there were combined programmes of both opera and ballet, for instance: *Pagliacci* followed by *Le Spectre de la Rose, Polovtsian Dances from "Prince Igor"*, and *Schéhérazade;* or *Il Segreto di Susanna* followed by *L'Oiseau de Feu, Le Spectre de la Rose* and *Polovtsian Dances from "Prince Igor";* or *Salomé* (Strauss) followed by *Le Carnaval.*

DIAGHILEV BALLET IN LONDON

The ballet season opened on February 4th, the programme being *Thamar*, *Petrouchka*, and *Les Sylphides*. This was the London *première* of *Petrouchka*, the theme being by Alexandre Benois and Igor Stravinsky, the music by Igor Stravinsky, the scenery and costumes by Alexandre Benois, and the choreography by Michel Fokine.

The principal characters were: *the Dancer*, Thamar Karsavina; *Petrouchka*, Vaslav Nijinsky; *the Moor*, A. Kotchetovsky; *Old Showman*, Enrico Cecchetti; *Coachmen*, Semenov, Romanov, Rakmanov, Oumansky, Ivanovsky; *Grooms*, Kremnev, Gavrilov; *Bibulous Merchant*, Serge Grigoriev; *Gypsies*, Mmes. Piltz, Astafieva; *Street Dancers*, Mmes. Jezerska, Gouluk; *First Organ-Grinder*, Tarassov; *Second Organ-Grinder*, M. Kobelev; *Old Father of the Fair*, Loboiko; *Picture-Showman*, Statkiewicz.

I well remember the startled expressions on the faces of the audience, and my own surprise, at the first hearing of Stravinsky's music, so wonderfully expressive of the raucous sounds and bustling movements of a fair, but which then sounded incredibly daring and uncouth to ears attuned to the melodies of classic composers.

Again, the setting, a Russian fair-ground in the 1830's, a charming composition in which primary colours, such as red, blue and yellow, played a prominent part, was in striking contrast to the romantic settings or Oriental scenes typical of former productions.

Except for the *Polovtsian Dances from "Prince Igor"*, the previous ballets had romance or passion for their theme; *Petrouchka*, however, was a tragi-comedy concerned, not with living persons, but with puppets, which their master, for a brief space, had endowed with human passions and emotions.

After the first shock of surprise had passed, I was soon captivated by the gay and ever-changing scene before my eyes—the nurses, in their full brightly coloured skirts, with one hand on hip, the other waving a handkerchief in the breeze; the coachmen, swinging to and fro to the well-marked rhythm of a dance, their long coats flapping as they stamped their feet and whirled round in time with the measure; the street-dancers with their tinkling triangle; and all the motley crowd of stall-holders, cossacks, soldiers, policemen, ladies and gentlemen passing backwards and forwards, intent on seeing the sights. Suddenly the flow of movement was abruptly stayed by the appearance of the old Showman who, having collected about him an eager audience with the strange melody which he played on his pipe, drew back the curtains of his booth and revealed the three puppets—the Dancer, Petrouchka, and the Moor.

Every ballet-goer knows that the three puppets are supported from the shoulders by an iron stand set at the back of each cell, which enables the puppets to execute the curious mechanical dance with which the first scene draws to a close. Nijinsky's dancing was unusual. When the Showman gave the signal for the puppets to dance, Nijinsky succeeded in investing the movements of his legs with a looseness suggesting that foot, leg, and thigh were threaded on a string attached

DIAGHILEV BALLET IN LONDON

to the hip; there was a curiously fitful quality in his movements, his limbs spasmodically leapt or twisted or stamped like the reflex actions of limbs whose muscles have been subjected to an electric current.

The whole production of the ballet was inspired. There was the blackout which brought the first scene to an abrupt conclusion, and the roll of drums that symbolised the passing crowd of sightseers outside the booth, and at the same time held the attention of the theatre audience, while the drop-curtain was lowered to permit of each change of scene, and then raised to disclose it.

There were four scenes, the first and last being the same, the scene of the fair; the other two showed Petrouchka's cell and the Moor's cell respectively. The second and third scenes were small ones set inside the main one, and since, in these, there were never more than three characters at one time, the contrasting gaiety of the outdoor scene with the comparative quiet of the indoor cells in which the puppets lived, was most effectively suggested.

The second scene, Petrouchka's cell, was the most unusual from the musical aspect, and at the first performance the members of the audience were considerably disconcerted by the piercing shrieks which conveyed Petrouchka's unhappiness. It was only gradually that it was seen how exactly right were those strident shrieks.

Nijinsky as Petrouchka dominated this and the last scene. He wore a thick white cotton blouse with a frilled collar edged with red, a red tie, satin trousers

NIJINSKY'S MAKE-UP AS PETROUCHKA

chequered in crimson and yellow, blue boots of soft leather, and a red and white hat with a tassel.

His features were made up a kind of putty colour, presumably a suggestion of wood; his nose was built up to have a thicker base; his eyebrows were painted out and replaced by a wavy line set half an inch higher; his lips were compressed together; his eyes seemed devoid of lid and socket, and suggested a pair of boot-buttons or two blobs of black paint; there was a little red on his cheeks. His features were formed into a sad and unhappy mask, an expression which remained constant throughout the ballet.

I have seen no one approach Nijinsky's rendering of Petrouchka, for, as I have said elsewhere, he suggested a puppet that sometimes aped a human being, whereas all the other interpreters conveyed a dancer imitating a puppet. He seemed to have probed the very soul of the character with astonishing intuition. Did he, in one of his dark moods of introspection, feel conscious of a strange parallel between Petrouchka and himself, and the Showman and Diaghilev?

Despite his set features he was, paradoxically enough, most expressive, his emotions being conveyed by the movements of his arms, the tilt of his head, and the various angles at which he bent his body from the waist. In general, his arms were stiff and extended like the arms of a puppet pivoted at the shoulder, but their meaning was plain. I well remember his dramatic entrance in the second scene when the double door leading to his cell burst open and he was propelled through it by the Showman's cruel boot. As if in acute pain, he tottered forward on his toes, flung up his arms, and threw back his head.

How vividly he presented his despair, his unhappiness, his misery, as he fingered and plucked at his clothes, the symbol of his servitude. Then he sank on his knees, and, with his stiff arms, now bent at the elbow, struck his neck first on one side and then on the other in a state of utter dejection at his pitiful lot.

Suddenly the folding door burst open and the Dancer appeared, to give him new hope. How excitedly he jerked his arms in greeting! But alas, the Dancer resented his strange manner of courtship and slammed the door in his face. Imagine his sorrow at this new affront. In a frenzy of rage and despair, he sought to escape from his cell and follow her.

Now I want to emphasise that this scene does not consist merely of kneeling at the bottom of the double door, making pattering movements of the hands up the wall and tearing at it until an opening is forced, through which Petrouchka's head and arms disappear, while his body remains within the room. To obtain the full dramatic value of this episode, the dancer must induce within himself a state of emotion such as a puppet temporarily endowed with life might feel under like circumstances, and then express it in terms of the movements designed by the choreographer. In most of the presentations of this scene I have been conscious of a certain casual approach, a sort of "now I do the business of pattering on the wall and bring the scene to a close". In short, you had a feeling that the movements were done because they had been prescribed,

NIJINSKY'S MIMING AS PETROUCHKA

and less with the realisation that they were the expression of a sudden mad moment of revolt on Petrouchka's part against the conditions which, when he was not performing to the public, reduced him to the status of a prisoner, confined within the narrow limits of his dark room.

Nijinsky gave an impressive performance of this episode. The Dancer's departure left him stunned for a brief moment, then he made you aware, through the almost imperceptible shaking of his head and body, and the twitching of his limbs, of the tumult of emotions stirring within him. Suddenly he flung himself on his knees by the doors, his gloved hands gliding ceaselessly up and down the jamb, higher and higher, as he tried to find an opening. Gradually he rose to his feet, still fingering the jamb more and more feverishly as his sense of frustration grew. Abruptly he rejected the door and passed his hands over the wall, faster and faster, while his head and limbs continually twitched from the intensity of his eagerness to escape. All at once his groping fingers found a weak spot and tore the paper apart—a piercing scream of triumph burst from the orchestra as his head and shoulders fell through the gap. His body went limp, curved in an inverted "v", as if he had fainted from exhaustion, while his arms, dropped in a vertical line, swung idly to and fro, as if still quivering from the violence of his efforts.

Another great moment occurred in the final scene when Petrouchka, struck by a blow from the Moor's scimitar, collapsed and sank on the snow-covered ground. He went inert like a broken doll. It was only with the greatest difficulty that he was able to raise himself from the ground. His head lolled to and fro as though attached to his neck by a piece of string. His arms jerked feebly. The green glare of a Bengal light turned his features a ghastly green. Then he fell back and rolled over on to his side.

Nijinsky's performance made a great impression upon me. As in all his creations, he absorbed himself completely in the character presented. His conceptions were illumined by genius; they were vital and memorable; and in the parts which he created he set a standard which his successors in those roles have never approached, let alone equalled.

Karsavina looked charming as the Dancer in her lace-fringed pantalettes, striped dull red and maroon, her pale mauve skirt, and her crimson velvet bodice with white sleeves trimmed with gold bands. Her hair, dressed in the short ringlets which became her so well, was crowned with a crimson velvet toque, trimmed with white fur. Her make-up was flesh-pink with a bright dab of red on each cheek. Her eyes were given an air of exaggerated surprise by short black lines painted ray-like about them.

She made the Dancer an impressionable, flighty young woman, and all her movements had a crispness and tautness which gave them a most attractively piquant quality. Her little dance with the trumpet was admirably timed and as gay and as sprightly as could be. Her daintiness made an excellent foil for the agitated, twitching, hypersensitive Petrouchka and the vain, lumbering, brutish Moor.

KARSAVINA AS THE DANCER IN PETROUCHKA

One of the most vivid of my recollections of Karsavina in this role is associated with the third scene, where she is captivated by the overwhelming personality of the Moor, so splendid a figure in his suit of emerald green and silver. When the Dancer paid him a visit, he dropped the cocoanut with which he had been playing, and, plumping himself on the divan, brazenly seized the Dancer and pulled her on to his knees. How delightfully she suggested by the particular tilting of her head and shoulders the nervous thrill she experienced from that bold attack. But when Petrouchka most inconsiderately burst upon the lovers and squeaked his indignation, her innate modesty returned and she quickly jumped to her feet, jerking up her hands to hide her burning cheeks.

Orlov created the role of the Moor when Petrouchka was first performed—at Paris; unfortunately, I never saw him. But Kotchetovsky, who played the Moor in the London *première*, has remained for me the best interpreter of that part, although Bolm ran him closely. Kotchetovsky made the Moor a big, burly, clumsy fellow, childishly vain of his physical strength and his imposing uniform. He made him a good-humoured lout with a child-like propensity for showing-off at the slightest provocation, yet he did the simplest movements with such a smacking of his thick lips, such rolling of eyeballs, such gusto, that you could not help sharing in his extravagant delight.

And I must not forget Cecchetti as the old Showman, a mysterious, enigmatic figure, his every movement timed to perfection. How calmly and carelessly he followed the policeman come to acquaint him of the murder of Petrouchka, an absurd notion he quickly disposed of by his contemptuous shaking of the limp figure to prove that Petrouchka was nothing more than wood and sawdust. Then came the dramatic moment when, as he strolled homewards, dragging the puppet's limp body behind him, preparatory to returning it to its cell, there was a succession of eerie squeaks and Petrouchka's ghost appeared at the top of the booth, to mock his master, who, shaken and terrified by this unexpected and inexplicable phenomenon, hastily took to flight.

I can still see the abrupt end of Cecchetti's leisurely walk as he jerked back on his heels, his whole body tensed in an attitude of listening. Then, as Petrouchka's mocking squeaks were repeated, there flashed over Cecchetti's features a look of mingled bewilderment and surprise, which swiftly changed to abject fear. Full of apprehension, he half-turned his head in the direction of the sound, and, as he caught sight of the roof of the booth with the head and shoulders of that ghostly figure gibbering with its stiff arms, a chill sweat broke out on his forehead. He smoothed his brow with his trembling hand, shaking so violently that his hat fell from his head. The sound of that object striking the ground startled him into immediate action, and, filled with a frenzied desire to escape, he scurried away, as fast as his trembling legs would carry him.

On February 11th I saw for the first time "*L'Oiseau et le Prince*", which was danced by Karsavina and

L'APRÈS-MIDI D'UN FAUNE

Nijinsky. This was the famous *pas de deux* best known as "*L'Oiseau Bleu*" from Petipa's ballet *La Belle au Bois Dormant*. The setting was a simple black velvet curtain surround.

I can still visualize the perfection of that dance partnership. I well remember Nijinsky's effortless ease and delightful *ballon*, and how, during one phase of the dance, he seemed not to touch the ground but to glide forward on air, his feet flashing to and fro in the brilliance of his *brisés* and *cabrioles*.

The next important production was *L'Après-Midi d'un Faune*, Nijinsky's first essay as choreographer, which had its London *première* on February 17th. This ballet, or *tableau chorégraphique* as it was termed, was arranged to Debussy's prelude of the same name, while the scenery and costumes were by Léon Bakst. The title-role was taken by Nijinsky; the nymphs were Mmes. Nelidova, Konietska, Tcherepanova, Maikerska, Klementowicz, and Kopycinska.

The ballet created a sensation both for its novelty of presentation and for the questionable character of Nijinsky's movements and poses immediately preceding the fall of the curtain. *L'Après-Midi d'un Faune* was quite unlike any other ballet previously presented by the company, for it contained practically no elements of academic technique and the track consisted of a single straight line bounded by the wings on either side. Faun and nymphs moved backwards and forwards in profile on that line, very like an animated frieze formed of figures inspired by the decoration of antique Greek vases.

DIAGHILEV BALLET IN LONDON

Contrary, however, to such figures, there were no poses or movements in which one leg was raised. The dancers remained "attached" to the ground, never rising in the air and always progressing by a series of half walking, half gliding movements, the heel of the rear foot being gradually raised and the foot passed forwards in the same straight line, then the new rear foot was similarly raised and passed forward likewise, and so on; a change of course was achieved by a sudden half-turn of the feet and body to right or left.

This method of progression appeared simple, and, once the convention was accepted, even natural; yet it must have required a nice sense of poise and contained many difficulties for dancers accustomed to turn their feet outwards.

How beautiful Debussy's silvery music was, with its hint of lazy streams and rustling leaves. But the music and movement did not blend to form an indivisible whole as in Fokine's *Petrouchka*, the melody served only as an accompaniment, the musical counterpart to the scenic setting against which the panorama of movement was displayed.

The Faun's costume consisted of cream-coloured fleshings splotched with brown; his bare arms were similarly treated. He wore a close-fitting cap of silver gilt hair, from the brow of which sprung a pair of horns, curving back and lying close to the head. The Nymphs also wore close-fitting caps of gold hair with spiral tresses falling midway between the waist and knee, and armless diaphanous robes, modelled on the

Greek peplum, of white pleated material bordered at the hem with tiny squares of blue or dull red, the white overskirt being decorated with a few wavy lines of the same colour as the squares.

When the curtain rose, an enchanting scene was revealed: a Grecian landscape in the tints of early autumn; a verdant hillside relieved with the yellow and reddish-orange foliage of the trees which scored its surface, and through which showed a narrow stream.

A little way up the hillside was a fallen tree-trunk on which the Faun indolently reclined, resting on his left elbow, his back half-turned to the audience, his right knee drawn up, and his right hand placed to his lips as if he were idly playing on a flute. Now and again he would cease his playing, and, taking up a bunch of dark grapes, whose fragrance he greedily inhaled, crush the fruit against his lips. The Faun's movements were so simple, so unaffected, so seemingly oblivious of any suggestion of a watching audience, that you had a feeling of being caught up in a time-machine and whirled back to the Greece of legend, on which you were permitted for a brief space to gaze in secret.

Presently a band of nymphs glided upon the stage. The Faun's quick eye swiftly discerned them and, after watching their arrival with intense curiosity, he made his way down the hillside, always moving in profile, until he was able to confront the startled nymphs, who at once retired in the opposite direction, their arms upheld in dismay. The Faun's movements were in profile, his arms extended before him with the hand flat and sideways to the audience, the thumb uppermost and separated from the other fingers, which were held together.

At the end of the ballet, the Faun returned to his fastness, bearing on his outstretched arms the scarf left by the leader of the nymphs. When he had caressed the extended scarf, and, with infinite care, lowered it to the ground, the symbolism was plain. And when Nijinsky proceeded slowly to recline, face downwards, on the scarf, the implication was obvious. I well remember the gasp that went up from the audience at Nijinsky's audacity. Yet the movements and poses were performed so quietly, so impersonally, that their true character, with their power to offend, was almost smoothed away. It was an intriguing study in erotic symbolism.

The ballet was received with rapturous enthusiasm mingled with some hisses, the expression of outraged feelings on the part of certain members of the audience, who thought that the Russian Ballet was going too far. But the final applause was so loud and so sustained that Diaghilev gave instructions for the ballet to be repeated, a rare occurrence on any night, but unique at a *première*.

Nijinsky's Faun was a curious conception, a strange being, half human, half animal. There was little of the sprightliness, lasciviousness, and gaiety which legend has ascribed to such beings. There was something cat-like about his propensity for indolence and the elasticity of his slow, deliberate, remorseless movements. His features were set and expressionless, and did not change throughout the ballet. By this means he suggested the brute, the creature actuated by instinct rather than by intelligence. Perhaps the most unusual characteristic of Nijinsky's portrait was this lack of emotion, all feeling being subjected to the exigencies of pure form.

During my visits to Covent Garden I made the acquaintance of a man in the forties, whom I frequently saw at the Ballet. His name was Gustave de Beer. He was of Belgian extraction, very fair, clean-shaven, ascetic-looking, slight, and of medium height. His sober and precise manner of dress combined with his charming old-world courtesy gave him the air of being "something in the law", but though I learned a little of his occupation he always remained something of a mystery.

He was a genuine lover of ballet, and rarely missed a performance of the Diaghilev Company, indeed, he even arranged his holidays to coincide with the troupe's Paris seasons. He was well versed in the technique of ballet. He was acquainted with Diaghilev, and on excellent terms with several members of the company. He knew Nijinsky, whom he revered as a god, and he did all he could to help him during his ill-fated season at the Palace Theatre in 1914. Diaghilev esteemed Gustave highly and I think I am right in saying that it was at the former's request that he later initiated Massine into the mysteries of the English language.

Gustave and I became great friends and night after night we sat together at the Ballet and exchanged views, and, as enthusiasts will, awarded praise or blame. A curious feature of the audiences of those days was the number of Japanese spectators, several of whom carried a miniature score of the ballet in which they were interested, which they followed throughout the performance with assiduous attention. In the intervals Gustave and I would repair to the refreshment bar at the side of the amphitheatre stalls which, being small and jammed with people of all nationalities, was a perfect babel of sound with passionate arguments and discussions in every language concerning the merits or defects of this or that production.

The performance over, my wife and Gustave and I, sometimes accompanied by other friends, would go to my shop, where I then had one of the downstairs rooms fitted up as a fantastic sitting-room, even containing a piano. Gustave would invariably produce a box of pastries and my wife would serve cups of chocolate in a service which had once belonged to Napoleon. There, until long past midnight, we would sit talking about the ballets and their interpreters. I had the pianoforte scores of several of the ballets, and, at Gustave's request, I would play some of the melodies of his favourite numbers, which he never tired of hearing.

That same season I also made the acquaintance of Thamar Karsavina, through her kindly autographing for my benefit a photograph of herself in *Le Pavillon d'Armide*. Those who only knew her in post-War years cannot conceive how beautiful she was in those early days, with her rounded features, her clear olive complexion, and her lustrous eyes. Her voice was low and musical, and had the sweetness and refinement of

ACQUAINTANCE WITH ADOLPH BOLM

one of Watteau's shepherdesses. Yet there was something exotic about her appearance, something enigmatic about her fleeting smile; she left you wondering whether she really was a mortal and not some peri who had assumed human guise.

One day Adolph Bolm looked in at my shop in search of some book, as a result of which I acquired one more friend. Bolm had a powerful personality, intensified by his fierce dark eyes and great shock of black hair. He was ever absorbed in the subject of Ballet, continually thinking out new steps, searching for themes that might be expressed in terms of choreography. Whenever he had a spare hour he was always adding to his store of knowledge, going to an art exhibition, attending a concert, or visiting a museum. Sometimes he would invite me to lunch and talk of his future plans and ambitions. Bolm always impressed me with his fire and enthusiasm, both on the stage and in private life; and, of the many dancers I have met, I set him apart as one of the most studious and intellectual, and among the most far-seeing in his estimate of the future trend of choreography.

The last new production of the season was *Le Dieu Bleu*, which had its London *première* on February 27th. The theme was by Jean Cocteau and de Madrazzo; the music by Reynaldo Hahn; the setting and costumes by Leon Bakst; and the choreography by Michel Fokine.

The principal characters were as follows: *the Blue God*, Vaslav Nijinsky; *the Goddess*, Lydia Nelidova; *the*

Young Girl, Thamar Karsavina; *the Youth*, Max Frohman; *Dancing Girl*, Alexandra Wassilewska; *High Priest*, Michel Fedorov; *Peacock Bearers*, Mmes. Piltz, Tchernicheva, Astafieva.

The best thing about *Le Dieu Bleu* was its setting, in which Bakst proved that while he could evoke all the cruelty and voluptuousness of the East, as in his setting for *Schéhérazade*, he could also, by a different combination of colour and design, conjure up the mystery and sense of awe produced by the East in a mood of religious exaltation.

Imagine a great orange-coloured cliff silhouetted against the deep blue sky of an Indian night, powdered with scintillating stars, and, jutting from the centre of the cliff, a group of gigantic heads hewn out of the rock, symbols of the deity worshipped by the natives and their priests. At the base of the cliff was a rock-girt pool, on the surface of which floated the sacred lotus.

The theme was undistinguished. A young man is received into the priesthood with appropriate ceremony. Among the bystanders he recognizes the girl he loves, and realises, too late, that he must renounce her for evermore, since he is now vowed to chastity. The girl, unable to restrain the ardour of her love, flings herself at his feet and implores him not to forsake her. The scandalized priests attempt to seize her, but the young man throws off his priestly raiment and hurries to her side, hoping that they may escape together. But they are quickly secured.

The priest is led away a prisoner. The girl is chained and left in solitude before the cliff. Terrified at her

LE DIEU BLEU

surroundings, she tries to leave by a door in the face of the cliff, but, in opening it, she releases a swarm of fearsome reptiles. As they encircle her, she kneels in prayer. To her amazement, the God and Goddess of the shrine appear, the former of whom, by means of a mystic dance, reduces the reptiles to a state of insensibility.

The deities are about to depart when the priests and their attendants return to gloat over the death struggles of their victim. On seeing the Divinities they fall prostrate before them. The lovers are restored to each other and receive the divine blessing on their union. The Goddess vanishes below the pool. The orange cliff splits asunder to reveal a flight of golden steps, which the Blue God mounts, and, playing on his pipe, ascends to heaven.

The music was dull and perhaps for that very reason Fokine's choreography for once seemed uninspired. One of the few interesting numbers was that danced by three temple-dancers each bearing a peacock on her shoulder. But, viewed as a whole, the ballet contained too much miming and posing, too many processions. What would have been a splendid climax to a play was insipid as a ballet, complete in itself. The demons and reptiles were too reminiscent of a Christmas pantomime; instead of creating an atmosphere, they merely provoked smiles.

Nijinsky was a striking exotic-looking figure. He wore a splendidly embroidered and bejewelled blue and gold tunic, with a short stiffened skirt of oriental design, and an elaborate headdress fashioned of gold wire; his face and limbs were coloured blue. His poses, for which Fokine had evidently sought inspiration from Hindu sculpture, were beautiful; but his role seemed to consist of posing, there was very little dancing. It was difficult to dispel the impression that for the first time Nijinsky's artistry and rare abilities had been wasted. Notwithstanding that the cast included Karsavina and Nijinsky, the ballet was an obvious failure, and, after two more performances, disappeared from the repertory.

That same evening I had my first sight of Fokine's *Cléopâtre*, which had not been given in London since 1911. The music was mainly adapted from Arensky's *Une Nuit d'Egypte*, with interpolated numbers, in the manner of the pre-Fokine ballet, by Taneyev, Rimsky-Korsakov, Glinka, and Glazunov.

The principal characters were: *Ta-Hor*, Sophie Fedorova; *Cleopatra*, Serafina Astafieva; *Amoun*, Adolph Bolm; *Favourite Slaves of Cleopatra*, Wassilewska, Gavrilov; *High Priest of the Temple*, Kovalsky.

Bakst's setting evoked the dramatic mood essential to the ballet. It represented a temple in the Egyptian desert. On either side were gigantic, sombre, basalt figures which dominated the scene and made the dancers seem insignificant in proportion. In the distance were the pink columns of a temple, while the horizon was bounded by the blue waters of the Nile.

Cléopâtre was one of Fokine's early compositions for, while it proved his admirable sense of stage effect, his command of mass movement, and his rare ability to make a drama expressed in terms of choreography no less gripping than one conveyed in terms of action and the spoken word, he had retained the traditional processions and mimed scenes characteristic of Ballet under Petipa.

The ballet was very popular in the early years of the Diaghilev Company; partly for its attraction as a colourful spectacle; partly for its powerful dramatic appeal; partly for its element of eroticism which, if treated boldly, was presented with tact; and partly because of the artistry of the interpreters of the principal roles.

The three principal characters in the ballet were Cleopatra, Ta-Hor, and Amoun. Astafieva's fine bosom and Junoesque figure were well suited to Cleopatra, whom she presented as an indolent, voluptuous woman, proud in the knowledge that her mere presence should cause Amoun to forsake his betrothed and barter his life for one night of love. Astafieva wore a simple, striped, close-fitting robe, in the Egyptian style, which became her well.

Fedorova remains for me the finest exponent of Ta-Hor. A slight, dark woman, with big expressive eyes and the vivid personality of a gypsy, her Ta-Hor was no pasteboard figure of a jilted maiden, but a credible being of flesh and blood. The part—all mime except for her single *pas de deux* with Amoun—offered many opportunities, and she made full use of them.

At her first entrance, when she came so joyously to keep her tryst with Amoun, there was something sublime in the half-shy, half-affectionate tenderness of her greeting. She made you aware of her deep love, not by any extravagantly passionate gestures, but by simple quiet movements full of poetry—an inclination of her head, a movement of her arm, a look in her eyes—the timing and quality of which made them no less forceful.

When Cleopatra made her regal entrance and Amoun betrayed by his ardent unyielding gaze the intensity of his desire, Fedorova showed by the look of fear and strained anxiety that passed over her face, and by the restless, nervous clasping and unclasping of her hands, her increasing apprehension that Amoun was lost to her.

She made you share in all the varied emotions that flooded her brain—her furious resentment, her grief that her lover should be so fickle. Those bitter thoughts were replaced in turn by a mounting sympathy for Amoun, born of her overwhelming love, and her final resolve to preserve him at the cost of no matter what humiliation to herself; a decision which impelled her suddenly to throw herself at the feet of majesty, to beseech with her whole being that her lover might not be taken from her, an entreaty received by the Queen with an indolent, half-pitying, half-disdainful smile.

Perhaps the most dramatic moment of all was when, Cleopatra and her suite having departed, Ta-Hor returned in search of her lover. The setting sun and the approach of night made the gaunt basalt figures still more sombre. The stage was empty, save for the black pall that covered the dead Amoun.

Fedorova entered almost imperceptibly, so closely did she hug the shadow cast by the giant figures. She

MORE ABOUT FEDOROVA

walked slowly and a little stiffly, as though her feet refused their office. Her face was set. One hand was clenched at her side, the other was pressed to her breast as though to quieten the pounding of her heart. She crossed into the open and, at first seeing nothing to disconcert her, her stern features relaxed a little. Then she caught sight of the pall. The hand at her breast instantly flew to her cheek in an access of terror. She hesitated, not daring to lift the pall, her hands clasped in a fervent prayer; then, very slowly, very fearfully, she drew back a corner of the dark coverlet, to reveal the still features of Amoun. She recoiled in horror, then, recovering herself with a great effort, bent slowly down and kissed his brow, cast off the fillet that bound her hair, and beat her breast in an agony of grief and despair.

Fedorova, like so many artists trained in the Imperial School of Ballet, had presence and a remarkable sense of timing. She also knew the supreme value of repose. So many dancers exhaust themselves with extravagant gestures which merely bore the spectator or leave him unmoved, even irritated. But a "happy few", as Stendhal has it, have only to raise a finger for the spectator's interest to be seized and held until the moment of the artist's exit. Fedorova belonged to that "happy few".

I have already related how my interest in the Diaghilev Ballet was first aroused by the sight of the Souvenir Programme issued in connection with their Paris season of 1912. The publisher was Maurice de Brunoff, then editor of the *Comœdia Illustré*, one of the best periodicals devoted to theatre activities in France ever issued, for the articles, illustrations, typography and production were all of a uniformly high standard.

Brunoff early recognized the importance of the Diaghilev Ballet and devoted considerable space to acquainting the Paris theatre-going public of the company's rare artistic merits. These issues were generally lavishly illustrated with reproductions in colour and monotone of the original designs for the settings and costumes for the latest productions. In recent years his publications have been imitated but never equalled, because they were produced without regard to expense, and with love and taste.

As I had purchased many copies of the Souvenir Programme for 1912, Brunoff sent me an advance copy of the Special Number of the *Comœdia Illustré* issued for the 1913 season. I was delighted with it and decided to purchase a number of copies of the issue if I could have a special new cover setting forth the various illustrations and articles devoted to the company, for the original cover gave no hint as to its contents. I resolved to go to Paris and discuss the matter with Brunoff, and take the opportunity of inspecting certain other French publications respecting the Diaghilev Ballet of which some details had reached me.

I called at the offices of the *Comœdia Illustré* in the Rue Louis le Grand and was courteously received by Brunoff, a handsome, well preserved, aristocratic-looking man of middle age, dressed with ambassadorial elegance, the opening of his waistcoat edged with the white slip then fashionable. He had a grey beard like a Russian admiral, which he wore parted in the middle and brushed to either side. I explained the purpose of my visit; he promised to see what could be done; and we agreed to meet again at 2 p.m. on the following day.

When I arrived, I was ushered into an office and informed that M. de Brunoff had still not returned from his lunch. I waited awhile and, for want of something to do, went to the window and looked out. At the end of the short street which connects the Rue Louis le Grand with the Rue de la Paix was a smart café, with a number of outside tables, at one of which I recognized Brunoff seated in company with two beautiful young women, actress written all over them. I sat down and looked at some issues of the *Comœdia Illustré*.

At 3 o'clock Brunoff burst into the room, panting and mopping his brow. He was *désolé* to be so late, but had been held up at an important interview. Now that he had come I had an intuition that our conversation would be brief, for I saw that he was dressed as for the races, with a pair of field-glasses slung over his shoulder. My foreboding proved to be correct, for he said that he would have no news for me until the morrow, and must now hurry away to another urgent appointment.

I returned the next day and found Brunoff in a mood of big business. He was seated in an office with a door on either side of him leading to smaller offices. At the edge of his desk was a run of six or eight pushbuttons. As soon as I sat down, his fingers played over the buttons as on the keyboard of a piano. Various men emerged from the outer rooms with a letter for signature or a proof to be passed for press. The hubbub and the rapid passing to and fro of all these people reduced me to a state of hypnosis. Then Brunoff struck his brow as a punishment for having forgotten me.

He pressed a button several times in succession, and, when it was answered, asked for the proof of the new cover. The proof was brought and I expressed my satisfaction. Again his fingers played over the buttons and the clamour was resumed. In the midst of this he suggested that I should take so many copies, about treble the quantity I had suggested. But I managed to keep calm and finally Brunoff agreed to supply me with the original number desired. If he had not chosen to be a publisher, I am sure he would have achieved eminence as an actor.

Another day I went to see another firm of publishers, La Belle Edition, directed by the author-poet, François Bernouard, which was in the Rue des Saints-Pères. Bernouard had lately published a charming album called *Vingt Dessins sur Vaslav Nijinsky*, a collection of drawings by George Barbier representing Nijinsky in his principal roles, with a Foreword by François de Miomandre.

So far as my memory goes, Bernouard had a large ground floor room, in one corner of which was a fair-sized machine press, and in the other portions there were a few tables and chairs. I suggested that he should print me a limited edition of *Vingt Dessins sur Vaslav Nijinsky* for England. Bernouard was interested and asked me to call back the next day as he wished to go further into the matter.

I paid my second visit and had just begun to discuss terms when a writer dropped in to see Bernouard, then an artist called, and so other matters intervened. Someone would be in the mood to write a poem, or an artist would have an idea for a decorative heading or tailpiece. Or perhaps someone would propose a suggestion for a book and an animated discussion would ensue. The subjects, I may say, were of a very diverse nature. It was all very bohemian and very stimulating, but the business of the English edition made little progress. However, in a few days, everything was settled and the edition put in hand.

How delighted I was when the copies eventually reached me in London. But the trade were less aware of Ballet then than they are now, and when I travelled the book among my fellow booksellers, some held it by one corner with expressions of deep misgiving as to its saleability. A year or so later, when the edition had been sold out, I had the satisfaction of supplying a copy at two guineas to one of the booksellers who had declined to purchase the book when it was available at the published price of ten shillings.

While in Paris I also went to the shop kept by Paul Iribe, a well-known designer and interior decorator, who had produced a little book of black and white drawings of Nijinsky, which I wished to purchase, but it was already *épuisé*. Iribe had a wonderful place with the most beautiful furniture and materials. I recall one magnificent writing-desk with a top in the form of a sea-shell. There also, hanging on the walls, were some framed photographs of Nijinsky by the Baron de Meyer. But I was overawed by the expensive air of the shop and feared to ask the price. I always regret that I never purchased at least one of those superb photographs, for they are almost impossible to find these days.

There was ample evidence in Paris of the influence of Léon Bakst on artists and designers. The windows of dressmakers, milliners, and interior decorators displayed dresses, hats, cushions, curtains, and furnishing materials in the bright colours and exotic patterns associated with his settings and costumes. Publishers of limited editions also brought out collections of costume plates in the same bright hues. Colour was everywhere to be seen and the people and streets of Paris had never looked gayer.

The second season began on June 25th, when the company appeared at Drury Lane in connection with Sir Joseph Beecham's Grand Season of Russian Opera and Ballet. The programme for the first night was *Le Pavillon d'Armide*, *Jeux*, and *Schéhérazade*, the second ballet having its first London performance. *Jeux*, Nijinsky's second essay in choreography, was arranged to music specially composed by Debussy; the scenery and costumes were by Bakst.

The cast was: *First Girl*, Thamar Karsavina; *Second Girl*, Ludmilla Schollar; *the Youth*, Vaslav Nijinsky.

The scene showed the private grounds belonging to some country mansion, where a young man and two girl friends appeared to have been enjoying a moonlight game of tennis. Such, at least, was the impression conveyed, for the ballet opened with a ball bouncing over an empty stage and disappearing into the undergrowth; then, following in swift pursuit, came the young man and his friends, all in white tennis kit.

The moonlight exercises its traditional enchantment and the young man pursues the girls in turn. Perhaps he is a little too boisterous, a little over-amorous, for his friends show signs of alarm. The sudden realization of sex disturbs their previous happy relationship, and the young people become self-conscious and ill at ease. Explanations are offered and accepted, and all ends happily in a little dance about the flower-beds until, breathless and exhausted, they all sit on the grass, each girl resting her head on the young man's shoulder.

I saw *Jeux* twice only, and, at this distance of time, my recollection of the choreographic structure is a little hazy. But, beyond the fact that the costumes were based on those used in tennis, the ballet might have been inspired by any other sport, for all the relation the dancers' movements bore to tennis.

The ballet contained, however, little dancing in the accepted meaning of the word. There were occasional leaps and bounds and turning movements borrowed or adapted from the classical ballet, but, for the most part, the ballet was concerned to express the theme of adolescence by a combination of plastic symbolism and taut, angular poses in the modernist spirit, with the head sometimes inclined to one side and the hands not free, but lightly clenched. There was another unusual movement which had a certain beauty from its display of muscle control, when Nijinsky turned his head to one side and tightened the muscles of his neck. The normally unusually expressive features of the dancers were here, as in *L'Après-Midi d'un Faune*, expressionless and set; doubtless this suggestion of a mask was to develop the sculptural convention.

Nijinsky had clearly studied the Dalcroze method, but had interpreted it in the letter rather than the spirit, the movements being so meticulously phrased with the beats in the music that the dancers were reduced to the level of automata. Moreover the music, except for a lively waltz movement in the centre portion, tended to be monotonous in itself. The ballet failed to attract, and, after having been given five times in all, was withdrawn from the repertory.

On this same date the Fine Art Society opened a Léon Bakst Exhibition, the designs including fantasies on modern costume, and settings and costumes for the ballet, *Jeux*, the opera *Boris Godunov*, and the plays, *Hélène de Sparte* and *La Pisanelle*.

During this exhibition the Fine Art Society announced the impending publication of two interesting works, *Studies from the Russian Ballet*, and *The Art of Léon Bakst*.

The first was a collection of fifteen photo-engravings after the photographs by E. O. Hoppé of Karsavina, Fedorova, Nijinsky, and Bolm in various ballets.

The second was and remains the finest collection of Bakst's work yet issued. Actually, it was an English edition of a work in course of preparation by Brunoff.

LA TRAGÉDIE DE SALOMÉ

It was a folio volume containing 75 full-page plates, 50 of which were finely reproduced in colour, each plate being mounted on a grey handmade paper. The edition was limited to 470 copies, 20 of which were bound in full vellum and contained an original drawing by Bakst.

June 30th saw the production of another new ballet, *La Tragédie de Salomé*, the music being by Florent Schmitt, the setting and costumes by Serge Sudeikine, and the choreography by Boris Romanov. I missed this ballet and cannot therefore record my impression of it. But Gustave told me that the "ballet" consisted almost entirely of Karsavina, attired in a fantastic costume reminiscent of a drawing by Aubrey Beardsley, who danced against a background of negro slaves, nude, except for a loin-cloth, their dark limbs set off by an occasional white ostrich plume worn as a bracelet or anklet.

It may be of interest to state that the music was not composed for the Diaghilev Ballet, but was originally commissioned by Loie Fuller, who produced her composition at the Théâtre des Arts, Paris, in 1907. Later, it was scored as an orchestral suite, when it formed the basis of another choreographic work by the dancer, Trouhanova; this, too, was presented at Paris.

One morning Nijinsky walked into my shop, attracted, no doubt, by the dance books displayed in the window. He uttered no word, but merely looked round. His slanting eyes were unmistakable, but not so fascinating as when emphasized with make-up. His head was rather large, his hair thin and dun coloured. He had the high cheekbones of the Russian peasant and seemed shy and even awkward. Nijinsky in private life bore little relation to the wonderful Nijinsky of the stage.

The final and by far the most important novelty of the season was *Le Sacre du Printemps*, which had its London *première* on July 11th. The music was by Igor Stravinsky, the settings and costumes by Nicholas Roehrich, and the choreography by Nijinsky.

The principal characters were: *An Old Woman*, Mme. Gouluk; *a Wise Man*, M. Woronzow; *the Chosen Maiden*, Marie Piltz.

That the production was unusual even for the Diaghilev Ballet, and that Diaghilev regarded its presentation as an important event, was implied in the fact that he had arranged for one of his friends, the music critic, Edwin Evans, to appear in front of the curtain immediately before the performance of the *Sacre* and explain the music and intention of the new ballet. But the audience, excited by the atmosphere of a first night and all eagerness to see the *Sacre* for themselves, became restive, and Evans was forced to curtail his introduction.

The first scene showed an expanse of wild hilly country intersected by innumerable streams; above the hills were great masses of rain-charged cloud.

It is a spring night and the young men of the tribe perform appropriate ritual movements under the guidance of an old woman, an aged seer. The women of the tribe enter and the men join them in simple dances and primitive games. Lastly come the elders, who bless the earth that the crops may be good and the tribe fruitful.

LE SACRE DU PRINTEMPS

The second scene presented the crest of a hill, seen against a vast expanse of sky.

Now begins the most important dance of all, the traditional dance for the selection of the Chosen Maiden, who is to be sacrificed as an offering to the goddess of Spring. As the maidens dance, one of their number falls into a trance. In a state of increasing ecstasy she begins to dance, faster and faster, her movements more and more violent, until, delirious and exhausted, she drops dead. The body is lifted up by her friends and borne out on their shoulders. The sacrifice is complete.

Le Sacre du Printemps, both in music and choreography, was and remains probably the most iconoclastic ballet so far presented. The music of *Petrouchka*, which had seemed so entirely new and so unusual, became almost conventional in comparison with that of the *Sacre*, which might be termed absolute music, music formed of pure rhythm, a rhythm sometimes dull and monotonous, but sometimes attaining tremendous force, bludgeoning the audience and driving the dancers to ever greater efforts.

The settings were suited to the required mood—dreary, half savage, half mystical landscapes, in the painting of which Roehrich is unequalled. The colours of the costumes, if I remember correctly, were flaxen and bright scarlet. The women wore simple smocks decorated at the hem with bands of simple designs in colour; their legs were wrapped in strips of cloth, cross-gartered, and on their feet they wore bast shoes. Their hair was twisted into long straggling pigtails; their cheeks were crudely daubed with red. The men wore a shorter smock, similar leg-coverings, and, I think, a pointed cap of some animal's skin.

The choreography was startling, being a complete negation of those rare qualities of *élévation* and *ballon* associated with Nijinsky. In the *Sacre* the dancers danced with their bodies seemingly weighed down, their movements often slow and heavy as though their feet were attached to the ground. The feet were turned inwards and the movements made inwards, in complete opposition to academic tradition. The arms and hands were cramped and the shoulders hunched. Everything possible seemed to have been done to make the poses as awkward, as uncouth, and as primitive as could be.

There was an element of counterpoint in the choral movements, in that now and again one group of dancers danced heavily in opposition to another group which danced lightly; or the seer moved with a curious shuffling movement, the rhythm of which was harmonized with the quick stampings of the young men.

Another innovation, which has been erroneously attributed to the later Massine, was Nijinsky's attempt now and again to imitate the orchestral pattern in his choreography, so that when a theme was given to a certain instrument, certain dancers would detach themselves from the mass and dance apart, the main body being used as a static or quietly moving background for the new dance.

Marie Piltz, as the Chosen Maiden, achieved a

MARIE PILTZ AS THE CHOSEN MAIDEN

triumph in her final dance of delirium, a difficult sustained dance, surcharged with emotion, and exhausting both mentally and physically. It was a magnificent performance and a remarkable feat of endurance, the dance being frequently interrupted by bursts of frenzied applause. When, at last, Piltz collapsed in simulation of death, the spectators showed the relaxation of the emotional tension produced in them by her dancing by giving involuntary sighs of relief.

Marie Piltz and the conductor, Pierre Monteux, were called before the curtain and applauded to the echo. But the ballet itself had a mixed reception. Those members of the audience who had gone to the theatre expecting to be charmed with light and graceful movements, and, instead, found themselves caught up in a maelstrom of rhythm, immensely vital and as dominating, as remorseless, and as irritating to the nervous system as the continuous thudding of a savage's tom-tom, bitterly resented Nijinsky's new production.

There were not a few members of the audience who in the interval after the ballet complained bitterly of splitting headaches. Others, none the less startled by this attempt to reproduce in terms of choreography the stark mood of primitive man, appreciated the sincerity of both composer and choreographer and applauded with fervour. It would be a fair estimate to say that the audience were about equally divided in their dislike and their appreciation. The ballet was given three times in all in London and then withdrawn from the repertory. I noticed with interest that at the final performance on the 23rd there were no expressions of hostility.

The season ended on the 25th, the programme consisting of *Schéhérazade*, *La Tragédie de Salomé*, *Jeux*, and *Le Spectre de la Rose*. That evening had a special significance, being the hundredth performance given in London by the Diaghilev Ballet.

CHAPTER III

~ 1914 ~

THE fateful year of 1914, destined to witness so many tragic events, opened with a dramatic surprise in the world of ballet—the appearance of Nijinsky, not with the Diaghilev Company, but with his own troupe.

I cannot remember now at what period I first learnt that Diaghilev, enraged by the news of Nijinsky's marriage at Buenos Aires in September of the previous year, when part of the "Ballets Russes" was on tour in South America, had expelled him from his company. I have no doubt that I had the news from Gustave. The outcome of Diaghilev's action was that Nijinsky determined to form and tour a troupe of his own.

The first intimation of the forthcoming appearance of the great dancer was contained in the advertised list of attractions at the Palace Theatre on February 23rd, at the end of which was the line—next week: NIJINSKY. On March 2nd the Palace Theatre advertisement in *The Times* bore the announcement—"First Appearance of Nijinsky, the famous Premier Danseuse [*sic*] in *Les Sylphides* and *Le Spectre de la Rose*."

The engagement was regarded as a wonderful coup

for the Palace, then directed by Alfred (later Sir Alfred) Butt, not only for securing the services of Nijinsky, but in overcoming his well-known objections to appearing at a music-hall. It was said, and I think with justification, that Nijinsky and his troupe received the then enormous fee of one thousand pounds per week. I believe the original engagement was for three weeks, which the management confidently anticipated would extend to twelve or sixteen weeks, as in the case of Pavlova's appearance at the same theatre. This hope, however, did not materialise.

The company consisted of Vaslav Nijinsky, his sister, Bronislava Nijinska, her husband, Alexander Kotchetovsky, and Mlles. Bonni, Jwanowa, Darinska, Jakowlewa, Krasnitska, Larionowa, Poeltzich, Ptitsenko, Tarassowa.[1] The composition of the troupe was unusual in that it contained only two male dancers.

I went on the opening night, the programme for the first week consisting of *Les Sylphides*, danced by Nijinska, his sister, and a *corps de ballet*; "*Danse Orientale*" (Sinding), a *pas seul* rendered by Alexander Kotchetovsky; and *Le Spectre de la Rose*, also danced by Nijinsky and his sister.

Les Sylphides, although clearly inspired by Fokine's original ballet of the same name, differed from it in the choreography and in the selection of compositions by Chopin, here, moreover, orchestrated by Maurice Ravel; the familiar setting by Benois was replaced by an exotic conception by Boris Anisfeld.

[1]The spelling of these names conforms with that in the programme.

NIJINSKY FORMS HIS OWN COMPANY

It may be of interest to give the musical structure of the ballet. There was an overture provided by an Etude, then a Nocturne (Nijinska, Nijinsky, and *corps de ballet*), a Mazurka (Nijinsky), an Etude (Mlle. Bonni), a Mazurka (Nijinska), an Etude (Mlle. Jwanowa), a Mazurka (Nijinska, Nijinsky), and a Nocturne (Nijinska, Nijinsky, and *corps de ballet*). It will be observed that the structure has some relation to that of Fokine's ballet, in that it consists of a *pas de deux* and several *soli* framed between two *ensembles*.

All eagerness to renew the glorious memories associated with Nijinsky, I anxiously awaited the rise of the curtain, but when the stage was revealed and the ballet proceeded I could not reconcile myself either to the new scenery, the different music, or the changed choreography. And when Nijinsky himself danced I have to confess that I was conscious of a pang of disappointment. He still danced with that rare *élévation* and feeling for line and style to which I have already drawn attention, but he no longer danced like a god. Something of that mystic fragrance which previously had surrounded his dancing in *Les Sylphides* had vanished.

The second number, "*Danse Orientale*", was excellently danced by Kotchetovsky. He was attired in a fanciful version of the costume worn by a Javanese dancer in the classic style. The costume was a dull red decorated with gold. The number was originally danced by Nijinsky and there is a well-known painting by J. E. Blanche depicting him in that character. The dance was executed entirely *sur place* and consisted of admirably harmonized, if restricted, movements of the head, body, and limbs, clearly inspired by the Javanese classical dance. Kotchetovsky was loudly applauded.

The third number was the famous *Spectre de la Rose*, presented, if I remember correctly, in a black velvet curtain surround. Both Nijinsky and his sister danced superbly, yet something of the old magic had departed.

There were many members of that first night audience who were well acquainted with Nijinsky's genius, and I think that they, too, were conscious of something changed in his dancing, for, although there was plenty of applause, it lacked enthusiasm, it was polite. As number succeeded number, the house became perceptibly colder. How far removed from those wildly enthusiastic audiences of a few months before!

It is possible that a certain innovation in presentation made by Nijinsky may have contributed to this coldness. Shortly before the first performance, the dancer informed the manager of the Palace, Maurice Volny, that he wished no music to be played between the numbers while the scenery was being changed, moreover, the house lights were to remain out during the three numbers and the two intervals. The manager asked Nijinsky how long the changing of the scenery would take and was told, "about ten minutes."

Volny, well aware of Nijinsky's great reputation, agreed to this innovation and gave instructions accordingly. Nevertheless, on the opening night, Nijinsky changed his costume in the wings to ensure that his wishes were carried out. But the audience, accustomed

NIJINSKY'S OUTBURST

to the lights being turned up and the interval for changing the scene being bridged by a snatch of lively music rendered by the orchestra, became exceedingly restive at being kept waiting in a silent and darkened theatre. Angry murmurs and expressions of disapproval broke the silence and the audience showed their resentment by a cold reception of the dancers' efforts.

On the second night, Nijinsky, after dancing in *Les Sylphides*, went up to his dressing-room to change for the *Spectre*. Volny, having observed the audience's reaction to the lack of music on the previous night, had instructed the conductor, Herman Finck, to play some appropriate music between the numbers. Finck chose a composition by Tchaikovsky. During the playing of the entr'acte, someone must have gone to Nijinsky's room and informed him of the change, for, soon afterwards, Volny received an urgent call to go and see the dancer who was reported to be behaving like a madman.

Volny told me that on entering the room he found Nijinsky's dresser and some of the company crying and wringing their hands, while the dancer himself, his costume dragged off, was rolling on the ground in a mad hysterical outburst of rage. Volny, fearing that Nijinsky was about to have a fit, snatched up a jug of water he saw on a table and, hurling the contents at the dancer, shouted, "*Lève-toi!*" This stern treatment had its effect, for the dancer got up. Then Volny barked a curt "*Habille-toi!*" and left Nijinsky to dress.

Nijinsky danced as usual in the *Spectre*, but the following morning, the dancer saw Butt and his manager, and made a strong protest at the introduction of music between the numbers. When informed that Tchaikovsky was the composer, he retorted that Tchaikovsky was no musician. When it was pointed out that Pavlova herself had danced to that same music, he made a caustic reply. This was the first of several disagreements with the management.

It may be of interest to mention that a souvenir programme was issued in connection with the season. This souvenir, priced at one shilling, contained a short appreciation of Nijinsky and four full-page camera portraits reproduced in photogravure. The programme attendants who offered this souvenir also carried copies of Geoffrey Whitworth's monograph, *The Art of Nijinsky*, published in 1913 at 3s. 6d.

The second week contained a change of programme. "*Danse Orientale*" was replaced by "*Danse Polovtsienne*". But I never saw Nijinsky after the first week. I preferred to keep intact my cherished memories of the Nijinsky of 1912 and 1913.

I saw little of Gustave at this time. He was mysteriously engaged in helping Nijinsky in some capacity or other, and, when I did see him for a few moments, I gathered that all was not going well. Nijinsky had been profoundly disappointed and hurt by his reception. His nerves were frayed by the innumerable cares of management and he detested the responsibility and the necessity for constant supervision of details that went with it. He became subject to moods of intense irritability and depression, and he flew into a rage over the most trivial incident. It was said that in one such

END OF NIJINSKY'S LONDON SEASON

fit of temper he had smashed a table. He became ill and Butt was often in doubt as to whether his star performer would be able to appear that night or not.

Yet a third week, beginning March 16th, was announced, with a new change of programme: *Le Carnaval*, "*L'Oiseau et le Prince*," and "*Danse Grecque*." But, a little before 9 p.m. on the 18th, Butt received a telephone message to the effect that Nijinsky would not be able to dance that night. Frantic telephonings enabled Butt to substitute a number of well-known music-hall turns for his star attraction. But Nijinsky, now seriously ill, was forced to take a long rest in the country; later, he went abroad. The ill-fated season had ended, and with it Nijinsky had made his last appearance in London.

During March the Fine Art Society held a most interesting exhibition of portraits of Nijinsky. The exhibits included some water-colour sketches by Valentine Gross of Nijinsky in *Le Carnaval* and *Le Spectre de la Rose*; some etchings and a statuette by Una Troubridge; the fine head and shoulders drawing by J. S. Sargent of Nijinsky in *Le Pavillon d'Armide*; three portraits in oils by J. E. Blanche, among them being the well-known one of Nijinsky in "*Danse Orientale*"; and another painting in oils by Glyn Philpot, a canvas radiating the glare of the stage, which showed Nijinsky as the Faun gliding from the curtain to the footlights to take his call.

The Diaghilev Ballet returned to London in connection with Sir Joseph Beecham's Grand Season of

DIAGHILEV BALLET IN LONDON

Russian Opera and Ballet at the Theatre Royal, Drury Lane, May 20th to July 25th.

The composition of the troupe showed some important changes; the absence of Nijinska, Fedorova, Nijinsky, and Kotchetovsky, and the addition of Vera Fokina and Michel Fokine. There was talk also of a new male dancer, little more than a boy, who was to make his début, a certain Leonide Miassine discovered by Diaghilev in Moscow.

The ballet season proper opened on June 9th[1] with *Thamar*, *Daphnis et Chloé* and *Schéhérazade*, the second ballet being given in London for the first time.

I believe this was the only season when Fokine danced to an English public; his wife, however, had previously appeared at the first London season of 1911. Fokina now shared with Karsavina the roles of Zobeida in *Schéhérazade* and that of Chloë in *Daphnis et Chloé*, while Fokine appeared as the Gold Negro in *Schéhérazade* and as Daphnis in *Daphnis et Chloé*. Fokine also resumed his position as choreographic director.[2]

Thamar, I noticed, had undergone a slight change in

---

[1] The dancers made their actual first appearance on June 8th when they rendered the Polovtsian Dances in connection with the performance of the opera, *Prince Igor*.

[2] Fokine had resigned his position as choreographic director to Diaghilev's "Ballets Russes" on June 5th, 1912, after the *première* of *Daphnis et Chloé*, which was originally presented at the Théâtre du Chatelet, Paris. Nijinsky's desire to achieve fame as a choreographer, an ambition which received every encouragement from Diaghilev, had the inevitable consequences of engendering friction in the company, which finally resulted in a complete break between Fokine and Diaghilev.

its ending. The Prince was now stabbed down stage and his dead body lifted up on the shoulders of a party of the Queen's retainers, borne to the secret opening in the wall, and cast into the depths below. It is true that this alteration gave Bolm an opportunity of miming the death scene at greater length, but the new ending was not nearly so effective dramatically; indeed, the lifting of the body and the ceremonious march towards the panel verged on the commonplace.

Daphnis et Chloé, in one act and three scenes, was arranged to music specially composed by Maurice Ravel, with scenery and costumes by Léon Bakst, and choreography by Fokine. The principal characters were as follows: *Chloë*, Thamar Karsavina; *Daphnis*, Michel Fokine; *Darkon*, Adolph Bolm; *Nymphs*, Mmes. Tchernicheva, Kopycinska, Pflanz; *Lisinion*, Mlle. Majcherska; *Old Man*, Kostecky. At subsequent performances the role of Chloë was sometimes taken by Fokina.

On the morning of the London *première* the following letter appeared in *The Times*:

SIR,

My most important work *Daphnis et Chloé* is to be produced at the Drury Lane Theatre on June 9. I was overjoyed, and, fully appreciating the great honour done to me, considered the event as one of the weightiest in my artistic career.

Now I learn that what will be produced before the London public is not my work in its original form, but a makeshift arrangement which I had agreed to write at M. Diaghilev's special request in order to facilitate production in certain minor centres. M. Diaghilev probably considers London as one of those "minor centres" since he is about to produce at Drury Lane, in spite of his positive word, the new version without chorus.

I am deeply surprised and grieved; and I consider the proceeding is disrespectful towards the London public as well as towards the composer. I shall therefore be extremely thankful to you if you will kindly print this letter.

Offering you thanks in anticipation, I remain, dear sir,
faithfully yours,
MAURICE RAVEL

Paris, June 7

The following day, the 10th, *The Times* announced that M. Ravel's letter had evoked a reply from M. Diaghilev, from which they quoted the following:

"Two months ago I produced *Daphnis et Chloé* with great success at the Théâtre de l'Opéra, Monte Carlo, and I presented the second version of that work, that is to say, without a chorus. After the first performance, I received a most gratifying telegram of congratulation from M. Ravel's publisher, and the composer until yesterday never seems to have had any idea of protesting against the manner in which his work was presented, the production, in fact, meeting with unanimous approval. The second version, without a chorus, is not a haphazard affair and was very far from being written with a view to production at small theatres. The experiment of giving *Daphnis et Chloé* with chorus was tried two years ago at the Théâtre du Chatalet [*sic*] and the Théâtre des Champs Elysées, and it was clearly proved that the participation of the chorus was not only useless but actually detrimental. ... I was, therefore, obliged to beg M. Ravel to write the second version, which was successfully accomplished by the distinguished composer. I had the pleasure of asking M. Ravel to write *Daphnis et Chloé* for my ballet; more, the composer did me the honour to dedicate this remarkable work to me, and it would be very extraordinary in view of this if I had not made every effort to present it in the most perfect manner to the London public to whom I owe a very great debt of admiration and gratitude."

I have retained no outstanding impression of the principal dancers and what they did. I recall that Karsavina was attired in a short white pleated tunic reaching to her knees, her dark hair flowing down her back, and I recall that Fokine wore a shorter white tunic, and danced with a long slender white wand. I remember that these two artists danced with lovely soft movements which were the embodiment of grace and poetry. I recall, too, something of Bolm's intentionally crude and clumsy dancing as the boorish herdsman, Darkon. But that is all.

In the same way, I remember little of the ballet proper, except two contrasting episodes. In the first scene, the procession of maidens in filmy robes of classic design, bearing offerings of wine, fruit, and flowers for the altar dedicated to the glory of the God Pan, a processional dance of almost celestial beauty, a Botticelli-like vision; then, in the second scene, the dance of the drunken pirates—picturesque bronzed ruffians—a dance which ended in a thrilling scene of quarrelling and discord, of savage fighting and wrestling, admirably phrased to the music and set against a background of orange-brown cliffs and a burning blue sky.

The next new ballet was *Papillons*, which had its London *première* on the 11th. It was set to Schumann's set of pianoforte pieces of the same name, orchestrated by N. Tcherepnine. The setting was by Dobuzhinsky, the costumes by Bakst, and the choreography by Fokine. The principal characters were: *First Young Girl*, Thamar Karsavina; *Pierrot*, Michel Fokine.

Dobuzhinsky's setting, like the ballet, was a study in romanticism. The scene represented a park. The wing on either side showed a circular domed building, perhaps a relic of that 18th century passion for decorating gardens with small edifices inspired by Graeco-Roman temples. The background was formed by a low stone balustrade, broken in the centre by another small domed temple containing a classic statue; above the balustrade rose on either side a tall tree, whose sprawling branches, banked with luxurious foliage, intertwined to form a natural archway, revealing a lake and the dark silhouette of trees on the opposite bank. The scene was flooded with a mellow moonlight. The foliage, in shades of chromium green, was painted in an impressionist manner, with a series of radiating brushmarks.

It is a Carnival night in 1830 and you see a melan-

PAPILLONS

choly Pierrot wandering in the park. A group of girls dressed in canary yellow crinolines, with tiny wings attached to their shoulders, enter and flutter about him. Pierrot is entranced and, believing them to be butterflies, seeks to attract them to him with the lure of a lighted candle. By this means he captures the prettiest; but handles her so roughly that her wings fall off and she sinks to the ground as if dead.

The young girl's companions hasten to her side, and, entering into the spirit of the game, lift up the butterfly and carry her off in a sad procession. Pierrot, grief-stricken, retrieves the fallen wings and beseeches the butterflies to try and revive his sweetheart. They succeed in re-attaching the wings and the "dead" butterfly is restored to life. Pierrot is overjoyed and the butterflies dance about the happy couple.

Suddenly a clock strikes to proclaim the end of Carnival. The butterflies hasten away and return walking decorously as befits modest young ladies, accompanied by their chaperons and servants. The last of the guests to depart is a young girl wearing a mask and escorted by a handsome young man. Pierrot, dazed by this sudden transformation, looks at her wonderingly. As she passes by, she turns her head towards him, half raises her mask, and smiles. Pierrot, slowly realizing that he has been tricked, remains staring after her, overcome with the bitterness of his fate. He turns, sways, and falls headlong to the ground, his body shaken with the intensity of his grief.

Papillons was an elaborated variant of the Pierrot-Papillon incident in *Le Carnaval*, while the episode of the butterfly's death from her wings dropping off and the subsequent funeral procession were presumably adapted from analogous incidents in Taglioni's *La Sylphide*. In *Papillons*, Fokine had hoped, I believe, to achieve a second *Carnaval*, but, although the new ballet was set in the same period and even had the same composer and designer, it remained nothing more than a dainty trifle. It had a definite charm of mood and was invested with poetry and lyricism; but it was too slight, too fragile, too intimate for a big theatre, and consequently failed to make a deep impression.

There was, however, one particular moment in the ballet which I always looked forward to seeing and which never failed to strike in me a responsive chord. This moment occurred at the end of the ballet when Karsavina, passing by Pierrot, half turned her head, looked back, raised her mask, and bestowed on him a friendly smile. Actually this incident could scarcely have required more than a few seconds, yet it seemed to last quite a long while, so intense was the effect produced. The whole ballet hinged on this poignant moment. To the young girl it was just a smile of gratitude to her partner in a playful conceit, but, for Pierrot, it was the collapse of his most cherished hopes.

During this season I formed a plan to write a book on Karsavina. I had studied her in all her roles in the Diaghilev productions, but I knew little of her early career. I wrote to her at the Savoy Hotel, where at this time she was staying, and, explaining what I had in mind, asked if she would tell me something of her

VISIT TO KARSAVINA

years at the School of Ballet and of the roles she danced in the Imperial Ballet at St. Petersburg.

I received a charming letter in return and an invitation to call on her on a certain afternoon. I remember that it was a warm sunny day when I set out for the Strand. Presently I arrived at the hotel and my name was sent up. This was my first experience at interviewing a *ballerina* and I felt a little self-conscious. Various questions formed in my mind. Did she have a suite? Would she ask me into her sitting-room? I began to picture the difficulties of trying to conduct an interview in a public lounge.

Presently the door opened and Karsavina, a vision of loveliness in her gay summery attire, glided into the room. She greeted me with that half sad, half whimsical smile which is her characteristic, offered her hand and invited me to be seated and to put my questions. So the interview was to be in public after all! But this momentary disappointment vanished when she produced a number of sheets of hotel notepaper on which she herself had most kindly set down the principal events in her career. This made an excellent basis for eliciting further information. And when it was time for me to take my leave, Karsavina crowned her kindness by presenting me with a Russian brochure, a collection of tributes to her art by a group of distinguished writers, painters, and composers who formed an artistic club called *The Wandering Dog*, whose headquarters were at St. Petersburg.

Having begun work on the text of the proposed book, I began to look about for suitable illustrations.

In this connection I was introduced to a Russian photographer who was travelling with the company and had taken a number of interesting studies. He was lodging in Bloomsbury and I made an appointment to call on him one morning at 11 o'clock.

The door was opened by a trim maid who announced my arrival. A little later the photographer himself appeared. I was a little surprised to see that he had evidently just got out of bed, for he wore nothing but a nightshirt, while his bare feet were thrust into slippers.

He was most affable and led me to his bedroom, where he produced a fine selection of photographs, upon which he discoursed pleasantly and with complete unconcern for his attire. I made a selection of prints which he said he would retouch before I took them away, and that he would do this as soon as he had breakfasted.

So saying, he went to the washstand on which stood a full jug of water, into which he paddled his hands, afterwards drying them on a towel. He produced a kettle into which, to my amazement, he poured some of the water from the jug, and set it on a gas-ring to boil. Meanwhile he crept under his bed and emerged with several paper packages from which he produced a French loaf, some butter, and a piece of sausage. He made tea, and, sitting on the edge of the bed, began his meal, which he courteously invited me to share. I hastily explained that I had already breakfasted.

The meal over he went to the mantelpiece, which was littered with bottles of photographic chemicals.

LE COQ D'OR

Impatient at finding the retouching medium behind some other bottles, he swept the offending bottles aside, remaining completely indifferent when some of them rolled to the floor. Then, sitting astride a chair, he retouched each print until he was satisfied. I describe this visit just to show that bohemianism did not die with Murger.

The proposed book, however, never materialized because, while I was still engaged upon it, Henry Bruce, Karsavina's husband, brought me the typescript of an important book on Karsavina which Valerien Svetlov, the eminent Russian critic, had just completed, and which Bruce thought I might like to publish. I agreed and gave up all thought of writing a book of my own.

On June 15th came the production of *Le Coq d'Or*, an opera-ballet in 3 scenes and a prologue, based on Pushkin's well-known poem, with music by Rimsky-Korsakov, settings and costumes by Natalia Goncharova, and choreography by Fokine.

Le Coq d'Or, certainly the most popular of the new productions, provided the sensation of the season. Not only was this work presented in a quite new manner, the action being simultaneously sung by singers and danced by members of the ballet, but the whole setting was most original, even startling in the fantasy and assumed artlessness of its conception, design, and colouring. As a decorative scheme the effect was stupendous, yes, that adjective might fairly be applied to it.

DIAGHILEV BALLET IN LONDON

The principal characters[1] were taken as follows: *Queen of Shemakhan*, Thamar Karsavina, Dobrovolska; *Amelfa*, Jezierska, Petrenko; *Golden Cockerel*, no dancer, sung by Nicolaeva; *King Dodon*, Adolph Bolm, Basil Petrov; *Astrologer*, Enrico Cecchetti, Altchevsky; *General Polkan*, Kovalsky, Belianin; *Guidone*, Serge Grigoriev; *Afrone*, Max Frohman.

The first note of strangeness was struck by the sight of the singers, uniformly dressed in dull red caftans and grouped to right and left of the scene in tiers, like an oratorio choir. This mass of colour suggested two sloping banks of flowers. Behind the singers rose a fantastic background of pointed towers, enormous houses, and giant trees with enormous blossoms, an arrangement of simple bright tones of yellow, brown, rose, white, and green, which, while crude, when considered in detail, collectively produced a richly decorative effect. Goncharova had sought inspiration partly from Persian painting, partly from Russian peasant art, but these elements had been transmuted through her own intensely personal and modern outlook and profound appreciation of stage effect.

The second scene was dismal in colour and mood until cheered by the appearance from the ground of the magic tent enclosing the Queen of Shemakhan. The third scene was another composition of fantastic buildings, turrets, and steeples, the colour scheme being pink, reddish brown, green and yellow.

Le Coq d'Or was a satire on the trials and tribulations of kingship. In expressing this theme in terms of

[1] The name of the dancer is given first, then that of the singer.

choreography, Fokine adopted a quite new plan, inspired, perhaps, by the final scene of all, when, after the ballet has apparently ended, the Astrologer appears before the curtain and announces that only the Queen and himself are real, all the rest was but a dream.

This difference was adroitly suggested in the movements designed for the other characters. All their actions were crude and burlesqued. There was something stilted about the peasants and the soldiers, even about King Dodon, his sons, and his courtiers. This was also conveyed in their costumes. For instance, the dresses of the maids were bunched and formless, despite their attractive pattern and colour; again, their faces were clumsily daubed with red. Thus they resembled nothing so much as highly coloured Russian peasant toys, temporarily endowed with life.

Bulgakov created the role of Dodon in the preceding Paris season in May, but Bolm played the part in London. It was all mime and well suited to Bolm's appreciation of style-atmosphere and sense of humour. He presented King Dodon as a portly, doddering old man, weighed down with his heavy crown and thick robe, who, exhausted by the trials of a long and difficult reign, yearns only for rest and sleep, instead of which he is continually being awakened to cope with fresh threats to his throne. Indeed, matters become so serious that he is forced to take the field to defend his kingdom.

Bolm's portrait was artistically conceived in an admirable blend of pathos and humour. Take, for instance, the episode when, in unwilling response to the tiresome call of duty, he mounts his huge charger (of wood). Stifled with his breastplate, encumbered with a sword in one hand and a shield in the other, grumbling and swearing and panting from his exertions, he does his best to climb into the saddle, with the help of a ladder and the support of his courtiers. Finally, after a supreme effort provoked by utter exasperation, he reaches the saddle, but the effort is so great that he promptly reels over to the opposite side, and is only just saved from falling to the ground. Bolm's expressive features and droll actions aroused roars of laughter. Yet humorous as this incident was, there was an undercurrent of pathos in this biting comment on the disabilities and infirmities of old age.

Karsavina wore an unusual costume, a white short-sleeved blouse decorated with vertical silver stripes, close-fitting trousers of brocade, and a very short skirt decorated with large floral designs and studded with jewels. Her hair was dressed in several long thin plaits reaching to the knee, and on her head she wore a crown of pearls and diamonds.

I remember few details respecting her dancing, except that she danced barefoot, and that there were several poses suggested by Asiatic art. But I recall clearly the manner in which she conveyed that the smiling enigmatic face she showed to King Dodon, with its hint of the exquisite delights in her gift, was only a mask for a sinister purpose, soon to be revealed, to judge by a tinge of mockery, a certain sly cynicism that hovered over her lips, as he fell more and more under the fascination of her spell. Her movements

MIDAS

reflected the same mood; those sinuous arms with their languorous movements could strangle as well as caress. And so, from the moment the Queen of Shemakhan made her appearance, her beautiful but mocking features dominated the piece, reducing the brilliant figures about her to the level of marionettes which she controlled with the skill of a puppet-master. This conception of the role, like so many other things, has vanished with the passing of the company.

On June 18th there were two more new productions: *Le Rossignol* and *Midas*. The first, an opera-ballet by Stravinsky, contained some charming melodies and some fine settings and costumes by Alexandre Benois. The story was an adaptation of Andersen's well-known tale. I remember little of the production, except that when the curtain rose on one act, the stage was dimly lit, doubtless to give full value to a chain of box-shaped lanterns, glowing blue, which were spaced out on the ground in a curvilinear design enclosing the stage area.

Midas was a mythological ballet in one act, arranged to Maximilien Steinberg's *Metamorphoses*, with setting and costumes by Dobuzhinsky, and choreography by Fokine.

The principal characters were: *Oreade*, Thamar Karsavina; *Midas*, Adolph Bolm; *Apollo*, Max Frohman; and *Pan*, B. Romanov.

The story, by Bakst, deals with a musical contest between Pan, who plays his pipes, and Apollo, who plays his lyre. The presiding deity decides in favour of Apollo, which verdict is acclaimed by all, save

Midas. He, alone, prefers Pan. Thereupon, Apollo decorates Midas with a pair of ass's ears in token of his stupidity.

The best part of this production was Dobuzhinsky's setting, inspired by certain early Italian painters; the music and choreography met with a lukewarm reception.

The last and most eventful production of the season, from the musical standpoint, was *La Légende de Joseph*, which had its London *première* on June 23rd. The theme was by Hugo von Hofmannsthal and Count Harry Kessler, the music by Richard Strauss, the setting by the Spanish painter, J. M. Sert, the costumes by Léon Bakst, and the choreography by Fokine.

The setting, which evoked an archaic period, showed a great hall, bounded on three sides by a wall of gold-faced bricks, that at the back having an arched recess. Above the wall was a loggia of massive convoluted columns, in colour a metallic blue shot with green, like the wing-case of a tropical beetle. Overhead was a deep blue sky, partly obscured by the heads of tall palm-trees.

For the second episode, the stage was dimmed and only the centre recess lit. This recess, furnished with a low couch, provided the setting for the attempted seduction of Joseph by Potiphar's wife. In the final scene the whole of the stage was used.

Bakst's costumes, however, did not harmonize as well as usual with the setting, for, with a few exceptions, they were in the manner of Paolo Veronese, and

LA LÉGENDE DE JOSEPH

therefore inspired by the slashed doublets and padded trunks of 16th century Italy. I can no longer remember what was the reason for Bakst's departure from his usual regard for period, perhaps he had simply adopted the convention favoured by Veronese which caused that artist to depict biblical episodes as if they were part of the splendid age of pageantry in which he lived.

Joseph, like *Le Coq d'Or*, suffered from over-concentration on spectacle, for it was a mime play interspersed with dances rather than a ballet. The dances did not always grow out of the ballet, rather were they imposed upon it, and not an essential part of the action as in *Petrouchka*. This weakness was definite and could be felt throughout.

The music was too turgid, too scientifically constructed, too reminiscent of a difficult exercise in harmony, to be really effective. One of the best pieces of descriptive writing in the score was that at the end of the first scene, which depicted the clearing away of the feast.

The chief interest of the ballet was that it afforded a vehicle for the début of Leonide Massine, then written Miassine. At this time he appeared little more than a boy, well formed, handsome, with curly black hair, swarthy features, and dark lustrous eyes. He suggested an Italian, a Neapolitan, rather than a Russian.

He made his entrance borne in a hammock. At a signal from his owner, he stepped to the ground, when it could be seen that his sole garment was a white goatskin. Then, to the sound of a pipe, he danced a few simple steps, travelling in a circle; and that was all.

To the best of my recollection that was the sole number danced by Massine. True, it was exactly suited to a shepherd boy, but, to the majority of the audience, who had been led to expect a successor to Nijinsky, it proved a great disappointment. As a dancer, the Massine of *Joseph* gave little hint of the Massine of the *Boutique*, of *The Three Cornered Hat*, and of *Pulcinella*.

In reality, the part of *Joseph* was a mimed role, and, in that capacity, Massine achieved a remarkable success. I heard that before his engagement by Diaghilev he had been a pupil at a Moscow Dramatic School and had been intended for an actor. When, as the shepherd boy, Massine stepped shyly into the hall of Potiphar's palace, that world of materialism and vicious luxury, he vividly conveyed the mingled bewilderment and embarrassment that might be expected. And when Karsavina, as Potiphar's wife, enamoured of the boy's beauty, clasped a jewelled collar about his neck, taking the opportunity slyly to fondle him, he permitted a momentary expression of loathing, instantly repressed from a dutiful sense of submission.

Another instance of this occurred in the second scene, when Potiphar's wife enters the room where he is asleep. Seeing her in her long white gown and loose hair, he at first takes her for an angel, but when she attempts to caress him, he flings off his tunic to which she desperately clings, and bids her begone.

To present a sophisticated Georgian audience with a picture of virtue resisting the temptation of vice, was a task that called for the most skilful handling, and Massine showed himself worthy of the confidence

VISIT TO BOLM

which Diaghilev had reposed in him, for the young artist invested his conception with a dignity and poetry that have not faded from my recollection.

The ballet season ended on Saturday, July 25th, the programme being *Papillons*, *La Légende de Joseph*, and *Petrouchka*. On that evening Sir Joseph Beecham was called before the curtain with the principal dancers, who presented him with a gilt laurel wreath.

A few days later I went to call on Bolm, at his flat near Marble Arch. I remember his receiving me informally, reclining on a sofa, while he dried his thick curly hair which he had just shampooed. He was strangely moody and reserved, for the political situation was changing rapidly and for the worse. There was an ominous portent in the air. Little did I dream that the First Great War was about to burst on the world and that four terrible and tragic years were to pass before the Diaghilev Ballet could return to London, the scene of its greatest triumphs.

CHAPTER IV

~ 1918–1919 ~

FOLLOWING the outbreak of the Great War, little had been heard of the Diaghilev Company. It was said to be touring in Spain and hard put to it to keep going. But, as war news took easy precedence over news relative to artistic matters, it can easily be imagined that there was little reference to the doings of the Diaghilev Company.

Some time in the summer of 1918 I had a surprise visit from Zenon, whose acquaintance I had made through our mutual friend, Gustave de Beer. Zenon had been a "non-com." in the Alexandrinsky Hussars. On leaving the army he had tried his hand at various jobs and finally came to be attached to the Diaghilev Company. A man in the forties, spare, dark, and with a bristling iron-grey moustache, his keen glance and determined manner smacked of military training. He was well informed about the business side of the theatre and carried out the most varied tasks for Diaghilev.

I remember his telling me on one occasion how, when the troupe was in Spain, Diaghilev confided his entire capital to his care—some four hundred pounds in notes—for fear that he himself might lose the money. So for days Zenon walked about with the notes sewn inside the lining of his waistcoat.

He hardly ever missed a performance by the company, and could usually be encountered somewhere at the back of the auditorium, contributing to the successful reception of the performance by clapping the entrance and exit of every soloist. He could produce a terrific measured hand-clap which could easily be heard above the general applause.

From Zenon I learned that Diaghilev, finding it more and more difficult to carry on abroad as a result of the War, was preparing to brave the U-boats and air-raids and bring his troupe to London, to which end Zenon, who spoke English well, despite a tendency to substitute "v" for "w", had been empowered to discuss preliminaries with Sir Oswald Stoll.

On Monday, July 29th, there appeared in the Daily Press, under the week's programme of the Coliseum Theatre, the following: "Next Week: The Original Russian Ballet from the Theatre St. Marie [*sic*], Petrograd, under direction of Serge de Diaghilew". This notice was soon altered to the more general announcement that the "Russian Ballet will shortly commence a season of ballets from their repertoire. Special bills will be issued shortly announcing date of arrival in England and date of first performance."

The weeks went by and on September 2nd a new announcement appeared in the press stating, "Owing to the non-arrival of essential costumes the Management reluctantly regret to have to postpone the first appearance to September 5th." The reason was that the difficulties of transport in wartime had proved almost insuperable, and that the company were able to arrive at all was largely due to the kind offices of the King of Spain.

Eager to renew acquaintance with Karsavina and Bolm, I went to the Coliseum to see if there were any new photographs of them. There were some photographs and a polished board bearing the names of the *ballerina* and *premier danseur*, and those of the soloists. Here is the list: Lydia Lopokova, Lubov Tchernicheva, Lydia Sokolova, Josephine Cecchetti, Felia Radina, Alexandra Wassilevska, Marie Zaleska; Leonide Massine, Alexander Gavrilov, Enrico Cecchetti, Nicholas Kremnev, Stanislas Idzikowsky, Leon Woizikowsky, Jean Jazvinsky. I was dumbfounded to discover that the well-known names of Karsavina, Fokina, Piltz, Nijinska, Fedorova, Fokine, and Bolm were absent, and in their place names which, with the two exceptions of those of Enrico Cecchetti and Stanislas Idzikowsky, were quite unknown to me.

On returning home I studied my programme of the 1914 season and wondered if M. Miassine, whose only appearance had been as Joseph in *La Légende de Joseph*, could have become Leonide Massine. Clearly there had been several promotions, for Mlle. Tchernicheva had become Lubov Tchernicheva, while M. Gavrilov and Kremnev had become Alexander Gavrilov and Nicholas Kremnev. Later I learned that Mlle. Munings had become Lydia Sokolova, the surname being borrowed from that of the celebrated Russian dancer of the 19th century.

As Diaghilev did not consider the small company which he had brought from Spain sufficiently large for a London season, he held, soon after his arrival and before the season began, an audition of promising British dancers. Among those engaged[1] were Vera Clark (a product of the Stedman School who, at a competition held on March 16th at the Olympia to find a British *première danseuse*, won "an easy first against all comers", to quote the terms of the award); Rachel Lanfranchi; Doreen Miller (Pavlovska); Dyta Morena (Istomina); Joyce Pettit (Petipa); and Laura Wilson (Olkhina).

One of the first tasks of the newly enrolled British dancers was to learn some of the *ensemble* work in *Cléopâtre*, in which connection Laura Wilson once told me an amusing incident. One of the Russian *corps de ballet* was detailed to teach the movements. Having expounded the first sequence of movements, she pointed dramatically to herself and announced, "Here, *me—solo!*" Then she taught the movements which followed the solo. On the night of their appearance in *Cléopâtre* the British girls all watched intently for the famous solo, which, somewhat to their amusement, proved to consist of a single crossing of the stage!

The British dancers, accustomed to the carefree spirit of rehearsals on the London stage, found work in the Diaghilev Company something of a strain, both mental and physical. It was not easy to grasp instructions given in a mixture of Russian, French, and broken

[1] See Appendix C for a typical contract.

English. Further, the dancers were expected to maintain a serious demeanour, a smile at rehearsal was thought to denote wandering attention or lack of intelligence. The rehearsals were carried out with the utmost vigour and the dancers exercised unceasingly and relentlessly until the particular quality of execution desired was attained.

There was a pleasant spirit of good comradeship among the members of the company, although the predominating Russian element naturally tended to draw together. The English dancers sometimes found the Russian dancers' outlook on the conventions a little difficult to grasp, for it was somewhat contradictory. Excessively modest in regard to some matters, they were very broad-minded in other respects. For instance, it was difficult for some of them to comprehend that a man or woman might prefer to live unattached to a member of the opposite sex.

In this connection I recall an amusing conversation related to me by an English *danseuse*, who happened to meet a Russian member of the "Ballets Russes" to which she had formerly belonged. Shaking her warmly by the hand, he enquired:

"And how have you been getting on after all this time?"

"Oh, not too badly. I've had quite a number of jobs, one way and another."

"I suppose you married long ago?"

"No, I'm still single."

"But you're living with someone, of course?"

"No."

MASSINE'S DEBUT AS CHOREOGRAPHER

"Dear, dear, I *am* sorry for you—and such a nice girl, too!"

The repertory for the first week was *Cléopâtre* (matinée) and *The Good Humoured Ladies* (evening). I saw the London *première* of Massine's ballet, the cast being as follows: *Marquise Silvestra*, Josephine Cecchetti; *Mariuccia*, Lydia Lopokova; *Constanza*, Lubov Tchernicheva; *Felicita*, Lydia Sokolova; *Dorotea*, Felia Radina; *Pasquina*, Hélène Antonova; *Marquis di Luca*, Enrico Cecchetti; *Leonardo*, Leonide Massine; *Battista*, Stanislas Idzikowsky; *Count Rinaldo*, Sigismond Novak; *Niccolo*, Leon Woizikowsky; *Count Faloppa*, Jean Jazvinsky; *Beggar*, M. Kostrovsky; *Street Musicians*, MM. Kostetsky, Mascagno.

This was Massine's first introduction to London as a choreographer and I came away with a divided opinion. I was not sure whether I liked the ballet or not. The unusual speed of performance was a little bewildering, and I could not get accustomed to the jerky, puppet-like quality of Massine's choreography, so different from the rounded and flowing movements of Fokine's compositions. Old Cecchetti as the Marquis di Luca had a part which suited him to perfection, but I was not quite sure whether I approved the other dancers. The fact is, I was still lamenting the absence of Karsavina, Nijinsky, and Bolm.

I went to see the ballet again and again, and the more I saw of it the more I liked the music—a selection by Vincente Tommasini from some 500 of Scarlatti's sonatas, with some portions rendered on a genuine eighteenth century spinet—which André Levinson so aptly likened to liquid sunshine; Bakst's setting with its reminiscence of the paintings of Guardi, Longhi, and Canaletto; and the appropriateness of Massine's choreography, whose beauties were gradually revealed to me.

I came to see that his dances did far more than accompany the music and accord with its rhythmical structure, they really translated the spirit of the music into terms of choreography. The miming, too, was quite unusual in that it was not separated from the actual dancing, but, so to speak, grafted on it. Thus the whole ballet was a continuous flow of expressive movement unbroken until the very end, the sequence being adroitly subjected to variations in mood and speed to afford contrast and variety. Finally, each artist danced in the very mood of Goldoni's comedy; their actions seemed spontaneous, bubbling over with irrepressible high spirits.

Was there ever a more rollicking number than the famous scene, half mime, half dance, at the supper-table, when the four revellers—the Marquis, Leonardo, Battista, and Mariuccia—while sharing the repast which Mariuccia has provided for them—clap their hands and stamp their feet, toasting first their pretty hostess and then in turn each other, banging their glasses on the table and clashing their knives and forks to the infectious lilt of the music.

Accustomed to the sweet sadness of Karsavina with her intensely poetical style of dancing, Lopokova's personality was such a complete surprise to me that, on first acquaintance, it was a trifle puzzling. She remains the first and only dancer I have ever seen who was a born comedienne. Petite and well formed, she was as lively as a London sparrow. She danced not only with her limbs, but with her head, her eyes, her shoulders, and even her lips.

Lopokova revelled in the part of Mariuccia and was the very incarnation of the vivacious maid in Pietro Longhi's painting, *My Lady's Toilet*. She was so full of vitality, so exhilarating, so ready to share in every prank, so spontaneous in all her actions and expressions, that she radiated happiness whenever she appeared. Yet, if she played the part of a soubrette, it was not a modern conception clothed in historical costume; her soubrette had a mellow quality, the glaze of a past epoch, a suggestion of period graces which gave a final touch to her performance, just as the passage of time confers a particular quality on the colouring of a painting.

I shall always remember her as Mariuccia, wearing her becoming white wig and paniered, ochre-coloured frock barred with red, and the violet bow at her breast; together with the little mannerism she had of tilting her head on one side and slightly arching her expressive eyebrows, while her lips perpetually trembled between a pout and a smile.

Later in the week I went to see *Cléopâtre*, now deprived of its original setting by Bakst, which always filled you with a sense of impending tragedy the moment you saw it. In its place was a new setting by Robert Delaunay, conceived in the violently contrasted colours and cubist shapes then regarded as the most advanced artistic expression. The setting was certainly striking and theatrically effective, but the colouring was strident and irritating. It contributed no mood and detracted from the ballet as a whole, since the blinding colours continually intruded upon one's vision. The majority of the Bakst costumes were not those of the original production, but a medley of dresses adapted from *Le Dieu Bleu* and other ballets, which, naturally, did not harmonize with the new setting. There was also a new costume for Cleopatra, designed by Sophie Delaunay; it was another vivid conception in yellow, red, and gold, not improved by a segment of mirror-glass affixed to the girdle, which winked like a heliograph every time it caught the light.

The cast was as follows: *Cleopatra*, Lubov Tchernicheva; *Amoun*, Leonide Massine; *Ta-Hor*, Lydia Sokolova; *Favourite Slaves of Cleopatra*, Felia Radina and Alexander Gavrilov; *High Priest*, M. Kovalski; the "*Bacchanale*" was danced by Lopokova.

Tchernicheva made a regal Cleopatra, whom she portrayed as a cold, enigmatic, sadistic being, quite different from the voluptuous woman presented by Astafieva. Massine was interesting as Amoun, though he did not convey the suppressed passion of Bolm's rendering; Massine was at his best in the death scene. Sokolova was a good Ta-Hor, and the episodes of her love for Amoun and despair at his death were well mimed, but not distinguished by any original touches. She lacked the range and subtlety of Fedorova, whose performance I have already described. Fedorova almost let you see her heart beating for her betrothed, and you could feel the dry sob that rose in her throat when, in an agony of fear and apprehension, she drew back a corner of the dark pall spread on the sand and looked upon the glazed eyes of her dead lover.

Lopokova appeared for a brief space to dance the "*Bacchanale*". Clad in a short white tunic, decorated with small green circles, and reaching just below the knees of her bare legs, she danced like a Maenad and electrified the audience with the sheer joy and seemingly boundless vitality of her movements.

Cléopâtre, however, was never a great ballet. A link between the old ballet and the new school of Fokine, it owed its success to individual performances rather than to the effect achieved by the whole, and its drama was heightened by Bakst's setting and costumes. The new setting and makeshift costumes made the ballet appear a little tawdry and the choreography seemed to date.

September 9th saw *Le Carnaval* added to the repertory. The cast was: *Columbine*, Lydia Lopokova; *Chiarina*, Lubov Tchernicheva; *Estrella*, Felia Radina; *Papillon*, Lydia Sokolova; *Harlequin*, Stanislas Idzikowsky; *Pierrot*, Alexander Gavrilov; *Eusebius*, Leonide Massine; *Pantalon*, Enrico Cecchetti; *Florestan*, Leon Woizikowsky.

The curtain was blue, and not green, as in pre-War times, while the famous little sofas had given place to others which were practical rather than decorative. The ballet was as lively as ever, but the role of Pierrot had shed something of the dramatic importance associated with Bolm's interpretation; and, with Lopokova and Idzikowsky as Columbine and Harlequin, the production took on the air of an innocent romp at a children's party. Even the entry of the Philistines suggested parents come to collect their offspring. In the pre-War *Carnaval*, the company, led by Karsavina and Nijinsky, suggested a costume ball, at which the dancers flirted and made love with a knowledge born of experience. On the surface, all was gaiety; but, beneath the maskings and dalliance, you were conscious of a certain mockery and cynicism, even a hint of tragedy.

Massine looked very poetic in his well-cut coat of crimson velvet. Tchernicheva made a tender Chiarina. But the chief attraction was Lopokova and Idzikowsky. Lopokova's fair hair, dressed in ringlets, was a novelty, for the other Columbines I had seen—Karsavina, Kshesinskaya, Fokina—had all been dark. Lopokova's Columbine was a lady of moods—by turns affectionate, piquant, playful, or teasing. Idzikowsky was a sprightly Harlequin, full of roguish pranks; moreover, he had the technical ability for the role and turned his *pirouettes*, especially the difficult *pirouettes à la seconde*, with admirable ease and finish. But he was puckish and impudent, where Nijinsky was cynical and sly. Idzikowsky's triumphant smiles at the success of his tricks were the smiles of a waggish schoolboy; those of Nijinsky were fleeting and tinged with mockery. Idzikowsky was inclined to exaggerate the shaking of the head, and swing it in a wide arc, whereas Nijinsky's

DIAGHILEV RENEWS HIS WARDROBE

head movement was so momentary and so exquisitely timed that it had all the force of a mark of exclamation.

I have referred to Diaghilev's having been hard pressed for money when in Spain, and when he landed in London the lounge suit and Homburg hat which he continued to wear were distinctly shabby. The success of the London season, however, enabled him to effect a complete renewal of his wardrobe, for one day he appeared in the theatre wearing a new bowler, new overcoat, new suit with dove grey spats, and carried an expensive-looking walking-stick. An eye-witness told me that when Diaghilev appeared that day behind the scenes after the ballet, the Russian members of the troupe crowded round him with expressions of admiration, fingering his clothes and praising the quality of the materials, while the director smiled proudly like an indulgent parent surrounded by his children.

September 16th saw the revival of the *Polovtsian Dances from "Prince Igor,"* with Lopokova and Tchernicheva respectively as a Maid and Woman of the Polovtsi, and Massine as the Chief. I do not believe that either the setting or the costumes were those of the original production. Certainly the costumes were not; they lacked the blending of deep ochres and dull reds and greens of the costumes worn by Bolm's warriors, which gave the dancers such an appropriately uncouth, earth-stained appearance.

Tchernicheva was languorous, Lopokova full of vitality, and Massine danced with appropriate vigour as the Chief, but, despite the forcefulness of his dancing, he did not realize that savage impetuous ardour which made Bolm's performance so memorable.

The *Polovtsian Dances* were preceded by a *pas de deux* styled "*The Enchanted Princess*," actually the "*Blue Bird*" *pas de deux* from Petipa's *La Belle au Bois Dormant*. The costumes, designed by Bakst, were not so attractive as usual. Lopokova wore a green pearl-embroidered turban, and a short mauve ballet-skirt with a green bodice. Idzikowsky was attired in a jewelled pink and white headdress and doublet which suggested Oriental inspiration; his tights were blue, later changed to dull red. It was a good performance in which Idzikowsky aroused great applause for his fine *élévation* and the precision and brilliance of his *cabrioles* and *brisés*.

Later in the same week, on the 19th, *Papillons* was given with the original setting and costumes. The cast was: 1*st Young Girl*, Lydia Lopokova; 2*nd Young Girl*, Lubov Tchernicheva; *Pierrot*, Leonide Massine.

It was about this time that a dapper Italian in the thirties, a most engaging and vivid personality, called at my shop in search of some book on dancing. We talked about Ballet and so came to discuss the Diaghilev Company at the Coliseum. On leaving he gave me his card, inscribed *Randolfo Barocchi*, and disclosed the fact that he was acting as business manager to Diaghilev. His final words were: "Do come round to the stage door whenever you are at the ballet and ask for me. I should like you to meet my wife—Lydia Lopokova."

Barocchi had an infectious charm which swept you off your feet. He had the expressive features of his race and walked with the light springy tread of a dancer. His head was most unusual in shape, due to the abnormally high forehead, and might fairly be compared to a marrow stood on end. This characteristic was the more pronounced because he was an unusually small man. His complexion was pale and heightened by his jet black hair. But while the hair on his crown was sparse, he could boast of a well-trimmed beard and whiskers. Although an Italian, there was something Oriental about him; he might easily have passed for a Persian.

When next I went to the Coliseum I encountered Barocchi in the foyer, and after the ballet he took me "behind" to make the acquaintance of Lopokova. That introduction led to a friendship which I am still privileged to enjoy to-day.

Lopokova off the stage was very much like Mariuccia on it. Under medium height, she had a compact, well formed little body which would have delighted Théophile Gautier. Her hair was very fair, fluffed out at the forehead, and gathered in a little bun at the nape of her neck. She had small blue eyes, pale plump cheeks, and a curious nose, something like a hummingbird's beak, which gave a rare piquancy to her expression. She had a vivacious manner, alternating with moods of sadness. She spoke English well, with an attractive accent, and had a habit of making a profound remark as though it were the merest badinage. And I must not forget her silvery laugh.

I went quite often to the ballet and from time to time I would pay a visit to my new friends. Lopokova had a very pleasant dressing-room off the passage leading from the stage-door to the stage, where most of the principals were accommodated. The room was well heated and comfortably furnished with a dressing-table, sofa, and various chairs, all covered with a gay cretonne. In one corner there was a wash-basin and in another a cretonne-covered hanging-space for costumes. There were also several mirrors of various sizes, that on the dressing-table having pinned to its frame two or three sketches of the dancer by Laura (later Dame Laura) Knight. Occasionally I was permitted to be present when Lopokova was making-up, and for me the rite of make-up is one of the most interesting spectacles to be encountered behind the scenes.

Sometimes, when the ballet was over, I would walk home with my friends to the Savoy Hotel where they were staying, and sometimes we would meet for tea or dinner. Lopokova had no exalted ideas as to her importance. As soon as she had taken leave of those who came to pay her homage, she would wipe off her make-up—she never put very much on—and change into a simple short skirt, woolly jumper, and tam-o-shanter, skipping home like a schoolgirl let out of school. She had an ingenuous manner of talking, but she was very intelligent and witty, and, unlike some dancers, her conversation was not limited to herself and the Ballet.

Barocchi was a whole theatrical entertainment in himself. He was a remarkable linguist and spoke English, French, Italian, Russian, Spanish, and, I believe, German, with equal facility. It was an amazing experience to see him receiving visitors of all nationalities who came to see Lopokova. He would greet one in English, answer another in French, crack a joke with a third in Russian, and so forth, and, at the same time, adapt himself to the company of the moment. He had an extraordinary range of anecdotes, some very amusing indeed, if not always suited to the drawing-room, which gained additional point from his graphic manner of description. Some of his stories concerned personalities in the world of dancing, whose mannerisms of speech and gesture he could imitate to perfection. For instance, in a flash he would compress his mouth into a certain shape, place an imaginary eye-glass in his eye, and give you Diaghilev to the life. And Barocchi had the Latin's admiration for the fair sex. The sight of a beautiful woman passing in the street made the day a memorable one; it afforded him a genuinely æsthetic, if sensuous, pleasure which added new zest to his already crowded life.

One night I went to the stage door to see Barocchi before the ballet, but he had not yet arrived. While I waited, I noticed by the stage-doorkeeper's office a large poster announcing some charity performance, at which Lopokova and Massine would appear. Lopokova's name, however, was in much larger type than that of Massine, due, as I afterwards learnt, to some misconception on the part of the organiser as to Massine's importance.

Presently Massine arrived. While he waited for his key, he caught sight of the poster and visibly snorted with indignation. He walked swiftly into his dressing-room at the head of the passage and closed the door. A little later Diaghilev came in. He strolled to Massine's room, turned the handle, and seemed surprised to find that the door remained shut. Thinking, presumably, that Massine had not arrived, he went down the passage in search of Grigoriev. While I was wondering whether I should continue to wait, Diaghilev re-appeared at the far end of the passage, accompanied by Grigoriev, both deep in conversation and looking anxious.

Grigoriev glanced at his wrist-watch, went to Massine's room, and tried the handle, but the door remained obstinately shut. Grigoriev, surprised in his turn, asked the door-keeper if he had seen M. Massine. When he replied that he had given him his key a quarter of an hour before, director and stage-manager looked at each other in amazement. Together they crossed to Massine's room and tried the door once more. They called to him, but all was silence. They banged on the door with their fists, but there was no reply. Still puzzled, tall, slight Grigoriev and massive Diaghilev, as though actuated by a mutual impulse, sank on their haunches and tried to peer through the keyhole, bumping their heads in the process. Their enterprise was rewarded, for Massine was evidently visible, to judge by the torrent of indignant Russian that followed. It was one of the most comical sights I have witnessed, to see those two important persons squatting before a keyhole like a pair of inquisitive schoolboys, alternately threatening, pleading, and cajoling, until Massine finally consented to open the door and go on the stage.

Schéhérazade was revived on October 11th. The Bakst scenery, however, was only a shadow of its former self. The lamps had vanished and the whole set appeared to have been crudely simplified, and to have lost its subleties of colour and lighting, in particular the mysterious shadows at the base of the walls, which hinted at so much.

The cast was: *Zobeida*, Lubov Tchernicheva; *Gold Negro*, Leonide Massine; *Shahriar*, Whitworth Jones; *Shah Zeman*, Jean Jazvinsky; *Chief Eunuch*, Enrico Cecchetti; *Odalisque*, Alexandra Wassilevska.

Karsavina had presented a clinging, indolent Zobeida; Tchernicheva portrayed a spoilt woman, but was so regal in her manner that it was difficult to imagine her giving herself to a negro, who, moreover, was one of her lord's slaves. She was particularly impressive in the closing scene where she stabs herself to death, which she mimed with poetry and feeling.

Massine's Negro was quite different from that of Nijinsky. He did not burst from the blue door like a wild animal released from a cage, then, with a sudden change of mood, indolently stretch his arms before he embraced his mistress; he hovered about Zobeida with quick nervous steps and caressing gestures in the manner of the true voluptuary, who finds pleasure in the excitation of desire, rather than in the satisfying of it.

On October 31st a new production, *Sadko*, was presented; it was preceded by the *pas de deux* styled "*The Enchanted Princess*", the third movement of *Antar* being played as an entr'acte. This was not the *Sadko* produced at Paris in 1910, with choreography by Fokine and setting and costumes by Anisfeld, but a new conception with choreography by Adolph Bolm and costumes by Natalia Goncharova. Although new to London, I imagine it was first produced in Spain during the War, when Bolm was acting as choreographer to the company. The ballet was based on the well-known Russian legend which forms the theme of Rimsky-Korsakov's opera of the same name, the music used being selected from the same source.

This is the story. Sadko plays so marvellously on his *gusli* that, when he goes to sea with his friends, the Sea King's daughter becomes enamoured of him. She causes a storm to rise and the vessel is like to be capsized when Sadko, to save his companions, leaps into the sea.

When he arrives at the bottom of the sea, he is invited to play at the Sea King's Court. He accepts and soon the King and all his subject creatures are dancing to Sadko's inspiring melodies. The dances become wilder and wilder, so that the sea itself is set in motion. Sadko, seeing that his playing is about to produce a new storm, snaps the strings of his *gusli* and returns to the surface, bearing with him the Sea King's daughter.

I remember a greenish-blue scene, formed of cut-cloths suggestive of sea-plants and inhabited by glistening figures costumed to represent goldfish, sea plants, fishes of various species, sea currents, and sea horses. In a misty light, Sadko, *gusli* in hand, was seen gliding

THE MIDNIGHT SUN

down to the sea bottom, when he was presented to the Sea King and his daughter. He plucked at the strings of his *gusli* and the various inhabitants began to dance, at first slowly, then with gathering speed. Finally, he cast away the *gusli*, and, taking the King's daughter in his arms, slowly ascended to the surface.

The principal characters were taken thus: *Sea King's Daughter*, Lubov Tchernicheva; *Sadko*, Jean Jazvinsky; and *Sea King*, Whitworth Jones; but the composition was really an *ensemble* ballet. The production was attractive, but I do not recall that it made any particular impression on me.

The Midnight Sun was produced on November 21st. This, although the second Massine ballet to be seen in London, was chronologically his first essay in choreography. It was not so much a ballet as a series of formal dances, founded on Russian folk dances, presented in a stylised Russian setting. It owed its success to the lively music by Rimsky-Korsakov, selected from his *Snegouroutchka*; the two *soli* by Lopokova and Massine respectively; and Larionov's gay setting and costumes, inspired by Russian peasant art.

The principal characters were: the *Midnight Sun*, Leonide Massine; *the Snow Maiden*, Lydia Lopokova; *Bobyl*, Leon Woizikowsky.

The production was suggested by the traditional dances held in certain parts of Russia in honour of the midnight sun, doubtless a survival of some primitive folk ritual, in which the whole village took part. The ballet opened with formal figures by dancers in exaggerated peasant costumes, with headdresses of deep red and gold. Then the dancers, joined by the shepherds in white smocks and the village fool, sat down in a circle to watch the dance of the Snow Maiden (danced to the *Song of Lel*, sung "off" by Zoia Rosovska). Finally, the Sun God appeared in a radiant costume of fire red and gold, his breast decorated with a giant sun and holding a resplendent red and gold sun in each hand, which scintillated as they were passed rapidly in front of each other or shot out at arm's length at various angles. The ballet ended with a well-arranged *ensemble* in which a number of buffoons entered and belaboured their friends with bladders tied to short sticks.

Woizikowsky was good as Bobyl (the Idiot), with his vacant stare and his curious manner of shuffling and hopping with bent knees, his arms hanging limply before him. It was a novelty to see Lopokova in stylised Russian peasant dress, white relieved with masses of vivid colour, and wearing bast shoes. How admirably she brought out the contrasting moods of the dance! First the slow dragging movements of the feet and the gradually extended arms, then the arms swept downwards over the shoulders, to be followed by a burst of lively footwork accompanied by the swift turning up and down of the wrists extended in a line with the shoulders. Massine was a fine figure as the Sun God, resplendent in red, yellow, and gold. I think it was in this dance that he first introduced that step of his own invention, in which, while leaping vertically upwards, he bent one knee under him and extended the other sideways—a kind of *prisiadka* step, executed sideways while in the air.

IMPRESSIONS OF THE RUSSIAN BALLET

The return of the Diaghilev Company, which revived so many memories, stirred me to attempt some publications dealing with the troupe, and I planned a series of monographs on each ballet, to be called *Impressions of the Russian Ballet*. Each booklet was to tell the story of a ballet and to be illustrated with one large and four small illustrations in the text, all to be coloured by hand. Colour was such a vital part of the ballets that I felt this to be imperative, and I decided on hand-colouring because it seemed to me so much brighter and so much more imbued with the spirit of the theatre than illustrations reproduced by the three-colour process. I decided to attempt the text myself, and I wanted to achieve not only a description of the ballet, but also to convey in words something of the movement of the dancers.

The first books to be planned were *Cléopâtre*, *The Good Humoured Ladies*, *Carnaval*, and *Schéhérazade*, and I chose Adrian Allinson to make the drawings. I remember quite well how delighted I was with his work, which captured both the colour and movement of the ballets. But it was a laborious task to colour the books, which work for a long time was done entirely by my wife and myself. Allinson also made drawings of *Papillons*, *Sadko*, *Igor*, and *The Midnight Sun*, but, as none of these furnished sufficient material for a whole book, they were never used.

On December 23rd a new Massine ballet was given —*Children's Tales*. The music was an arrangement of Liadov's melodies on Russian themes. The cast was as follows: *Dance Prelude*, Leon Woizikowsky; *Kikimora*,

Lydia Sokolova; the *Cat*, Stanislas Idzikowsky; *Swan Princess*, Lubov Tchernicheva; *Bova Korolevich*, Leonide Massine; *Baba Yaga*, Nicholas Kremnev; *Little Girl*, Hélène Antonova. The peasant dance at the end of the Dragon's Funeral was danced by Sophie Pavlovska and Leon Woizikowsky.

The London production differed from previous presentations abroad, in that it was revised and enlarged by the addition of two comic interludes newly composed by Massine.

The ballet made a considerable impression and it had many claims to success. It was intended to be a kind of folk play expressed in dance-mime, inspired by Russian legends and fairy tales. The scenery, by Michel Larionov, was quite unusual, being conceived in the vivid colouring characteristic of Russian peasant decoration, but interpreted in the modernist spirit. The designs and colouring were full of fantasy. Every ballet-goer will remember the great yellow wall, green stove, and orange beams of the Kikimora episode; the decorative blue, grey, and green drop-curtain which symbolized the mysterious lake where the Swan Princess watched at night for the coming of her longed-for deliverer; the Bova Korolevich scene with its green scaly dragons and pink palace set against a blood-red sky; and the fantastic blue-green grove where the horrid Baba Yaga lurked in ambush to seize stray children.

The ballet was intensely Russian in spirit, and, with the exception of the classical number for the Swan Princess, with its exhausting pose *en arabesque*, all the

NOTABLE PERFORMANCES IN CHILDREN'S TALES

choreography was based on Russian folk-dance technique, although every dance had some twist, a Massine flavour, as it were, which gave it originality of expression.

The most unusual number was the Kikimora scene, an extraordinary presentation of venomous hate, most forcibly rendered by Sokolova, whose striped make-up gave her a fiendish appearance. Idzikowsky's remarkable *élévation* was admirably suited to the Cat, and his miming was excellent, especially his sorrow at the death of the dragon. The whimsical manner in which he despondently shook his head, and dabbed his eyes with an orange handkerchief dangling from a trembling hand, used to make Diaghilev shake with laughter.

Woizikowsky rendered his lively dance with a captivating phrasing and feeling for choreographic colour which were a joy alike to the eye and ear. Massine made a knightly Bova Korolevich, his dexterous sword play contrasted with archaic poses inspired by ikon decoration. Kremnev, as Baba Yaga, evoked a nightmare vision, with his humped back, hooked nose, and awe-inspiring twirl on the "bone" projecting from his heel, and his sudden rise and poising on it.

So much for the ballet. Perhaps this little anecdote may also be of interest. The awesome masks worn in the Baba-Yaga scene by the wood-demons, with their long straggling beards of bast, were kept in a room at the end of the passage from the stage-door, which room served as a combined office and store-room. Barocchi was greatly attached to these masks and would sometimes amuse himself by putting one of them on, and then, suddenly peeping in at the door of Lopokova's room, startle friends come to visit her.

During the new year, two more ballets were revived—*Les Sylphides*, on January 20th, and *Thamar*, on March 17th. In *Les Sylphides* the male dancer was alternately Massine or Gavrilov, but the traditional fair wig did not suit the former. The three soloists were Lopokova, Tchernicheva, and Radina, an Italian dancer. Tchernicheva was not the best technician of the three, but I think she came nearest to the attainment of that sweet melancholy which is the keynote of the ballet. The performance on the whole was good, particularly with Gavrilov, an excellent classical dancer, but I missed the lovely Benois setting, for which a design by Socrate had been substituted, an avenue of green trees relieved by a stone fountain set in the central pathway.

Thamar, with Tchernicheva and Massine as Thamar and the Stranger Prince respectively, was given with the original setting and costumes, but the vital spark had gone from it. To be frank, what had once been a choreographic drama, a kind of Russian *Tour de Nesle*, had become rather obvious melodrama, charged with a fatal element of humour, due to the disproportionate heights of Tchernicheva, who was tall, and Massine, whose slight build made him appear boyish. When the splendid Bolm was ensnared by the appropriately smaller Karsavina, the situation became dramatic, but, with Tchernicheva and Massine, you could not help thinking of the latter as a boy led astray.

I have said little about the *corps de ballet*, yet that

IMPORTANCE OF THE CORPS DE BALLET

hard-working group had had a new importance ever since 1914, when the Diaghilev Company had been newly constituted as a complete and separate organization. No matter how much the choreographers and soloists might change, a trained and well-rehearsed *corps de ballet* was the keystone of the enterprise. It included several dancers destined in after years to achieve varying degrees of success, for instance, Allanova, Evina, Istomina, and Klementowicz, not to mention Nemchinova I, who, as Vera Nemchinova, was destined to achieve the rank of *ballerina* in the troupe, and Clark, afterwards Vera Clark, and later known as Vera Savina, who was the only dancer of British origin in the Diaghilev Company to dance the principal role in *Les Sylphides*.

The season, which lasted for over six months, surely a record for an engagement of a company of dancers, ended on March 29th, with *Schéhérazade* (matinee) and *Les Sylphides* (evening).

CHAPTER V

~ 1919 ~

EXACTLY one month had elapsed when the Diaghilev Company, flushed with its success at the Coliseum, began, at the Alhambra Theatre, again in association with Sir Oswald Stoll, a new season which was to run from April 30th to July 30th. The troupe was the same with the addition of Nicholas Zverev and Anatol Bourman, while Vera Nemchinova and Leokadia Klementowicz were promoted to soloists. It was also announced that Thamar Karsavina would rejoin the company, while Lydia Kyasht, Karsavina's bosom friend at the time they were pupils of the Imperial School for Ballet, St. Petersburg, and Alice Vronska were also to appear. To the best of my recollection, however, Vronska did not dance at all.

The repertory was to be the same as at the Coliseum, but, in addition, four revivals were promised, namely, *Petrouchka*, *L'Oiseau de Feu*, *Narcisse*, and *Daphnis et Chloé*; then *Parade*, hitherto only given at Paris, was to be performed in London for the first time; while three entirely new ballets—*La Boutique Fantasque*, *The Three Cornered Hat*, and *The Gardens of Aranjuez*—were to be presented for the first time on any stage.

LOPOKOVA AS THE DANCER IN PETROUCHKA

The season began on April 30th with *The Good Humoured Ladies*, *Petrouchka*, and *Les Sylphides*. Lopokova was the *Dancer*; Massine, *Petrouchka*; Zverev, the *Moor*; and Cecchetti, the *Old Showman*. The ballet was given with the original costumes and scenery.

Massine was good as Petrouchka, but he remained a dancer, he did not give you that uncanny feeling of a puppet trying to be a human being, which was so characteristic of Nijinsky's interpretation. I liked Lopokova very much as the puppet Dancer, her doll-like eyes (the result of eyelashes painted ray-like about them) and plump cheeks made her look the part to perfection, while the drollery of her vacant stare, contrasted with the expression she achieved by the angle at which she tilted her head and body, was most entertaining. Zverev was an excellent mime and character dancer.

The soloists in *Les Sylphides* were Lopokova, Kyasht, and Tchernicheva.

On May 8th *L'Oiseau de Feu* was revived with Lopokova in the title-role; the role of the Tsarevich was taken alternately during the season by Massine or Gavrilov. The original setting and costumes by Golovine and Korovine were used, but Bakst had designed new costumes for the Bird of Fire and the Tsarevich; unfortunately, they were inferior to the original conceptions.

For instance, Lopokova's costume consisted of a short yellow ballet skirt, decorated with orange and gold motifs, and trimmed with orange feathers, while on her head she wore a white tinselled cap, trimmed with long orange feathers; the general effect suggested the old Alhambra Ballet and not that of Diaghilev. Similarly, the Tsarevich's costume, with its long-skirted caftan, wired to make it spread, was marred by an obvious staginess.

There was another innovation in the actual production. No longer did the Bird of Fire make her first appearance flashing across the sky like a fiery comet; that effect was omitted, she just flitted by *sur les pointes* against the background of shadowy trees.

Barocchi asked me what I thought of the new Bird of Fire, and I had to confess that I was a little disappointed. Lopokova was at her best in the scene where the Bird of Fire forces Kostcheï and his demons to dance until they fall exhausted; but, in the first part of the ballet, she seemed just a dancer, she did not give you that suggestion—achieved by Karsavina—of a bird in human guise; and, in the episode where she is caught by the Tsarevich, she did not make you realize, as Karsavina did, something of the agony that a bird must feel when suddenly bereft of its freedom. Nor, when she was released, did Lopokova make you utter an involuntary sigh of relief and share in her happiness. The changes of mood and fluttering of the arms seemed to be done because such movements were laid down by the choreographer, to me they were not felt, they lacked conviction.

Barocchi promptly communicated my observations to Lopokova, who, however, took them in good part, and asked me about Karsavina's rendering of the role, which I described as fully as I could. In subsequent appearances, Lopokova greatly improved on her first performance, but, if she happened to see me, would often ask, with a wickedly assumed anxiety, "Was I better to-night?"

Lopokova and Barocchi were most kind to me, and from time to time I would accompany them home after the performance, and, if it were not too late, I would be invited to sit with them in their suite at the Savoy, where we would discuss the inexhaustible subject of Ballet. Lopokova would bring out biscuits, and, having learned that I was fond of chocolate, she would produce milk, chocolate powder, and a saucepan, and prepare us each a cup of that beverage. There were two other guests at these "banquets", a pair of canaries which were Lopokova's particular joy. She would open their cage, when they would alight on the table, and daintily accept any biscuit crumbs that might be offered them.

What happy days they were! Diaghilev presented me with a pass which enabled me to watch every performance, and, when I wished, to bring an artist with me for the purpose of making drawings for my publications. Grigoriev gave me the freedom of the stage, so that I could go through the pass-door that admits to the stage from the auditorium. Thus, I could enjoy the show, and, during the intervals, sit in the greenroom or watch the scene being set for the next ballet.

The greenroom was on the left-hand side of the stage, entering from the auditorium, and was situated between the stage and the dressing-rooms. It was a small, rectangular, low-ceilinged apartment, to which access was gained by a short flight of steps. The furniture was simple and consisted of a large mirror and two small tables at the far end of the room, a large table in the centre, and a few chairs. This apartment served as auxiliary property-store, office, and green-room. But its particular interest was the fact that it was used by Diaghilev as his headquarters in the field.

During the interval he would enter the room accompanied by Derain or Picasso, and they would discuss details of the forthcoming productions with which they were associated. At this time there was great enthusiasm about the new ballet called *La Boutique Fantasque*. One night I saw in the green-room the pinkish-brown wheelbarrow with its quaint load of green melons; another night, I encountered a long pole with a bunch of dolls tied to one end; these and other strange objects greatly aroused my curiosity.

Diaghilev would put up his eyeglass and inspect these objects with the utmost deliberation, considering their value as decoration, their practicability, and so on. Sometimes Derain would bring for Diaghilev's approval a sketch for a costume or a curtain.

Lopokova told me that she thought I would like the ballet when it was completed, but, beyond the fact that it was about a toyshop, details were very secret. One evening, however, Diaghilev showed me an advance proof of a little illustrated monograph he had prepared, which dealt in a witty manner with the new ballet, its music, its setting, and its choreography.

On some evenings the agenda would be concerned

with administrative problems. Diaghilev would discuss expense sheets prepared by Grigoriev and approve the plans for music rehearsals and ballet rehearsals. Another night Grigoriev would produce a great wad of banknotes, which Diaghilev would push into an inside pocket as unconcernedly as though it were a bundle of programmes.

Derain was a charming personality, radiating a bluff good humour; but you would never have thought him an artist from his appearance. Tall, fair, and massively built, with his huge hands and ruddy complexion, he looked more like a farmer.

At one of the smaller tables you might see one of the two conductors—Defosse or Ansermet. Defosse was a short, dark, dapper, clean-shaven Frenchman, who wore his hair *en casque*. Courteous and reserved, he had something of the dreamy preoccupation of a poet. Ansermet, except that he was also dark, was the exact opposite. Tall and spare, with a pale face, high brow, luxuriant tapering beard, and magnetic eyes, he had a Svengali-like air. He was a dominating, energetic personality. He was often to be seen in the interval sitting at one of the smaller tables, and, before him, the open score of the ballet he was soon to conduct. As he turned the pages with one hand, he would beat time with the other while he imitated the sounds of the instruments carrying the principal theme—Pom! Pom! Pom! Deedle! Pom! Pom! Pom! Pom-pom, pom-pom, pom-pom, pah! Pom-pom-pom! Pah! Pah! Pah!

As the time drew near for the next ballet, some of the dancers taking part in it would step into the room,

DIAGHILEV BALLET IN LONDON

to try a pose in the mirror, or give a shake to their skirt, or a final pat to their hair, or test the ribbon of a shoe, before going on to the stage. It was very interesting to see the costumes at close quarters, and especially the make-up, which gave some of the dancers a most exotic and fascinating appearance.

On May 23rd *Narcisse* was revived, and, on June 4th, Karsavina made her promised re-appearance, the ballets for that evening being *Petrouchka*, with Lopokova, and *Carnaval* and *Schéhérazade* with Karsavina as Columbine and Zobeida. Karsavina had a splendid reception, but she was not the Karsavina of pre-War days. I am not speaking of her technique but of herself. She looked thin and sad, and there was a tragic look in her eyes; her sufferings and losses in Russia as a result of the Bolshevist Revolution had left her with bitter memories not lightly to be dispelled.

At last, on June 5th, came the great night of the *première* of *La Boutique Fantasque*, in reality an adaptation of the theme of the old German ballet *Puppenfee*, set to an arrangement of lively airs by Rossini, which Diaghilev had discovered in an album preserved, I believe, in an Italian library. The settings were by André Derain. The *Boutique*[1] was preceded by *L'Oiseau de Feu* and succeeded by the *Polovtsian Dances from "Prince Igor"*.

I had expected a full house, but I was not prepared for the enormous audience that had gathered. The promenade at the back of the stalls was so packed that

[1] See Appendix D for cast.

you could hardly cross from one side to the other. I visited the other floors and found every available space crowded with people. Everywhere you looked, you could see nothing but rows of white faces blurred by the haze of cigarette smoke. It was a critical audience, too, for I recognized many faithful ballet-goers and many well-known music critics, painters, sculptors, and composers. There was an air of jollity and buoyancy which seemed to promise success before even the ballet had begun.

The first ballet was well received, but it was obvious that everyone was impatiently awaiting the *Boutique*. I crept through the pass-door and was immediately conscious of an atmosphere of nervous calm. The large table in the greenroom had been covered with paper, on which the evening's bouquets were set out in order. In a corner there was a silent sewing-machine, indicating that last-minute touches had been put to some of the costumes.

As the dancers emerged from their dressing-rooms and came on to the stage, Derain passed them in review. He was very particular on the subject of make-up and each artiste had placed on his or her dressing-table a tiny sketch of what was required. There was a shout of *orchestre!* a flash of white shirt-front, and Defosse appeared and hurried away to the orchestra-pit. I went back into the auditorium where the buzz of conversation was almost deafening. There I came across Barocchi who was smiling and shaking his clasped hands in anticipation of the success to come.

Suddenly the house-lights began to dim and the frail silhouette of Defosse passed through the musicians to his seat. Three metallic raps of his baton on the iron frame of his desk and there commenced the lively pizzicato notes of the *"Marche Slave"* which forms the overture. The heavy curtain swung upwards to reveal the drop-curtain. The naïve treatment of the two figures posed against the broad masses of harmonious earth reds and browns resembled the decoration of an early Victorian pencil-box.

The drop-curtain rose and there was the quaintest of toyshops bathed in the sunlight that streamed through the windows overlooking a bay, where a paddle-steamer floated lazily in the distance. The shopkeeper and his assistant opened the shop, customers arrived, and dolls were brought out and set in motion. From that moment the ballet was danced to continual applause, sometimes crackling like rifle fire, sometimes exploding into a roar. When the Can-Can Dancers appeared there were terrific shouts of *Lopokova! Massine!*

With the fall of the curtain the applause was literally deafening. But when the collaborators came forward to take a call in their turn, Derain was frightened at the warmth of his welcome and had to be dragged upon the stage; Massine made repeated graceful bows; while Lopokova, half-crying, half-laughing, seemed divided between sadness and delight.

As soon as the house-lights were on, I returned to the stage with Barocchi, and together we went to Lopokova's dressing-room to congratulate her. Flushed

NOTABLE PERFORMANCES IN BOUTIQUE

and very excited, she was suddenly sick. We induced her to lie down for a few minutes, there was no time for a real rest as she was due to dance in *Igor*, which followed.

Where everyone was so good it is difficult to single out any dancer for detailed description. Of the mimed parts I liked best Cecchetti's benevolent and whimsical shopkeeper; Gavrilov's quaint Assistant—he remained for me the best interpreter of that role; Jazvinsky and Alanova as the American and his Wife, with Bourman and Evina as their naughty and fidgetty children; and Grigoriev and Mme. Cecchetti as the Russian Merchant and his Wife—Mme. Cecchetti was particularly good, when, in well simulated horror, she prudishly shrank from the unwelcome attentions of the Snob.

Of the Dolls, my favourites were Sokolova and Woizikowsky as the Tarantella Dancers, their number being admirably timed and danced with a gusto—not to be seen nowadays—which made you long to join them; Idzikowsky as the Snob, an excellent character study danced with the exact precision of the clockwork figure he was supposed to represent; Zverev as the Cossack Chief; Clark and Kremnev as the Poodles, in which the feminine character of the one was well contrasted with the gruff masculine attributes of the other—the final pose, however, was too closely related to actuality to be pleasing; and, of course, the Can-Can Dancers, presented with the utmost brilliance and fire by Lopokova and Massine.

Before I discuss the Can-Can Dancers, I want to say something about the Poodles. Although the white poodle and the brown poodle are always associated with a man dancer and woman dancer respectively, the costumes were not so distributed at first. Diaghilev offered Vera Clark her choice of the two costumes and she chose the brown dress, simply because it was the smaller. Originally, the costume included an attached property muzzle and a short pleated skirt. At the dress rehearsal, however, it was found that the muzzle prevented the dancer from breathing and so it was discarded, likewise the skirt, which Diaghilev considered ineffective.

Vera Clark danced the Brown Poodle number as you can no longer see it danced to-day. She was so light, so playful, so delightfully wanton. Moreover, the dance had a particular technical difficulty in the second phrase of the *pas*. This began with two steps diagonally forward, ending in a *demi-plié*, followed by a spring on the front foot, with a kind of back-bend, at the same time sweeping the back leg outwards and inwards so that the toe touched the back of the head. This movement required the most supple body, while the difficulty was increased when the dance had to be executed to 3/4 time.

The Can-Can Dance was not the Can-Can of the Bal Mabille, but a balletized version designed to exploit its frivolity rather than its coarseness. None the less, on this first night there were some gestures by Massine —particularly when he slipped to the ground and his partner whirled her leg over his head—which, to say the least, were inelegant.

Lopokova looked charming in her pale blue bodice

and white skirt trimmed with black lace and blue bows, while her hair, dressed in her favourite ringlets, was bound with a garland of cornflowers and marguerites. Massine, dressed entirely in black velvet, save for his light waistcoat, looked, on the contrary, a decidedly raffish figure with his black curly hair and moustache and dead-white make-up.

Lopokova had an extraordinary resemblance to a doll, for which her rounded limbs, plump features, curved lips, and ingenuous expression were admirably suited. You could easily imagine her squeaking *Mam-ma! Pa-pa!* She whirled her leg and flirted her skirt with the utmost abandon, yet there was nothing vicious, nothing inelegant in her presentation, it was all deliciously mischievous, exuberant, light-hearted.

I must record that at one point, for a few minutes only, her ingenuous expression did change. This occurred when, after the shop is closed, she is raised high in the air on the crossed sticks of the Cossacks. As she was temporarily parted from her sweetheart, she gazed at him with a look of ineffable love, which seemed to light up her whole face.

With the performance of *Igor* a wonderful evening came to an end and henceforth I could boast, "I was there, I saw the first night of *La Boutique Fantasque*." I went on the stage and took leave of Lopokova and hurried down the stairs to the stage door. But it was a long time before I could get out, the entrance was jammed with a struggling mass of people waving arms, hats, and umbrellas, anxious to pay tribute to Lopokova and Massine. Although it was almost midnight, I felt so gay that I scorned a taxi and walked home with Rossini's sparkling melodies still echoing in my ears.

Soon after the production of the *Boutique* I observed the beginning of a certain coolness between Lopokova and Barocchi. The reason for this change need not be discussed here, but undoubtedly a contributory cause was the strain of overwork. When, from time to time, I went to greet Lopokova in her dressing-room, she would sometimes lean back in her chair, a wave of weariness would pass over her features, and she would murmur half plaintively, *Kak yah oustal!* (How tired I am!)

With the passing of the days, however, the breach, so far from healing, widened, and one night—Thursday, July 10th—Lopokova did not appear at the theatre; she had fled everything and gone to stay with some Russian friends, and nothing would alter her determination to dance no more that season. Lopokova's sudden disappearance caused a minor sensation, dispersed by a notice from the management to the effect that she was unable to appear owing to indisposition caused by the strain of her work.

Lopokova's part in the *Boutique* was given to Vera Nemchinova, who thus secured her first big chance. She had a good strong technique, but at this time her movements were inclined to be masculine rather than feminine, and one thought of her more as a character dancer. Her rendering of the Can-Can Dancer was well received, but she danced it without that piquancy, that gaiety, that paradoxical combination of innocence and provocativeness that made Lopokova's presentation so captivating. Karsavina, too, danced the role, but her poetical nature, tinged with melancholy, was temperamentally unsuited to the part. She made it over-refined, almost precious. Those who never saw the Can-Can in *Boutique* danced by Lopokova and Massine will never know that dance as it was, or appreciate how exhilarating it could be.

I planned two more *Impressions*—*Petrouchka*, the illustration of which I entrusted to a Russian artist, Michel Sevier, and, of course, the *Boutique*, for which Ethelbert White made the drawings. Few of those who have read those little books would realize the work that went into them. Once the episodes for illustration had been chosen, my collaborator and I had to watch the ballet night after night until the particular group or pose appeared, and during that brief moment check up all the details of the poses. In the interval, we would go behind and sketch the scenery while it was being set, and note the details of the costumes from the dancers, as they strolled on the stage before the ballet. In the case of the more important dresses I would beg the loan of them after the ballet and we would wait outside a dressing-room until the dresser, or a white arm, presented us with the costume still warm from its wearer. I fear that in our passion for authentic detail we may occasionally have been regarded as harmless pests, but, as a general rule, our victims were most courteous and gave us every assistance.

I also brought out some new wooden figurines,

DIAGHILEV BALLET IN LONDON

more elaborate than those early ones[1] which Allinson had designed for me. When I had chosen the pose, I asked the dancer concerned to assume, when convenient, the desired attitude. These "sittings" or rather "standings" took place in all kinds of odd corners, on a stair landing, in a dressing-room, behind the back-cloth, or in the greenroom. Sometimes the pose was difficult to hold for the required length of time, and I had to afford support by holding the dancer's foot, or waist, or knee. The new figurines were variously designed by Randolph Schwabe, Michel Sevier, Ethelbert White and Vera Willoughby.

I also planned an album devoted to Lopokova, to be illustrated with, among other drawings, two portraits, one by Picasso and one by Glyn Philpot. I remember how we set off one afternoon for Philpot's studio in Tite Street, and how charmed Lopokova was by an extraordinary painting of his which depicted life beneath the sea. The painting emanated a soft translucent light in which you could almost feel the water quivering to the passage of some fish or from the opening of some flower of the sea. He told us that he had once sold the painting but had bought it back as he missed it so much. He drew a fine head of Lopokova in sanguine,

[1] I see that, in dealing with the pre-War years, I have forgotten to mention that in 1913 or 1914 Allinson designed for me some wooden figurines of Karsavina and Nijinsky in their principal roles. These figurines were inspired by those of soldiers which Caran d'Ache delighted to fashion and paint. My figures, like those, were cut out of plywood by means of a fretsaw and coloured by hand. They were some eight inches high and were pegged in a base of the same plywood.

PREMIÈRE OF THE THREE CORNERED HAT

but I remember that he several times re-drew her elusive nose before he was finally satisfied.

A friend of Philpot's, Vivian Forbes, wished to paint Lopokova as Mariuccia, and so one day we visited his studio, but the proceedings were a little marred because, although Lopokova had secured the costume, which we took with us, she had forgotten all about the wig, and the whole effect was spoilt, much to Forbes's disappointment.

One of the two remaining new ballets did not materialize, the exception being *The Three Cornered Hat*, which had its first performance on July 22nd, in practically the last week of the season. The music was by Manuel de Falla, the setting and costumes by Pablo Picasso, and the choreography by Massine.

The principal characters were: *the Miller*, Leonide Massine; *the Miller's Wife*, Thamar Karsavina; *the Corregidor*, Leon Woizikowsky; *the Corregidor's Wife*, Mlle. Alanova; and *the Dandy*, Stanislas Idzikowsky.

While I watched the stage being set for the first performance of the new ballet, Picasso strolled into view, accompanied by a stage-hand carrying a tray of grease-paints. Picasso was short and stocky, with pleasant, sunburnt features. His smooth dark hair, parted at the side, with a strand falling over his brow, was a little reminiscent of Napoleon, and would have been more so, had Picasso's nose been less broad at the base.

One of the dancers, dressed as an Alguacil, came on the stage, walked towards Picasso, bowed, and waited. Picasso made a selection of grease-paints and decorated the dancer's chin with a mass of blue, green, and yellow dots, which certainly gave him an appropriately sinister appearance. As he went off, another Alguacil appeared, and I well remember his startled look on seeing his fellow-artiste.

The ballet began in an unusual manner with a fanfare of trumpets followed by the slow thunderous beats of a big drum. But, before the curtain rose, there was a volley of enthusiastically shouted *olés*, immediately followed by a burst of heel-tapping and the dry rhythmic clicking of lustily shaken castanets.

Picasso's scenery, a remarkably successful attempt to express the sun-scorched mountains of Spain in the simplest terms, was acclaimed by painters as a masterpiece. Brevity is the soul of wit, and, it might be added, of good stage decoration. In essence, the scene consisted of a white back-cloth with a patch of blue sky at the top and a few grey lines suggesting distant mountains; before the back-cloth was a white cut-cloth in the shape of a great arch, its edges shaded with grey, and, inset, a practicable semi-circular bridge stretching from one leg to the other. The costumes were also effective, but the stripe motif, for instance, green and white, black and pale blue, red and yellow, was inclined to be carried to excess.

De Falla's music was most attractive. Invested with a rare impish humour, it offered a mocking comment on the characters of various personages and the nature of certain incidents in the ballet.

Karsavina looked charming in her pale blue dress and pink shawl, and danced with animation and spirit.

MASSINE'S DANCING OF THE FARRUCA

The one criticism that might be made was that she was a little too refined to suggest a miller's wife.

Massine was superb as the Miller and dominated the ballet throughout. In his hip-tight and ankle-tight black silk trousers and purple waistcoat edged with white, he danced like one possessed, and received a tremendous ovation.

Few of those who saw that first night will have forgotten the colour and bravura with which he invested his Farruca, the slow snap of the fingers followed by the pulsating thump of his feet, then the flickering movement of his hands held horizontally before him, palms facing and almost touching his breast. All at once this gave place to a new movement in which his feet chopped the ground faster and faster until he suddenly dropped to the ground on his hands, and as quickly leapt to his feet and stopped dead, his efforts greeted with thunderous applause.

Woizikowsky was admirable as the Corregidor, especially in the scene where he dances with the miller's wife, at the conclusion of which he becomes overbold and is pushed into the river. His mimed despair at his discomfiture and his terror at the threatened return of the miller were excellent.

So passed another memorable night and a few days later, on the 30th, the season came to an end, the final programme being *Carnaval*, *The Three Cornered Hat*, and *Children's Tales*.

The company went on holiday and returned in September for a season under Alfred Butt at the Empire Theatre, which began on the 29th. The company was the same, with Karsavina, Tchernicheva, and Massine as principals, for Lopokova still declined to return to the ballet-stage. A new dancer, Veceslav Svoboda, appeared during the season; he made his début in *Cléopâtre*.

I saw a good deal of Idzikowsky at this period. We often lunched or had tea together, sometimes accompanied by Wanda Evina. I frequently went to the Empire and during the intervals would sit with him in his dressing-room. It was a joy to me to watch him make-up and dress, even to the squeezing of seccotine into his ballet-shoes before finally pulling them on, a device which ensured the sole's sticking to the dancer's foot. Dancers of the opposite sex, who have the additional support of ribbon ties, generally content themselves with a little homely spit.

But the process of make-up, varying from "straight" to "character", was an education in itself. Few things are more fascinating to watch than the widening of an eye, or the thinning or broadening of a nose, by the adroit disposition of certain lines of colour. Then there were times when a wig had to be fitted, the edge carefully aligned to the forehead with spirit gum, or it might be that he was to play Harlequin, which requires a black mask to be painted on the face.

Apart from the actual difficulties of make-up there was the all-important element of speed. Imagine the dancer returning to his room, still panting from the exertions of the ballet just ended, who must change his costume while his skin is still sticky with perspiration, and effect a quite different make-up. To the audience

A BLAKE VISION BEHIND THE SCENES

the interval seems long; to the dancer, racing against time, it seems to be momentary.

On certain nights, in a room not far from that of Idzikowsky, you could see an unusual sight. There, whenever *Cléopâtre* was to be performed, you would catch sight of a dozen or more wooden bath-tubs set on the floor. At a fixed time the tubs were filled with steaming water. As soon as the ballet was over, you would see a crowd of male dancers, changed into Egyptians by the application of a brown solution, come bounding up the stairs to slough their bronzed skins in readiness for the next ballet. Clouts were removed and hung on hooks, and lissom brown limbs stepped into the smoking tubs. It was a curious scene reminiscent of a painting by William Blake.

One fateful evening Idzikowsky and Evina called at my "Boutique Fantasque" about half-past seven, when I was working at my hand-press. They watched me "make-ready" and run off some sheets, by which time it was well past eight. Surprised that Idzikowsky made no attempt to leave, I reminded him that it was time he was at the theatre, but something had annoyed him and he said that he preferred to watch my printing. Evina pleaded with him to go, but, finding him obdurate, went off alone.

The clock ticked on and it was now past nine. I could see that Idzikowsky was concerned about the theatre, although he affected to ignore it.

I decided to make up his mind for him and said, "I'd better tell Grigoriev that you're here, or he'll be worrying about your absence."

DIAGHILEV BALLET IN LONDON

I took Idzikowsky's silence for consent.

I went to the Empire stage-door and the first person I met on the stage was Diaghilev, who immediately asked me if I had seen Idzikowsky.

"Yes," I said. "I came to tell you that he is at my shop."

"What the devil's he doing there!" he snapped.

"Printing," I replied.

"*Printing!*" echoed Diaghilev, opening his mouth and screwing his eyeglass into his eye, with a gasp of mingled rage and astonishment.

He signed to Zenon, who was standing in the wings, and ordered him to go with me and return immediately with Idzikowsky. On the way out I learned that the atmosphere on the stage had been highly charged, and that the dancer called upon to deputize for Idzikowsky, had caused Karsavina some anxious moments.

When we arrived at the shop there was a brief colloquy between Zenon and Idzikowsky and they at once set out for the theatre. There was an unpleasant sequel, for Diaghilev gave instructions that in future all Idzikowsky's roles were to be doubled.

On November 1st the ballet was honoured by the presence of H.M. the Shah of Persia, who occupied a box with his suite. The door leading to the box and its immediate vicinity was thronged with his own detectives who, curiously suggestive of Heath Robinson's conceptions, wore fezzes and carried umbrellas, with the points of which they seemed pre-occupied to trace designs on the carpet.

The one event of the season was the long-promised

performance of *Parade*, given on November 14th. The ballet had first been given at Paris in 1917. The book was by Jean Cocteau, the music by Erik Satie, the scenery and costumes by Pablo Picasso, and the choreography by Massine.

The present cast was as follows: *Chinese Conjurer*, Leonide Massine; *Acrobats*, Vera Nemchinova, Nicholas Zverev; *Little American Girl*, Thamar Karsavina; *Manager in Evening Dress*, Leon Woizikowsky; *American Manager*, M. Statkiewicz; *Manager on Horseback*, MM. Oumansky, Nova[k].

At the time *Parade* was first produced the circus and music-hall were favoured vehicles of artistic expression, and *Parade* was a ballet fashioned from such elements. The ballet satirized a number of well-known types and the dances were based on the movements and gestures associated with such characters.

Picasso designed a fine drop-curtain for the ballet, the base of which represented some circus artistes sitting at a long table, above them was a stretch of curtain, against which was posed a ladder and a winged horse balancing on a sphere.

The best dance was undoubtedly that of the Chinese Conjurer, in which Massine wittily parodied the movements associated with pseudo-Oriental conjurers of the music-hall stage.

I recall one point of interest concerning the acrobats' costumes. Lopokova, who was one of the original acrobats, told me that she was asked to put on white fleshings, which Picasso himself painted with the blue lines and whorls which form the decorative scheme.

DIAGHILEV BALLET IN LONDON

The production seemed rather obviously planned *pour épater les bourgeois*, to which end Picasso had designed cubist costumes for the several managers, which produced a curious effect of false realism, so that the real dancers resembled puppets, while Satie's often interesting music was spoilt by such "signature noises" as the clicking of typewriters for the American Girl and the humming of an aeroplane engine for the acrobats. The ballet was mildly amusing as a joke, but should never have been put forward as a serious choreographic work. It had a lukewarm reception.

The season ended on December 20th, the final programme being *Schéhérazade*, *L'Oiseau de Feu*, and *Les Sylphides*.

CHAPTER VI

TO go behind the scenes at the theatre at which the Diaghilev Ballet was appearing, was to enter a rare and magical world whose fascination never palled and whose aspect changed with every moment.

Most stages seen from behind the curtain have a certain similarity—they are rectangular and vary merely in the size of the proscenium opening and in their cubic content. In essentials they are the same, but in details there are countless differences. In order to give a more intimate atmosphere to my description, let us assume that the historic past has become the immediate present.

The visitor who passes behind the stage some time before the performance is due to begin will find the opening scene set, but all is dark save for a tiny pilot lamp which sheds an eerie glow. Everything is as depressing and as cold as though you had stepped at night into an empty warehouse. Nothing seems more incredible than that a performance should ever take place.

Sometimes the space behind the back-cloth is clear, sometimes it may contain portions of built-up scenery, such as the puppets' booths for *Petrouchka*, or the

DIAGHILEV BALLET IN LONDON

bridge for *The Three Cornered Hat*, or some important property such as the sedan chair used by the Corregidor's wife in the same ballet. All these objects have naturally a quite different appearance when seen in semi-darkness.

As the zero hour approaches there are unexpected signs of activity. Stage-hands assemble under the direction of the carpenter. The electrician switches on a few lamps, while some of his men drag out portable "floods" with their lengths of heavy cable which writhe over the boards like so many snakes. There is a tinkle of metal as the lids of small square traps in the stage are jerked open and the cables plugged in.

The tall spare silhouette of the company's *régisseur*, Grigoriev, appears near the prompt corner. He strolls on to the stage and inspects the setting of the scenery. If there are properties to be used, he checks them over. The electrician gives his men their orders and now some lamps are dimmed, and others brought up, until the requirements of the lighting plot are fulfilled. Grigoriev glances at his wrist-watch, peeps unseen into the auditorium, and, finding the majority of the spectators seated and expectant, gives the signal in broken English—"'ouse lights out", then flashes another warning to the conductor at his desk in the orchestra-pit, whereupon the overture begins.

Meanwhile the dancers begin to arrive in ones and twos and little groups, some chatting, some laughing, some with a serious look of concentration on their faces. Some smooth the folds of their dresses, some pull up their tights, some indulge in a few *échappés* and

JUST BEFORE THE CURTAIN RISES

changements to work in a new pair of shoes. Most of them take the opportunity to "warm up", that is to say, to execute some of the traditional exercises to make the muscles supple and elastic, holding on to a vertical batten, a piece of scenery, or a fixed ladder for support. To attempt to dance without such preliminaries might induce muscular cramp or strain a tendon. Some dancers prefer to "warm up" in their dressing-rooms, others choose the stage.

In odd corners you may come across a dancer rehearsing a phrase of steps. Suddenly a pair of soloists bound on to the stage to put the final touches to their *pas de deux*, which is rehearsed with an astounding sense of detachment, as though they had a whole month before them.

As the overture draws to its climax, the dancers take up their positions on the stage or in the wings, as the case may be, ready to dance their respective roles. It might be thought that at the first note of the overture every dancer was keyed up, waiting for the curtain to rise. Far from it, they are often strolling about the stage, chatting or comparing notes, as if they were taking a walk in a park. If there are chairs in the opening scene as in the *Boutique*, the dancers often calmly sit down in them. Only at the very last moment, when it seems that nothing can prevent their discovery by the audience, do they swiftly vacate the stage and take up their positions for their entrance.

Sometimes last-minute renovations are being applied to the scenery. There would be Komishov, the machinist, paint-brush in hand, touching up some portion of the setting. On one occasion, during the actual playing of the overture to *L'Oiseau de Feu*, I recall his being mounted on a tall pair of steps while he adjusted a small flood lamp above the "golden tree", to bathe it in appropriate amber radiance. Every moment I expected the curtain to rise and the proceedings to be revealed to the spectators.

Once the ballet has begun, the watcher must take up his post near the wings. It is not, of course, possible to see the ballet in profile, as it were, because such a clear field of vision is unobtainable, being partly obstructed by the angles of the wings, while what space is available between them must be reserved for the men handling the "floods", since it is essential that the way should be clear for dancers making their entrance or their exit.

A dancer making her exit with a *grand jeté* or a series of *petits tours* arrives with an appreciable momentum. Again, dancers wishing to discard a property which they no longer need, usually toss such objects through one of the entrances, and it is well to be prepared for such moments. For instance, in *Papillons*, the Pierrot flings his lighted candle into the wings, and, during the Khorovod in *L'Oiseau de Feu*, the Tsarevna disposes of her two golden apples in the same manner.

The watcher in the wings has his vision bounded by the size of the gap between each two wings. But it is possible to see *soli* and *pas de deux* at curious angles, or to witness, as in *Les Sylphides* or in *Le Lac des Cygnes*, a chain of dancers in white ballet-skirts flash past like a flock of seagulls.

VIGNETTES BEHIND THE SCENES

And even when there is no dancing to be witnessed, there is still much to be seen. For instance, the dancer taking up her position for her entrance, moistening her lips with the tip of her tongue, and invoking God's blessing on her work by devoutly crossing herself, an action no less characteristic of Russian male dancers.

Conversely, there is the dancer making her exit, her bosom palpitating, her facial make-up flecked with minute beads of sweat. In the shadows stands a dresser in sober black. With a resigned air she waits in attendance, holding a powder-puff or small bottle of eau-de-Cologne, or perhaps a plate with a sliced orange to refresh parched lips, or a glass of water for the dancer to rinse out her mouth; such cares and attentions are reminiscent of a second preparing a boxing champion for his next round in the ring.

From the wing nearest the back-cloth it is possible to see in profile such exciting moments as the Corregidor in *The Three Cornered Hat* toppling over the bridge into the river, when, once out of sight, he quickly changes his coat for another sewn with sequins, which admirably suggest dripping water. Or perhaps you may see the famous moment at the end of the second part of the *Boutique*, when the Can-Can dancer is raised higher and higher in the air, delicately poised on the "carbines" of the Cossacks.

Then there is the entrancing fragrance compounded of the mingled odours of size, hot metal, grease-paint, and the varied perfumes used by the dancers; the strange grating noise made when a dancer rubs her shod foot in the rosin-box. There may be little quips to be overheard such as old Cecchetti saying to one of the dressers called Margaret: "If you will be my Margaret, I will be your Faust." Finally, it is most interesting to study the dancers' faces with their make-up, which, at close quarters, suggest the faces of insects seen beneath the microscope.

Perhaps the most stirring experience of all is to gaze upon the celestial beauty of beams of vari-coloured light, sometimes co-mingling to form a new tint, sometimes producing curious high-lights where they impinge or reflect upon the faces, limbs, or costumes of the dancers.

Even when the ballet comes to an end there is still much to see. If you are lucky enough to stand near the controls in the prompt corner, you will observe the long stretch of curtain rise and fall, the bowing dancers, and the flashes of white which mark the clapping hands of the white-fronted and bare-necked spectators beyond.

"'Ouse lights on!" directs Grigoriev, for it is the turn of the principals to take a call before the curtain. He pulls back a part of the curtain where it laps over the centre join, on which the *ballerina* and her partner, floral tributes in hand, glide through the tent-like aperture to show themselves once more to the applauding audience. Presently they are back. If you are lucky enough to know the *ballerina*, and she is pleased with her reception, you may be the envied recipient of a flower from her bouquet.

But while the principals are bowing their acknowledgments before the curtain, behind it, all is activity.

STRIKING THE SCENE

The white and amber lamps are switched on, the stagehands hurry on to "strike" the scene—to remove the properties, carry off built-up pieces, fold up the stage-cloth, and roll up the back-cloth. Wings glide upwards, new ones glide down; loops and lines of rope, some ending in a sandbag which serves as a counterpoise, hurtle through the air.

Presently the dancers, refreshed and redressed, trickle on to the stage for the second act, or the second ballet. A dancer bends down to adjust her shoe-ribbon, it is a charming gesture which has been recorded by numerous artists over many years. Another dancer rehearses a tricky "lift" with her partner. Still another practises a difficult *enchaînement*, the while she counts the appropriate number of beats, or hums the corresponding melody.

Sometimes, the choreographer of the ballet to be performed—Fokine, Massine, Nijinska, or Balanchine—comes to give last minute instructions to a dancer, to polish up some detail, or to supervise the arrangement of the group with which the ballet begins. Another time you may see choreographer and conductor, seated on a skip, going over, phrase by phrase, some portion of the score, the *tempo* of which on the last occasion did not satisfy the choreographer.

It is perhaps unnecessary to state that the success of a ballet depends a great deal on the *tempo* at which the music is taken. Movements intended to be full and expressive become fussy and irritating, just as movements which were originally quick and sharp become soft and dragged. Again, if a dance be taken too slowly, the dancer must fill out the movements to fit; conversely, if the dance be hurried, he is obliged to quicken up all his movements in order that they may correspond. Nothing provokes trouble more quickly in a ballet company than a bad conductor, for the dancers will vent their displeasure in no uncertain terms.

When the curtain has fallen for the last time that evening, the stage quickly reverts to its normal resemblance to a vast and lofty warehouse, with one brick wall masked by the lining of a curtain. Who would credit that, a short while before, this austere prospect had witnessed such glorious visions, such scenes of transcendental beauty?

CHAPTER VII

~ 1920 ~

THE Diaghilev Company gave one season only in 1920, and that was in conjunction with the season of Italian Opera at the Royal Opera House, Covent Garden. The constitution of the troupe remained practically the same, with the exception of some minor changes. It may be mentioned that among the recruits was Addison—Errol Addison—an English pupil of Maestro Cecchetti's, who, under his guidance, gradually acquired a remarkable technique, particularly in all kinds of turning movements. The principals continued to be Karsavina, Nemchinova, Tchernicheva, and Massine.

The ballet season opened on June 10th with *Contes Russes*, *Pulcinella*, and *Les Sylphides*, the second ballet being given in England for the first time. The ballet was set to an arrangement by Stravinsky of melodies from Pergolesi's operas, the scenery and costumes were by Pablo Picasso, and the choreography by Massine.

Picasso's setting, a cubist study in black, blue-grey, and white, admirably conveyed with a remarkable economy of means a moonlit street overlooking the Bay of Naples.

The ballet was based on a theme taken from a manuscript book of comedies, dated 1700, and found by Massine, I believe, in Naples. The choreography was interesting, but lacked the spontaneity and continuity of *The Good Humoured Ladies*.

The whole production was dominated by Massine as Pulcinella, for which character he had invented all manner of grotesque steps, obviously inspired by a careful study of the many pictorial representations of the Mask in question. Massine's dancing was particularly interesting for the way in which he caused certain steps to be expressive in themselves. Remember, too, that his features were almost hidden by his bird-like mask. Yet it was extraordinary to observe how, by the tilt of his head and the angle of his body, and by the varying speed and variety of his movements, he was able to suggest his thoughts and emotions. When I saw his subtle, intensely expressive, and beautifully timed dancing, I was reminded of Garrick's comment on the Italian harlequin Carlin—"Behold how the very back of Carlin has a physiognomy and an expression."

A minor sensation occurred in the scene where Rosetta and Prudenza, leaning out of their windows, rout their serenaders, Caviello and Florindo, by pouring water on them. On the first night the ladies displayed actual chamber-pots, from which sand was poured. I can still hear the audible gasp that went up from the occupants of the stalls. At the next performance these domestic articles were replaced by modest pitchers.

LE ASTUZIE FEMMINILI

On June 22nd there was another new production, Cimarosa's *opera buffa* in three scenes, *Le Astuzie Femminili*. The settings and costumes by the Spanish painter, José Maria Sert, were as charming as they were unusual. The first two scenes were entirely opera, the third was a moonlight fête at which the guests were entertained by a ballet—a *ballo russo*. Except for a brief sung introduction, the ballet or rather series of *divertissements* constituted the whole of the scene. The choreography was by Leonide Massine.

The dances and their interpreters were as follows: *Pas de Trois*, Lubov Tchernicheva, Vera Nemchinova, and S. Novak; *Pas de Six*, Mmes. Klementowicz, Wassilevska, Bewicke, MM. Kremnev, Zverev, Bourman; *Tarantella*, Lydia Sokolova, Leon Woizikowsky; *Contre-Danse*, Mmes. Allanova, Pavlovska, Mikulina, Zalevska, Komarova, Forestier, Slavinska, Istomina, Evina, and MM. Jazvinsky, Statkiewicz, Kegler, Kostetsky, Pavlov, Elmuzhinsky, Ribas, Addison, Mikolaichik; *Pas de Deux*, Thamar Karsavina, Stanislas Idzikowsky.

Imagine the dances set against Sert's lovely panorama of Rome at night—a broad terrace relieved by stone pedestals bearing groups of statuary and bounded by a low balustrade, and, in the distance, the cupolas and spires and hills of Rome. The whole was bathed in yellowish-green moonlight, with here and there patches of velvety shadow.

Of the five dances I liked best the *Pas de Trois*, *Tarantella*, and *Pas de Deux*.

The ladies in the *Pas de Trois* had particularly charming costumes in black and yellow adorned with tiers of flounces in a manner reminiscent of one of Gillot's designs for Folly.

The *Tarantella* was a character dance, obviously inspired by the *Commedia dell'Arte*. Woizikowsky wore a brimmed hat, with coat and breeches of dark velvet, the coat being stuffed out at the waist like the curved paunch of a Pulcinella. Both melody and dance had an infectious lilt reflected in the vivacious and admirably timed movements of Sokolova and Woizikowsky.

The *Pas de Deux* was classical in feeling and full of a refined grace and charm. The woman's role was worked out by Massine on Vera Clark who, however, was told that Karsavina would dance it. Here, again, the costumes were most original, a delightful confection of *chinoiserie*. Idzikowsky wore a circular hat with a spire—suggested perhaps by the *mokot* of Cambodian dancers—and pink fleshings decorated with wedgwood blue cameos, looped with tasselled cord. Karsavina's costume consisted of a cap like a fuschia flower, trousers with the ends slashed in points, and a close-fitting bodice which at the waist jutted out to a ruff-like shape; the colours were pink, blue, black, and green.

A few days later I had a visit from a young man representing a firm of West End photographers, who wished to photograph leading members of the Diaghilev Company, and asked me if I could help them to secure sittings. I suggested that they could not do better than begin with Mme. Karsavina and M. Idzikowsky, to which he agreed. I spoke to the artists

LAMENTABLE EPISODE AT A PHOTOGRAPHER'S

concerned and it was decided that they should be photographed in the *Pas de Deux* from *Le Astuzie Femminili*, while Karsavina should also be taken as Pimpinella in *Pulcinella*. Permission was obtained to borrow the costumes and one sweltering morning we all went to the studio.

We were welcomed by the same young man who presented his partner, a rather stout lady of uncertain age, who, he informed us, was the camera artist. She seemed rather agitated and was perspiring freely, partly from the heat, and partly, perhaps, from the responsibility of her task. The first hitch occurred in regard to dressing-rooms. There was a pleasant room for Karsavina, but no provision for Idzikowsky. I wondered if the photographers thought that ballet-dancers all undressed together in the manner of old-time strolling players in a barn, as recorded in 18th century memoirs.

It was then suggested and decided that Idzikowsky should change in the studio. Alas, he had only just taken off his collar when the perspiring lady returned to prepare the camera. For one who on occasion had changed in the wings of a theatre, Idzikowsky became ultra-modest and declined to be photographed at all, unless he could have the room to himself. Crisis! The situation became difficult, but improved when the young man proposed that Idzikowsky should change in the dark room upstairs, which was agreed.

I accompanied Idzikowsky to the room, ready to assist him with his costume if desired. Needless to say the red light—which was almost useless as illumination—was received with great disfavour, but, after scratching myself with embroidery, and doing the same for Idzikowsky, he was dressed and ready. He opened his make-up box, and, with more abuse of the light, added a few touches to his features.

We returned to the studio, the walls of which were hung with a single row of framed photographs, while at one end was a folded canvas screen. Karsavina being ready, the two artists took up their pose, and the photograph was taken. Idzikowsky departed upstairs to change.

Karsavina went to put on the costume of Pimpinella and on her return expressed an unexpected wish to be photographed in a particular attitude, which necessitated her being placed on a raised platform.

Since nothing of the kind was available, some boxes were borrowed from neighbours. These were built up to the requisite height and Karsavina climbed upon them and took her pose. The perspiring photographer, however, found it most difficult to focus her camera as she wished, because she could not get far enough away from the subject, owing to the smallness of the room. Almost flat against the wall, she was soon half out of the window. At last, with many sighs, she had the camera focussed to her satisfaction, and asked her partner to place the screen so that it formed a background for the dancer.

But just when all was ready, the boxes shifted and Karsavina was almost flung to the floor, while the nervous young man dropped the screen, which fell sideways, taking with it several of the pictures on the

DIAGHILEV'S OFFER TO VERA CLARK

wall. Karsavina became very pale. Aware that most Russians are highly superstitious, I hastened to assure her by pointing out that the pictures had been knocked down and had not fallen of themselves.

Karsavina replied:

"Oh, I'm not concerned for myself, but I do hope that nothing dreadful will happen to the owners of this studio."

Both partners looked very apprehensive.

I decided that enough photographs had been taken for one day and Karsavina went to dress.

I returned to the dark-room to see how Idzikowsky was progressing. He was in a very bad temper, having discovered that, while he was being photographed, someone had entered the room, upset his make-up box, and spilt a box of powder. Worse still, some hurried attempt had been made to put the powder back and it was full of dust off the floor.

A few days later the photographer brought me some rough proofs. I will only say that I did not show them to either of my friends. Idzikowsky was very anxious to see the proofs when they were ready, but I told him that they had turned out unsatisfactorily. Since that day, I have never taken any dancer to be photographed, one unfortunate experience was sufficient for me.

At the conclusion of the London season, Diaghilev complimented Vera Clark on her work and promised her that she should have more important parts in the near future. He also told her that under these circumstances it was essential that she should appear to be

Russian, and so he changed her name to Vera Savina, after the famous Russian tragedienne, because, he said:

"You are petite, fair, and lively, just the opposite to her."

The company went on a provincial tour when Savina was billed more prominently and given the *Pas de Deux* in *Le Astuzie Femminili*, now consisting of the last act only and re-named *Cimarosiana*, and the "*Mazurka*" and "*Valse*" in *Les Sylphides*.

Events outside London are really beyond the scope of this book, but I shall make an exception in this instance in order to explain the events which resulted in the loss to the company of both Savina and Massine.

When the troupe was in Liverpool, Savina noticed that Massine paid her many little attentions and helped her in her dancing. She accepted these kindnesses in a spirit of comradeship, without ever thinking that there was more in them than that. At this time she greatly admired Massine, the choreographer and dancer, but had no particular interest in Massine the man.

However, as the months went by and the company travelled from England to France and then to Italy, the friendship gradually ripened into mutual affection. But in January (1921), when the troupe was appearing at the Constanza Theatre, Rome, Diaghilev summoned Savina to his hotel and expressed his disapproval of her friendship with Massine, which, he said, had come to his knowledge. He wished her to concentrate on her dancing and insisted that she should renounce Massine,

SAVINA AND MASSINE LEAVE THE COMPANY

promising that, if she did so, he would make her his leading *ballerina* and give her all the roles that went with that position.

During the next week or two Diaghilev frequently asked her to dine with him, always using these meetings to urge her acceptance of his plan. On the 30th he told Savina that he would have a contract drawn up immediately in accordance with the proposed terms, and invited her to dine with him that evening, when she could sign it. Savina, very distressed at this forcing of a decision, hardly knew what to do, swayed between her affection for Massine and her natural ambition to attain what was then the most coveted position in the world of ballet.

But she felt that she could not give up Massine and so did not attend the dinner. Diaghilev promptly gave evidence of his displeasure, for the very next day Savina was ruthlessly deprived of all her important roles and told that in future she was to dress with the *corps de ballet*; moreover, a bill announcing her appearance in *Les Sylphides* was cancelled. Massine, too, had been billed to dance in *Petrouchka* on February 2nd, but was not allowed to appear in that role.

At the beginning of February both Savina and Massine resigned from the company. They secured a three months' contract to appear in South America as *première danseuse* and *premier danseur* with the famous Walter Mocchi Opera Company, and, after rehearsing in Paris, left Geneva on May 27th to fulfil their engagement. At the conclusion of their contract, they formed a small ballet company, with which they successfully

DIAGHILEV BALLET IN LONDON

toured South America for a further three months. The repertory included *Papillons, Le Carnaval, The Midnight Sun,* and some 30 *divertissements.* Savina and Massine returned to London in 1922 and were married at the Fulham Registry Office on April 16th.

It was during this year, I think, that I first began work on the *Manual of Classical Theatrical Dancing.* I remember that soon after I saw the Diaghilev Ballet I was seized with a fervent desire to know something of how the dancers moved, in short, to acquire some knowledge of the mechanics of dancing, but I could find no book which afforded such information. So there gradually formed in me a most ambitious resolve to write one myself.

From time to time opportunities occurred for me to see dances given by various teachers and gradually I arrived at the studio of the famous Cecchetti, whose school was then situated on the first floor of 160 Shaftesbury Avenue, now occupied by the well-known firm of printers: Hazell, Watson, and Viney.

I had seen and admired so many of Cecchetti's pupils, that I was delighted to be able to set foot in the workshop of that great master, a Coppelius in real life, for Cecchetti truly did fashion dancers. He gave me the inestimable privilege of his friendship and was kind enough to allow me to watch his classes, a concession of which I took full advantage. Enchanted by the lovely lines and the harmonious co-ordination of the movements of the body and limbs of his pupils, I resolved that, if ever I compiled a book of dance technique, it should be that of the Cecchetti Method.

MY INITIATION IN THE CECCHETTI METHOD

One day, while having tea with Idzikowsky in the prosaic surroundings of a Bloomsbury tea-shop, I was moved to tell him of my ambition, and after he had recovered from his surprise at my audacity, I was happy to find him most sympathetic to the enterprise. We discussed the matter and he agreed to initiate me in the technique of classical ballet, according to the Cecchetti Method. We arranged a succession of meetings and I worked hard to try and grasp the principles propounded. Sometimes we met at my shop and sometimes at Idzikowsky's rooms in Bloomsbury, where, with a chair or bedstead serving as a bar, he demonstrated the movements for my benefit.

Idzikowsky's thin, sallow features, short stature, and slight build gave an illusion of under-development. Only when he sat down did the ripple of muscles under his close-fitting trousers suggest that he might be stronger than he looked. But when he was stripped he revealed an extraordinary muscular development. The position of the knee is an important factor in some dance exercises, and I remember that one of my first troubles was to discover where Idzikowsky's knee was, for he appeared to have several.

Two of the main characteristics of the Cecchetti Method are, first, that it makes use of a series of eight imaginary fixed points—the four corners of the practice-room or stage, and the centre of each wall—for the dancer's body to align upon; second, that every movement is considered in relation to the whole body. Thus it is not enough to watch, for instance, the movement of a leg, it is imperative to see what is happening to the other leg, the arms, the head, and the torso—and all in relation to the imaginary points at the self-same moment.

I worked ceaselessly on this self-imposed task, so obsessed was I with the necessity to try and preserve this system of training for the benefit of all dancers, and particularly for those of British nationality. But, as the work progressed, I must confess that, more than once, I thought of abandoning the whole project, the difficulties seemed insuperable. It took me hours to set down in simple language the most elementary movement, though Idzikowsky performed it many times, for, as I have stated, it was necessary to watch and record a number of things all happening at once, including, moreover, some movements executed very quickly.

As the book progressed I soon realized that it was essential that my descriptions should be accompanied with illustrations, and to that end I commissioned first one artist, then another, to make the desired drawings. One of the trials I early encountered arose from the fact that it was sometimes difficult for the dancer taking the pose to hold it long enough for the artist to complete his drawing. So the dancer, becoming wearied, unconsciously lapsed into positions which were technically incorrect, and which, at this period, I often failed to detect, with the result that the drawing, when completed, was useless.

Idzikowsky was very patient in his explanations and demonstrations and I studied hard to grasp the intricacies of technique. No doubt my former training in

THE MANUAL CONTINUED WITH CECCHETTI

physics and mechanics helped me in the analysis of dance movement. But the time came when Idzikowsky had to leave London with the company and I was left on my own. I tried to carry on by corresponding with him, but, as can be imagined, I made little headway and was soon brought to a standstill.

Not knowing when Idzikowsky might return to London, and fearing that if the work were once abandoned I might never have the opportunity or the inclination to resume where I had left off, I decided to approach Cecchetti himself. He was greatly interested in the work and offered to demonstrate his method to me and to supervise and assist that the book might be brought to a conclusion.

He told me that, in years gone by, he himself had once devoted much time to the recording of his system of training, which descriptions he had carefully written out in ink. One afternoon, when he was seated at a table looking over the pile of sheets and making final improvements, he was suddenly called away. On his return he found that one of his children had climbed upon the table in his absence and upset a large bottle of ink all over his manuscript, moreover, to his horror, the paper being porous, the ink had soaked through and rendered much of the writing illegible. He was distressed for days at this loss, the bitter memory of which so affected him that he could never bring himself to attempt the task afresh.

Whatever misgivings he himself may have felt concerning my capacity and staying power to accomplish the proposed work, they remained unspoken. But I think he was happy in the mere possibility that the essence of the book he had laboured so hard to write, and which had been lost in a moment of ill fortune, might yet be recovered and given permanence in print and paper.

The 1920 season, which ended on July 30th, saw a third and final new production, *Le Rossignol*, a ballet version of Stravinsky's opera, with settings and costumes by Henri Matisse and choreography by Leonide Massine. Unfortunately, I did not see this ballet and must therefore limit my comments to the mere mention of it.

CHAPTER VIII

ENRICO Cecchetti was born in the dressing-room of a theatre; his parents were both dancers of repute. He, himself, was the greatest of male dancers in the eighties and nineties, and had been both *premier danseur* and *maître de ballet* to the Imperial Russian Ballet, St. Petersburg. Among numerous personal triumphs it may be mentioned that he was the first to dance the *cavalier* in the famous *pas de deux*, "*L'Oiseau Bleu.*" Pavlova engaged his exclusive services as her teacher for a period of years, but he had to beg her to release him from his contract, as so many dancers besought him to give them lessons. From 1909 he was attached to the Diaghilev Ballet as mime and *maître de ballet*, and in the latter capacity was therefore responsible for the technical efficiency of the entire company. But, by 1918, he had grown weary of touring Europe and definitely decided to settle in London. There he opened a school, but he continued to give lessons to the company and to appear with them during their seasons in the capital.

When I first met Cecchetti, or "Maestro", as he was known to all his pupils, he was in the late sixties. He was a tubby little man with a figure like a peg-top, a slighter and shorter counterpart of Mr. Pickwick. His back was broad but a little rounded. He had a fine large head, fairly covered with white hair, which he wore close-cropped. He was, however, bald where the crown met the forehead. His plump, clean-shaven features were the colour of old ivory, save for a slight ruddiness at the cheek-bones. His eyes were blue-grey, very bright and alert like those of a large bird, and they sparkled with a fatherly benevolence or a whimsical air of mockery, according to his mood. His expressive features, typically Italian, radiated intelligence and personality.

His studio in Shaftesbury Avenue was reached by a flight of narrow, well-worn stairs. It was a large, rectangular, white-walled room, spoilt a little at one end by the presence of some columns supporting the ceiling; the studio was lit by four windows facing the street and masked for half their height by a glazed, transparent paper patterned with roses and their leaves.

The room was bare except on the side opposite the entrance door, where there was an upright piano, a large mirror, a revolving chair sacred to the use of Cecchetti, a table set with vases filled with flowers, and, lastly, a comfortable settee. Along the three remaining walls was fixed the all-important bar, above which hung photographs of Karsavina, Pavlova, Trefilova, Nijinsky and others of Cecchetti's famous pupils.

Cecchetti was so busy in his studio that he worked from nine in the morning until six at night, when he went home to dine. Between the time he arrived and the time he left he often ate nothing but a banana and a few biscuits.

He was nearly always the first to arrive. He entered with a brisk step, took off his coat, picked up a malacca cane, and sat in his chair waiting for the class to assemble. It was the invariable custom for every pupil, immediately on his or her arrival, to greet him with a kiss on both cheeks, which he returned. He prolonged the greeting with pupils he liked, whereas in other cases he granted only the briefest salutation.

Regular class pupils were expected to pay weekly in advance every Monday, and all such fees went into one trousers' pocket, as did payments for odd class lessons. This method made for simple and efficient accountancy. The fees for private lessons went into the other trousers' pocket. On his return at night he would take out all the money from one pocket and count it, and then do the same with the other. Thus he could ascertain with ease his receipts which he banked every few days.

Speaking of financial matters, I remember how shocked he was one day at the arrival of an unexpected demand for income tax, the basis of which, while highly gratifying to his pride, was deeply wounding to his pocket. Only in Italian could he find words adequate to express his indignation. Expostulations having failed, he announced to me his magnanimous resolve.

"I realize," he said, "that since I am living in this country, I must abide by its laws, and I shall therefore tell the authorities that I am quite willing to give five pounds for the use of the government!"

Cecchetti taught dancing with a deep understanding and a profound reverence for beautiful movement. He knew the long travail that must be undergone before a human being is formed into a dancer. He had no use for pupils whose mothers thought them prodigies, or for pupils obsessed with ideas of their own importance, or for those so eager to arrive at success that they expected to be finished dancers after three months' training. Such applicants for tuition he flatly refused to teach. Brought up in a hard school, he was well aware that there was only one road to the acquisition of technical ability—work, more work, and still more work.

He permitted no privileged pupils in his classes. He treated all alike, whether the pupil was a comparative beginner or a *ballerina* of the Diaghilev Ballet. He was always brutally frank and to the point. He would say to his class:

"Whatever the difference in your status outside, here you are all my pupils and I shall make no distinctions."

The relation between master and pupil was that of a father and his children, but he was none the less exacting. He conducted the lessons with the discipline and rigour of a drill-sergeant, whistling a set melody to each movement, and emphasizing the time with vigorous taps of his cane on the floor. These melodies were extracts from classical composers, or quotations from well-known operas and famous old ballets.

Now and again he would step forward and correct the curve of an arm, the placing of a head, or the position of a leg. It was an inspiration to watch him demonstrating a movement, to see the actions of his wonderfully expressive arms and hands, to witness how his whole body shared in the movement, even to his very breathing. When the movements were executed to his liking, his face took on a beatific expression and he seemed to be lost in a dream. Suddenly, he would note a careless movement. In an instant his manner would change. He would dart forward with contorted brows, fix a glaring bloodshot eye on the culprit, and loose a searing spate of mingled Italian and Russian, the precise nature of which it would be unwise even to guess at.

There was no modern pampering of inhibitions, no slacking in Cecchetti's classes. He would insist on a movement's being repeated until he was satisfied. Many a time have I seen a famous dancer practising *pirouettes*, over and over again, until the beads of perspiration on her brow flew off and bedewed the ground like the drops from the rose of a watering-can.

On one occasion when his upbraidings had reduced a pupil to tears, he patted her cheek affectionately and observed:

"My dear pupil, I had to scold you because you were doing your work badly, and I shall continue to do so until you improve. Here, in class, it is *my* business to teach and *yours* to learn, and if the good God Himself were my pupil, and His work did not please me, I should treat Him just the same!"

Cecchetti had a robust and satirical humour which he vented on pupils with whose work he was dissatisfied. For instance, he would say, "I asked you for an *attitude croisée*, but what you are doing reminds me of a dog lifting its leg!" He had an equally pungent remark for the pupil who had difficulty in holding her stomach in (a common occurrence with beginners), but this I can quite easily leave to the reader's imagination.

When he was in a particularly good humour and expansive mood, he would promise an interesting anecdote concerning Henri Quatre of amorous memory. But, by some curious coincidence or intuition, Mme. Cecchetti would always arrive at the moment of revelation, for, almost before the door opened to announce her presence, her voice would be heard raised in remonstrance, "*Non, non, Enrico, pas l'histoire de Henri Quatre!*

Cecchetti resided on the first floor of 21 Wardour Street, his rooms being above a tobacconist's shop. The tenants of the floors above were also professionals of diverse kinds, including a trombone-player, a pair of tap-dancers, and a strange individual who wandered in and out with a couple of huge dogs.

Cecchetti's dining-room, like his studio, radiated an air of homely comfort. By the window stood a piano, the top groaning under bronze statues of dancers, vases of flowers, and piles of music. The mantelpiece was crowded with signed photographs of dancers. There were several comfortable chairs, a table covered with a chenille cloth, and a massive sideboard on which gleamed bottles of wine and more vases of flowers. From the ceiling over the table hung a cluster of electric lamps whose illuminating power was positively blinding. Cecchetti, so long accustomed

CECCHETTI AT HOME

to the glare of the footlights, seemed to insist on a like brilliance in his home.

I shall always remember those evenings at Wardour Street. Both Cecchetti and his wife were kindness personified. They had nothing of the lofty airs and graces that characterize petty talents; every visitor, whether she were a little child learning her five positions, or a *ballerina* of international reputation, received the same genial welcome. No sooner did one cross the threshold than Madame would proffer a box of chocolates or a jar of biscuits, or Cecchetti would pour out a glass of vermouth. Then he would talk while Madame sat sewing by the fire; and presently their cat, Mami, would scramble up on the table and listen with eager ears and wise eyes.

I used to visit Cecchetti almost every evening about seven, except when he asked me to call for him at his studio, when I would accompany him home. There, an excellent meal, prepared by his wife, awaited him. When he had dined and rested, the table would be cleared, and work on the book began, so vigorous and indefatigable was the Master. I rarely left before midnight.

Cecchetti would explain or demonstrate, the conversation being mainly in French, while I made my notes in English. Now and again he would be at a loss for a word and give its equivalent in Russian or Italian which I could follow but seldom. Hence my place at the table was flanked by two dictionaries, Russian-English and Italian-English.

The evening usually commenced with an examination of my description of exercises in accordance with the teaching of the night before. I would read out my text, rendering it in French, while Cecchetti moved accordingly to see if I had correctly interpreted the movements and their sequence. One of my principal difficulties was to describe a movement in such a way that it could not be performed in any other manner but the right one. To this end I tested my descriptions on young students of my acquaintance and was often dismayed to find that a foot or arm could be placed in so many positions but the right one. So I had continually to revise the text in order to prevent all possible misinterpretations. Things did not always proceed smoothly, for Cecchetti had a quick temper and at the shortest notice would fly into such a rage that, literally, lightnings seemed to flash from his eyes. But the storm generally ended as quickly as it had begun, to be accompanied by a smile of such beauty that all differences were at once forgotten.

From time to time, in the explanation of a *pas*, Cecchetti would recall the movements of one or other of the countless dancers he had known; this would lead to anecdotes of some phase of his theatrical life which he would relate with rare gusto. On such occasions it was easy to imagine what magnificent performances the actors of the *Commedia dell'Arte* must have given. A wink, a sniff, a pursing of the lips, a scratching of the ear, a tapping of the nose, could, in his hands, supply all the elements for the telling of a tale without words.

The question of illustrations for the book was almost the last problem to be tackled. It was in the winter that

CECCHETTI POSES FOR THE MANUAL

I discussed the matter with Cecchetti. I decided to scrap all previous sketches, some three hundred in all, and to have new ones drawn. This difficult task I entrusted to Randolph Schwabe, now the head of the Slade.

Some of the illustrations were kindly posed by Lopokova, but the model for the majority was Cecchetti himself. I recall that the first sitting took place one bitterly cold Sunday morning. In order to concentrate on the essential line of the various positions, Schwabe and I made delicate hints as to whether it would be possible for Cecchetti to remove some of his clothing. Full of enthusiasm, he responded readily, but, owing to the then shortage of fuel, the room, despite the small fire in the grate, was too cold to keep him standing dressed only in his underwear.

Cecchetti, however, with Napoleonic decision, resolved to produce a fire. He dragged two perfectly good chairs from his kitchen, and, to our amazement, broke them up. Then, by placing some of the pieces in the existing fire, and holding the lid of a dustbin before it, a strong draught was created which speedily fanned the fire into a roaring blaze. Having proved the success of this method, Cecchetti put on his fur overcoat and waited until Schwabe had his pencils sharpened and sketching block to hand. Then, at a given signal, wood was packed into the grate and blown into a blaze; I immediately whisked off Cecchetti's coat and he assumed the desired pose until the fire subsided. The whole process was then repeated.

I studied with Cecchetti on and off for some two

years, and, I fear, almost ruined my business as bookseller, for lack of time to attend to it. I spent most of the day assembling, clarifying, and writing out what I had learned the night before, and in revising the notes I had discussed with Cecchetti. And these revisions were never-ending, there was always some touch to be added, some loophole for error to be closed.

The reader will appreciate that with so many obstacles and difficulties to overcome, there were often times when I was haunted with the fear that the book never would be completed, but, at long last, the day came when I could write at the bottom of the page, with a sense of deep satisfaction not unmingled with intense relief—*finis coronat opus*.[1]

[1] The book is entitled *The Manual of Classical Theatrical Dancing (Cecchetti Method)*.

CHAPTER IX

~ 1921 ~

THE year 1921 found the company still without Massine. His roles were taken by Leon Woizikowsky, a good choice since many of them had been worked out on him. He was a short, dark, stocky young man with sallow features that might almost be described as nondescript. He looked like so many other young men that in private life he would hardly have occasioned a second glance. On the stage, however, he was a character dancer of the first rank. He seemed possessed of a tireless energy and danced with a vitality, an ease, a poise, and a sense of timing which were remarkable; added to these qualities he had a wonderful memory for steps, and could, I am sure, have danced almost any role in any ballet in the repertory. His appreciation of the most subtle rhythm can be grasped only by those who have seen him in action. An important addition to the male soloists was Pierre Vladimirov, a fine classical dancer.

The first Diaghilev season of the year took place at the Prince's Theatre, under the management of C. B. Cochran, and opened on May 26th, the programme being *Children's Tales*, *La Boutique Fantasque*, and *Les*

Sylphides. The part of Bova Korolevich was taken by Jean Jazvinsky. In the *Boutique* the Tarantella Dancers were Sokolova and Novak, while Jazvinsky was the King of Spades, and Vladimirov the King of Diamonds. The male dancer in *Les Sylphides* was Stanislas Idzikowsky.

The first night was marked by a considerable event, the return to the company of Lydia Lopokova, who danced the Can-Can Dancer in *Boutique*, and was the leading soloist in *Les Sylphides*. She received a great ovation and had innumerable curtain calls after *Boutique*. In *Les Sylphides* she was again continually applauded and called before the curtain. It was almost as though the spectators vied with one another to show their joy at her return.

But even theatres must close and so the footlights were put out and the safety-curtain lowered. Still the audience clapped for Lopokova. Diaghilev went behind the scenes and returned with the *ballerina*, then in her dressing-gown. He ushered her into a box on the stage level and led her forward until she was in full view of the audience, and, as she smilingly bowed her acknowledgments, affectionately patted her shoulder.

The first novelty of the season was a suite of Andalusian dances, called *Cuadro Flamenco*, which had its London *première* on May 30th. The setting and costumes were designed by Picasso. For the first time in the history of the company, the numbers were danced not by members of the ballet, but by a group of Spanish gypsy dancers, whom Diaghilev had brought over from Spain. The music was provided by their own guitarists.

MARIA DALBAICIN

Picasso's setting consisted of a small, square, raised platform placed in the middle of the stage and set within a false proscenium frame with a decorative scheme in red, yellow, and black. A number of chairs were arranged on three sides of the platform, the open side facing the audience. The dancers and musicians were seated on the chairs, the former rising when they had to dance and sitting down again at the end of their number.

The curtain rose in comparative silence, while the musicians strummed on their guitars and the dancers smoothed their skirts, or tested their castanets. The performance opened with a *Malaguena* rendered by the singer of the troupe. This song was an acutely shrill and discordant wailing which was more curious than agreeable. Then came the dances—"*Tango Gitana*", "*Farruca*", "*Allegrias*", "*Garrotin Grotesco*", "*Garrotin Comico*", and, finally, the "*Jota Aragonesa*". I do not recall the numbers sufficiently well to attempt to describe them, but I can still remember something of the appearance of the dancers, whom Goya and Zuloaga would have loved to paint.

One of the dancers, Maria Dalbaicin, still in her 'teens, was one of the most beautiful women I have ever seen. She had a fine figure, regular features of classic beauty, and a complexion smooth as marble, bronzed by the sun and set off by a wealth of dark silky hair which gleamed like old lacquer. But with all her beauty there was something strangely sexless about her. I could have sat and gazed at her for hours, not as a desirable woman, but in the same way that one admires a fine bronze or an exquisite piece of porcelain.

At the other end of the scale was a male dancer who, having lost both legs, danced on the stumps of his thighs, which were encased in stout leather sheaths. To see him "dance" was rather a horrifying spectacle, and there were so many protests to the management that after a while he ceased to appear.

The men wore sober clothes, the typical open shirt, waistcoat, and hip-tight and ankle-tight black trousers; the women's dresses were of light colours. One dancer wore a white dress adorned with tiers of wide flounces ending in a long train which, on turning, she deftly kicked behind her.

This was the real thing. You forgot the well appointed theatre, with its conventional plush and gilding, and seemed to be transported to that land where things beautiful, sinister, sensual, grotesque, and macabre are to be found in such strange proximity, their very qualities stressed by such vivid contrasts.

Dalbaicin danced with a pure, if cold, classic grace. The other dancers, emphasizing the rhythm with the staccato stamping of their heels, were passionate or lively. As each dancer rose, those seated incited their companion to greater efforts by rhythmic claps of the hands and shouted imprecations and encouragement. The troupe had an enthusiastic reception and at the end several of the women demonstrated their appreciation by leaning over the footlights towards the audience, placing their hands on their well developed breasts, so that they stood out in sharp relief, and then jerked their bodies so that their breasts shook violently, a form of acknowledgment quite new to a ballet audience.

When I went behind the scenes I often encountered the members of this strangely assorted group, sullen, quarrelsome, and passionate by turns. Sometimes they would pass from words and violent menacing gestures to blows, a man would suddenly twist sideways and lash out with his foot at a woman's stomach, from which blow she would just save herself by a swift backward arching of her body. When Diaghilev crossed the stage while they were there, he was greeted with, presumably, friendly words and gestures. But I noticed that he invariably hurried quickly past the Spaniards, half alarmed and half embarrassed.

Diaghilev tried an interesting experiment by giving Dalbaicin the role of the Miller's Wife in *The Three Cornered Hat*, in which she made her début on June 2nd. A genuine Spanish dancer and a lovely woman, her success appeared a foregone conclusion. Actually, she did not seem to fit into the ballet at all, and the experiment proved only too clearly that to dance one's national dances well is insufficient to achieve success in Ballet, which demands not only a thorough training in classical technique, but the ability to project oneself into the very core of a part, and to work with others for the success of the whole.

June 9th saw the first London performance of *Chout*, the production of which Diaghilev, who for some months past had lacked an experienced choreographer, had entrusted jointly to Michel Larionov and Thadeus

Slavinsky. Slavinsky was an excellent character dancer and Larionov was the Russian painter who had already achieved success with his designs for *The Midnight Sun* and *Children's Tales*. I never saw the ballet in rehearsal, but I should say that Larionov conceived the ballet and that Slavinsky was expected to give practical expression to his ideas. Larionov certainly had many ideas for the poses and groups which, as they occurred to him, he would record in a pocket-book by means of stick figures.

I made his acquaintance through Barocchi. Larionov was tall and strongly built, with fair hair and typically Russian features of the broader type. His head was large and his cheeks plump and clean-shaven. He had a strong, even slightly aggressive, personality, and he had a disconcerting mannerism of placing his face close to yours when he wished to emphasize a point.

One evening, as I was coming from the stage through the pass-door, I met him just at the bottom of the stairs leading to the stalls. He began to talk about Ballet and, becoming enthusiastic, spoke so loudly that we were almost turned out for creating a disturbance. But, stripped of his formidable exterior, he had a generous and kindly nature, and was a great student and admirer of everything to do with Ballet.

Chout was in six scenes, with music by Sergey Prokofiev. The scenery and costumes were by Larionov.

The principal characters were: *the Buffoon*, Thadeus Slavinsky; *the Buffoon's Wife*, Lydia Sokolova; *the Merchant*, Jean Jazvinsky; *the Bridesmaids*, Mmes. Nemchinova, Zirmundska. The London *première* had an additional cachet in that it was conducted by the composer himself.

The book of the ballet, adapted from a Russian legend, was one of those examples of tortuous Russian humour which strike no responsive chord in our breasts.

A Buffoon pretends to kill his wife (also a Buffoon), then, with a crack of a whip, he apparently restores her to life. The pre-arranged trick is performed successfully before an audience of seven other admiring buffoons. Impressed by the magic qualities of the whip, they purchase it for a goodly sum (that is the purpose of the trick), and set off for home. There they kill their own wives and hasten to restore them with the whip, but without avail.

The angry buffoons return, determined to punish the Buffoon for having played them such a trick. Terrified, he hides his wife and disguises himself as a cook. The buffoons, failing to discover the Buffoon, carry off the cook, who pleases them.

The seven buffoons have seven marriageable daughters. A rich merchant, attended by two bridesmaids, comes to choose a wife. But, to the chagrin of the buffoons, he decides on the cook.

The merchant, having returned home, takes his wife to his room. The pretended cook, hoping to save the situation, pretends to be ill and clamours for fresh air. The merchant obligingly lets her out of the window by means of a sheet.

When he eventually pulls the sheet back, he finds a goat tied to the end. The bridesmaids and servants rush in with the news that his wife has been changed into a goat. At this point the Buffoon enters with seven soldiers and demands the return of his cook. The bewildered merchant proffers the goat, but the Buffoon forces him to pay a fine of 100 roubles on pain of imprisonment. The Buffoon and his wife enjoy themselves on the money they have acquired, and the seven soldiers make love to the seven daughters of the buffoons.

The best part of the production was the setting, the rest fell flat. Larionov's settings, inspired as usual by Russian peasant art, interpreted in the spirit of cubism, were brilliantly conceived, but the colour contrasts, accentuated by the angular shapes composing the design, were so vivid and so dazzling that it was almost painful to look at the stage, and the position was not improved when brilliantly clad figures were set in movement against such a background. I would say that the effect on the eyes was almost as irritating as those flickering streaks of coloured light so characteristic of early colour films. Again, some of the costumes exceeded the limits of fantasy, for instance, certain of the women wore high-heeled satin shoes with their peasant dresses.

The music was a medley of folk airs and jazz rhythms. The ballet itself had a few good moments when Slavinsky danced the character steps which he had devised for himself as the Buffoon, but as a whole the choreography was disconnected and lacked design.

On July 9th, *L'Oiseau de Feu* was revived, the part of Ivan Tsarevich being taken by Pierre Vladimirov.

DIAGHILEV PLANS A NEW SURPRISE

On the 29th the Miller's Wife had a new interpreter in the person of Lydia Sokolova. She danced well and gave a good robust performance. But while Karsavina always struck me as being a little too refined, Sokolova seemed to err in the opposite direction, and to make the character a little too rough.

The season ended on July 30th, the programme being *The Good Humoured Ladies*, the *pas de deux*, "*The Enchanted Princess*"; the *Polovtsian Dances from "Prince Igor"*, with Vladimirov as Chief; and *La Boutique Fantasque*. In the last named the role of the Shopkeeper's Assistant was taken by Zverev and that of the Cossack Chief by Addison.

Soon afterwards, the company disbanded for the holidays and I heard no more of them until September, when I was delighted by a visit from Barocchi, who told me that Diaghilev was planning a new surprise. Having accustomed his audiences to expect each season some new sensation inspired by the latest movement in art or music, he was going to execute a *volte face* and produce one of the most famous of classical ballets—Petipa's masterpiece, *La Belle au Bois Dormant*, for which Tchaikovsky wrote the score. Moreover, Sir Oswald Stoll, on behalf of the Alhambra Co. Ltd., had agreed to finance the venture, the capital sum to be repaid by the setting aside of a certain proportion of the weekly receipts. The ballet was to be given at the Alhambra, where it was confidently expected to run for at least six months.

Barocchi told me that Diaghilev had a plan for giving the ballet a touch of modernity by having each scene introduced by a boy and girl of 1921, who, acting as a kind of *compère* and *commère*, would speak appropriate lines. Diaghilev, Barocchi said, had thought of asking Bernard Shaw to write the dialogue. What did I think of the plan? I expressed strong disapproval of the proposed introduction of contemporary children in a ballet set in the 17th and 18th centuries, and said I disliked still more the use of dialogue which, while it might be used to introduce a dance scene in a revue, would have a most disagreeable effect in a ballet, and was unpardonable in a great classic ballet. Whether other opinions were sought in this matter I do not know, it is sufficient to record that this scheme did not materialize.

Presently I heard more details. Stravinsky was editing Tchaikovsky's score and restoring it to its original state. Bakst had been commissioned to design the settings and costumes, and, full of enthusiasm, was inventing more wonderful designs each day. Sergeyev, former *régisseur* of the Maryinsky Theatre, was to reconstruct the ballet from his choreographic records of the production as originally composed by Petipa; while Nijinska was to devise certain *ensembles* and special interpolated numbers. Finally, the whole was to be produced under the direction of Léon Bakst.

Barocchi, with his usual kindness, said he would let me know when there were to be specially interesting rehearsals, and, kinder still, promised to take me along to see them. Thus I was privileged to see that memorable production in the course of preparation.

The company was practically the same as that which

had appeared at the Princes, except that the principals had been reinforced by the engagement of Olga Spessiva (Spessivtzeva), the greatest of Russian *ballerine* at this period, Bronislava Nijinska, Carlotta Brianza (the Princess Aurora of the original production at St. Petersburg in 1890), Lubov Egorova, Ludmilla Schollar, and Anatol Vilzak. The *corps de ballet* showed a few additions, including some promising English dancers, for instance, Hilda Bewicke, Ursula Moreton, Dorothy Coxon, and Patrikieff, who is best known by the name he later assumed and made famous—Anton Dolin.

The Alhambra had been closed for the rehearsals and there I spent many enjoyable and instructive evenings. The nights were cold and it seemed colder still in the theatre, with the heating cut off and the stalls shrouded in white dust-sheets. There were no lights in the auditorium, which was as dark as the proverbial tomb; only the stage was lit and that by footlights alone.

There were barely a dozen people in the stalls. You could recognize Diaghilev by his broad back, the strangely flat contour of the back of his head, and the astrakhan collar of his overcoat which he had slung round his shoulders. At his side would be Stravinsky, with his slender, stooping shoulders, egg-shaped head, big nose, straggling moustache, and globular eyes peering owlishly through horn-rimmed spectacles: he reminded one of a harassed headmaster.

They would be joined by Bakst, a brisk, blue-eyed, dapper little man—what a fine Pantalon he would have made—who walked with that elastic poise which comes from daily fencing exercise. His hair was auburn, his complexion fresh-coloured, and he sported a fine auburn moustache. He wore gold-rimmed spectacles. In the lapel of his coat was the red ribbon of the *Legion d'Honneur*. When Bakst had taken his seat he would rest his head on his chin and gaze at the proceedings with a cold and critical gaze which missed nothing. Sometimes there would be a fourth personage: Sergeyev, short, spare, grizzled, and grim of expression.

The stage itself was bare except for a piano (played by the diminutive, grey-haired, and admirable pianist, Mrs. Lucas) placed near the prompt corner, and a cluster of dancers. The women wore pink tights and shoes, and short skirts of various colours; the men were attired in close-fitting black breeches, white shirts and socks, and black shoes. They all looked cold and many of the women had knitted footless stockings drawn over their tights and one or more woollen jumpers tied round their shoulders.

As the pianist rendered the air of a *pas seul* or *pas de deux*, the mass of dancers would move to the sides, and Lopokova or Vladimirov would dance separately or together. If the group of critical watchers in the stalls were pleased, there would be a few discreet handclaps, which the dancers would acknowledge with an exaggerated mock obeisance. Despite the severe discipline of the proceedings, the dancers were so bound up with the theatre that, even at rehearsal, they could not resist an opportunity to indulge in a little stage play.

DIAGHILEV HOLDS A LIGHTING REHEARSAL

Sometimes the rehearsals would concentrate on an *ensemble*, when the main body of dancers would swirl into long sinuous lines, combine into one throbbing mass, divide, form circle, revolve, then dash from sight. The proceedings were directed by Nijinska. In her dark practice clothes, with her pale features and straw-coloured hair, she seemed like a goddess as she stood near the footlights, bending this plastic, infinitely responsive material to her will, staying it, urging it on, guiding it through evolution after evolution with dramatic gestures of her white arms, faintly luminous in the half light.

Another evening there would be a lighting rehearsal. I remember how thrilled I was when the curtain went up on the setting for the first scene, with its suggestion of the Palace of Versailles. Here was true grandeur and magnificence, without vulgarity or ostentation. Then began the business of lighting. Diaghilev would remain hunched in his seat with an electrician to relay his instructions to the stage, first, pink in this flood, amber in that, then the whole "washed" with white. He would spend hour after hour dimming this, "bringing up" that, until he was satisfied and the weary light-men could plot the lighting. Even then he would have the curtain lowered and, after a few minutes' interval to banish the memory of the lighting from his mind, would order the curtain to be raised again so that he might judge how the effect appealed to him, when revealed afresh.

Those who had never been present at one of Diaghilev's lighting rehearsals did not know what they were in for. The rehearsals went on half the night if need be. At such times he cared nothing for the mounting cost of overtime, the passing of the hours, or the fact that he had not eaten for a long period. If the men showed signs of revolt, he would grant a ten or fifteen minutes' rest interval. As soon as the interval was up, he would utter a curt, *"Continuez, s'il vous plaît"*. The men would glare and curse under their breath, but they did his bidding.

On yet another evening I saw a trial of some of the special scenic effects, the climbing arabesques of green plants charged with lilac blossoms which the Lilac Fairy (desiring to protect the Princess Aurora after she has pricked her finger and fallen asleep) brings into being with a flourish of her wand. This effect, which Bakst had designed with such loving care, was not easy to realize. The plants were meant to sprout from the ground and rise higher and higher until the wooded garden with its sleeping princess and her courtiers was quite hidden by the climbing tendrils; but some part of the machinery always failed, so that the plants, having once sprouted, remained obstinately still. At the first rehearsal, the flymen and the machinists beneath the stage began to blame each other for the constant mishaps, and almost came to blows in their bitter exasperation.

One afternoon I watched a costume rehearsal. The dresses were made of the finest materials and in some instances cost from forty to fifty pounds apiece. Certain of the more historical dresses were made by Mrs. Lovat Fraser, the wife of the designer of the

DIAGHILEV AT A COSTUME REHEARSAL

setting and costumes for Playfair's revival of Gay's *Beggar's Opera*.

A chair was placed with its back to the footlights and there Diaghilev sat in judgment while Grigoriev summoned dancer after dancer. Each was completely dressed in the costume to be worn and carried Bakst's original design, framed in talc. The dancer under inspection handed the design to Diaghilev, who compared it with the finished costume. When he had passed or criticized the dress, as the case might be, he would ask the dancer to execute a phrase of steps from his or her *pas*.

I well remember Vladimirov, who might have stepped from a painting by Le Brun, with his splendid gold-laced suit of red and broad-brimmed feathered hat. But when he was asked to dance, the fine *élévation* I had remarked at rehearsal had greatly diminished. Diaghilev's treatment of the costume reduced the tailor to the verge of tears, for he shortened the skirts of the coat, altered the sleeves, stripped off gold braid, until the dancer no longer felt he was tethered to the ground. So each costume was rigorously subjected to the dual test of accuracy of reproduction and dancing practicability.

In the foregoing paragraphs I have attempted to describe some of the stages attendant on the production of this ballet, since they are typical of Diaghilev's methods and prove his supervision at every stage of the evolution of the ballet in preparation. He worked no less assiduously on the literary structure of the ballet. *The Sleeping Princess* was much more than a reconstruction of Petipa's ballet. Diaghilev had edited it. For instance, a hundred years is supposed to elapse from the time when the Princess Aurora falls asleep to when she is awakened by the kiss of Prince Charming, and in the original production the first scene was set in the reign of Henri IV and the later ones in the time of Louis XIV. Diaghilev chose the periods of Louis XIV and Louis XV.

Diaghilev also eliminated those dances which are feeble, for instance, *"Cinderella"*, and replaced them with others such as the *"Dance of the Sugar Plum Fairy"* from *Casse Noisette*. He also took the melodies of the *"Danse Arabe"* and *"Danse Chinoise"* from the same ballet, and commissioned Nijinska to devise new dances to them. He could never have countenanced such abominations as Ivanov's burlesque imitation of an Ouled-Naïl dancer, or his pair of pseudo-Chinese knockabout comedians, whose proper place was in Widow Twankey's laundry, in some fifth-rate production of a pantomime based on the story of *Aladdin and the Wonderful Lamp*.

Instead there was a Mandarin who made love to two Porcelain Princesses who hid their blushes behind their trembling fans, and a Schéhérazade, borne in a Persian version of a sedan-chair, who was allowed to take a short walk always moving with a staccato heel-tapping borrowed from the Moors, and watched by the jealous eyes of the Shah and his brother, each bearing an upraised scimitar.

Similarly, in the final scene, Diaghilev refused to permit Prince Charming and Princess Aurora to dance to a certain boisterous melody which occurs after the *grand pas de deux*. This melody was certainly not suited to a classical *pas de deux*, and Nijinska used it for a character number, "*Innocent Ivan and his Brothers*," based on Russian folk dance measures, whose vigour and animation invariably "brought down the house".

Genius has been defined as an infinite capacity for taking pains. Diaghilev had this quality in large measure and to it he joined knowledge, taste, and inspiration. He seemed to feel instinctively what was good and what was bad, and, when he was preparing the *Belle*—as he always referred to the ballet—for production, he did not hesitate to remove some of the weaknesses of the original version, such as I have instanced. How right he was is proved clearly by a quite recent revival of this ballet, the defects of which are only too obvious. But he made one mistake in regard to the financial side of the production; he expended far more than the sum[1] agreed with Sir Oswald Stoll, a reckless action which was to have serious consequences later.

[1] Quite recently I learned from a former member of Diaghilev's staff that the original sum guaranteed by Sir Oswald Stoll for the production of the "*Belle*" was £10,000. Diaghilev, however, was so extravagant that before the production was completed, he had to confess to Stoll that his commitments already exceeded that amount, and that he could not complete the ballet without the outlay of a further £5,000. This sum, too, was exhausted and an additional £5,000 declared to be imperative. Stoll was exceedingly displeased at this second demand which, however, he was forced to concede, since the recovery of the capital invested depended on the production of the ballet.

DIAGHILEV BALLET IN LONDON

At last came the first night, originally announced for October 31st, but postponed to November 2nd. Only then could one receive a complete impression of that superb production, to my mind the finest exposition of classical ballet that London of the present century has yet seen. Bakst had steeped himself in the *Grand Siècle*, had studied such masters as Berain and Martin for his costumes, and had sought inspiration for his settings from the portfolios of the Bibienas, which he transmuted into lovely conceptions of his own. The curious may examine many of these designs for themselves in the volume entitled *L'Œuvre de Léon Bakst pour la Belle au Bois Dormant*, which contains 54 reproductions in colour of Bakst's designs for settings and costumes and a preface by André Levinson; it was published by Brunoff, Paris, in 1921.

Diaghilev had produced the ballet in a manner worthy of Fouquet's entertainments at his Palace of Vaux. The cast is so long that I have relegated it to the Appendix,[1] where it may be studied at leisure.

The atmosphere of the *première* of *The Sleeping Princess* was like that of *La Boutique Fantasque*. There was the same packed house, the promenades almost obliterated by the throng of expectant bystanders. Everywhere there was tobacco-smoke, chatter, and surmises.

I hurried on to the stage because I was anxious to renew acquaintance with the greenroom. The mirrors had disappeared. The contents of the room were a strange admixture of poverty and wealth. To the left,

[1] See Appendix E.

a much-used sewing-machine; to the right, along the whole side of one wall, a row of faded deck-chairs. Every conceivable space was piled high with beautiful flowers and gigantic laurel-wreaths.

The stage was filled with scene-shifters and workmen putting the finishing touches to the scenery. The machinist, Komishov, very tall, with an imposing red beard, was transforming a wooden balustrade into stone by means of a brush filled with grey paint. Some of the dancers appeared. Lopokova, serious and reserved. Spessiva, a beautiful, shy creature, thin and frail as an ivory statuette. They passed to the centre of the stage to rehearse a few difficult steps.

Until then, there was always the atmosphere of *behind the scenes*. Yet in a moment all was transformed. It became impossible to move. Everywhere one encountered proud and richly costumed ministers of state, courtiers, maids-of-honour, and ladies-in-waiting. As the bewigged figures strutted to and fro you were reminded of a page of Dumas awakened to life, a picture by Vanloo or Charles le Brun. There was nothing of the tawdriness, the unreality that invariably greets the spectator who, charmed by the stage picture, seeks to touch, only to have the illusion destroyed.

But, despite the rapturous applause with which the ballet was received, the production was slightly marred by two failures of the stage machinery at critical moments. At the end of the second act, the climbing tendrils, having raised their heads, remained in a state of suspended animation, and ignored the summons of the Lilac Fairy, who waved her wand in vain. Again, at the end of the third act, when the Prince steps into the Fairy's frail barque to be carried to the mysterious abode of the sleeping Princess (an effect produced by a panoramic background which is eventually blotted out by a deepening mist, simulated by the lowering of a succession of gauze curtains), the machinery failed. Instead of the gauzes descending one behind the other, they piled up on a piece of projecting scenery until they resembled a monster bale of muslin on the shelf of a draper's shop. Diaghilev paled with anger at these blemishes and during the intervals burst upon the stage like a Fury.

I can still see that magnificent first scene of the Christening, the rich stonework and marble walls and columns lined with gorgeous negro guards in white and gold, and black and silver, the Marshal of the Court greeting the guests—lords and ladies, and fairies with their pages bearing charming gifts for the baby Princess. The aristocracy bore themselves with distinction, while the fairies invested their movements with an austere nobility which set them apart from the most honoured mortals. So life moved at a stately pace until suddenly interrupted by the appearance of the Wicked Fairy, who arrived in her coach drawn by rats. But she, too, had dignity; she was majestic even in her wrath.

It is not my intention here to describe the ballet, for that I have done elsewhere and at length. I only wish to emphasize the dignity and good taste which graced the production from the moment the curtain rose until it fell for the last time. Nothing is more difficult to produce than a classical ballet founded on a familiar fairy tale, it can so easily become a Christmas pantomime, which is danced instead of being spoken.

Petipa's classical numbers are most difficult to dance properly. I am not thinking primarily of their technical difficulty, often considerable, because that is only the framework of the dance, but of the *manner* in which they are danced. Those dances are full of subtleties of choreographic colour, a slow phrase contrasted with a quick one, the timing of a particular movement which must be held so long and not a moment longer, the carriage of the body, the poise of the head, the very control of the features—it is the attention paid to such details as these which makes the dance a work of art and not a mere combination of steps and *port de bras* rendered by a woman in ballet costume. Most of Petipa's *variations* were composed for dancers of distinction who spent months and even years polishing and perfecting the numbers they had made their own. This was the spirit which dominated Diaghilev's presentation.

The three principals were Olga Spessiva as the Princess Aurora, Lydia Lopokova as the Lilac Fairy, and Pierre Vladimirov as Prince Charming.

Spessiva was a superb dancer in the classical style, slight in figure with pale wistful features, her smooth dark hair parted in the middle and brushed flat to her head in the romantic manner. She had a splendid technique which she displayed with art. Style, line, timing, poise, control—such were her attributes. Her *pirouettes*, her *batterie*, and her *développés* were models.

Her poise and control when extending her raised leg in a *développé* were quite remarkable.

Lopokova, though possessed of an excellent technique, was not a great classical *ballerina* like Spessiva, but she made her Lilac Fairy charming, generous, and impulsive like herself.

Vladimirov brought style and nobility to his Prince Charming and was particularly good in his scenes with the Lilac Fairy and in the *grand pas de deux* in the last act.

When all was so excellent it seems invidious to mention names, but among portraits which I felt to be very well done were Zverev's Gallison, a masterly impersonation of a wine-bibbing courtier, and Tchernicheva's Countess, which created a real nostalgia of unrequited love.

The dances given by the hunting party in Scene III were beautifully arranged by Nijinska; the figures, obviously based on dances of the period, were conceived in a mood of elegance and refinement well suited to the occasion.

Among the individual dances of the final scene I liked best the Carnation Fairy's *variation* and "*Columbine*", both danced by Nemchinova; the *variation* of the Fairy of the Humming Birds, danced by Nijinska, whose movements were often reminiscent of her famous brother; the "*Blue Bird*" *pas de deux* by Lopokova and Idzikowsky; the Puss in Boots and White Cat of Addison and Schollar; and the Red Riding Hood and Wolf of Sokolova and Mikolaichik.

Fired by that wonderful evening I decided to add *The Sleeping Princess* to my series of *Impressions of the*

BEHIND THE SCENES AT THE SLEEPING PRINCESS

Russian Ballet, but, as the ballet required a whole evening for its performance, I resolved to devote two books to it. The illustrations I entrusted to Randolph Schwabe.

I went almost every evening to *The Sleeping Princess* for the whole of its run. Sometimes I watched the ballet from the auditorium, while during the intervals I went and sat in the greenroom, where another unrehearsed ballet could be seen, little pages in blue and silver watching in admiration the famous soloists as they came into the room to give a final glance at their appearance. There would also be members of the *corps de ballet* chatting, exchanging confidences, or indulging in light-hearted banter.

On other nights I went "behind" long before the curtain was due to rise. The unlit stage made a most eerie impression. The walls of blackness formed by the wings and backcloth seemed to stretch to infinity. The palace scene of the first act was set, but all was dark and ghostly except for a tiny pilot lamp suspended above the golden cradle of the Princess Aurora. The dim stage seemed like a room out of a macabre tale by Edgar Allan Poe, a haunted palace which the stranger entered at his peril, a feeling heightened by the vague outline of Carabosse's sinister black coach which lurked behind the backcloth.

As the time drew near for the curtain to be rung up, Grigoriev would appear, glance at his wrist-watch and make a signal, when, as though at the waving of another fairy's wand, the darkness immediately gave place to the palace gleaming with light. It was a wonderful spectacle to see the ballet from the wings, to stand amid the throng of splendidly dressed men and women in their lovely silks and satins, slashed with gold or silver, waiting their turn to enter, and try to throw one's thoughts back in conjecture as to what the *levées* at Versailles had really been like.

Schwabe shared all my enthusiasm for the life behind the scenes. There was so much that I wanted him to sketch in his notebook. But, before he had time to set pencil to paper, I would see something which seemed still more desirable. To tell the truth, there were too many things to sketch and so we had to choose, but, during that brief moment of reflection, the magic had passed, perhaps never to return in quite the same guise.

Among a myriad recollections I recall two great moments. First, the end of the second act, when the Lilac Fairy conjures from the ground the climbing net of tendrils with their purple blossoms; at that same moment there were floods of lilac light from above and below the swiftly rising plants. It was an enthralling sight to look through the transparent columns of light at the dancers moving beyond.

My other recollection is associated with the end of the third scene, when the hunting party leaves the moody Prince to his thoughts. As the light slowly faded you could see emerging from the darkened wings the pearly gondola bearing the Lilac Fairy, and, in the shadows beyond, a band of nymphs, phantom-like in their white ballet-skirts, awaiting her summons to enter, a lovely vision still imprinted on my memory.

ROYALTY VISITS THE SLEEPING PRINCESS

One night after the performance I took Schwabe to Nijinska's dressing-room, to make a drawing of her in the part of the Lilac Fairy. We chose the pose in which she holds her wand between her clasped hands. As the narrow room made it difficult for Schwabe to see his subject in the right perspective, Nijinska quickly took the things off her dressing-table and posed stand-on the top of it. The "sitting" was varied with little rests, during which Nijinska talked about ballet, a conversation so interesting that we lost all count of time, until we were sharply reminded of it by the abrupt turning off of the lights in the dressing-room. Startled, I hurried to the stage door where I found the door-keeper, believing that all the artistes had gone, was on the point of departure.

It was not yet possible to forecast the staying power of *The Sleeping Princess*, for, after the first few weeks, the "houses" varied considerably; sometimes they were full, and sometimes they were patchy.

On December 12th the ballet received the royal patronage of Their Majesties King George V and Queen Mary, the Duke of York, the Queen of Norway, the Princess Victoria, the Princess Mary and Lord Lascelles.

The theatre became a kind of ballet club, for night after night you would see the familiar faces of certain enthusiasts come to relive the ballet and enjoy its enchanting melodies and compelling rhythms, music that dancers could feel with all their bodies and which inspired them to exert their talents to the utmost.

This interest was stimulated by slight changes in

the cast so far as the two principal roles were concerned. For instance, the Princess Aurora would be taken by Spessiva one night, and by Lopokova another. A little later the *ballerina*, Vera Trefilova, came over from Paris at Diaghilev's invitation to dance the same role, a greatly appreciated performance which she repeated several times. Later still, Egorova danced the part.

Trefilova, petite, slight, and dark, with thin muscular limbs, dark eyes, and pale, expressive features, was at this time no longer youthful. But, when she danced, her fine school and the nobility and grace of her movements were immediately apparent. She danced with such poise, such steadiness, such lightness, such admirable timing, such complete subservience of the body to her will, that she made you realize as seldom before how beautiful is the geometry of dancing in the hands of a genuine *ballerina*, a term which meant something in the days of the Imperial Russian Ballet. I have to observe that the term has been so loosely used of late years that its true significance and importance have long since been lost.

The part of the Lilac Fairy was alternately danced by Lopokova and Nijinska. The latter presented a very interesting conception of the role, and her large eyes and pale features, crowned with her eighteenth century wig, gave her the appearance of a rare immortal.

As Christmas drew near I planned a few presents for some of my friends in the company. To Lopokova I gave a little work-box in the form of the crown she wore as the Lilac Fairy. This round tapering box,

EXCURSIONS INTO BIJOUTERIE

made of wood and covered with deep lilac leather, was tooled in gold with an outline design of the crown. The lining was of pale lilac silk and contained pockets for reels of cotton or silk. The lid, padded to hold pins and needles, was tooled with Lopokova's initials in Russian script, grouped about a tiny wand of mother-of-pearl. The two shades of lilac corresponded to the actual colours of the Lilac Fairy's costume.

For my other friends I planned little treasury-note cases of vellum tooled with an appropriate design and lined with silk of suitable colours. For instance, the case for Nemchinova, the Carnation Fairy, bore a carnation in pink and gold and was lined with carnation pink silk. These excursions into *bijouterie* were admirably carried out by my friend, George Sutcliffe, the binder of the volumes which adorn the Queen's Dolls' House.

A very important event occurred on January 5th, 1922, when Cecchetti appeared for one performance only in the part of Carabosse, which he had created thirty-two years previously. This was in celebration of his jubilee.

Some days beforehand a deputation from the company asked me to prepare for them some brief address in honour of Cecchetti which all could sign. I planned a vellum scroll to be headed with portraits in watercolour of Cecchetti in his most famous roles, below this came a short address, the precise wording of which I do not now remember. The scroll was laid between two pieces of silk, the lower green, the upper red, a delicate allusion to his Italian nationality.

Schwabe painted the figures, while the text was written out by one of Sutcliffe's scribes. As soon as this was done, the scroll was hurried to the stage-door of the Alhambra Theatre. There it was placed in a tiny room off the stage, to which the members of the company were summoned one by one, in great secrecy, to append their signatures. I noticed that the least important members of the troupe wrote the largest hand. The signatures were so many, and so interwoven and intercrossed, that at first sight the scroll resembled a piece of black lace.

At the end of the second act, when Cecchetti was taking his call, the curtain was raised and he was presented with a heavy silver tray from the company and many individual souvenirs of the occasion from his fellow artists. Lydia Kyasht, for instance, presented him with a silver fruit dish which she bore on one of Bakst's cushions.

The curtain was then lowered and a moving scene enacted. Imagine some hundred dancers grouped in a circle. In the centre stood Cecchetti and opposite him one of the company who read out a long speech in Russian, which set forth his history, his triumphs, the love and honour they bore him as a great artist and kindly teacher, and, lastly, their congratulations to him on that night of his jubilee. The old man listened with bent head, then, as the words conjured up vision after vision of dancers: some passed down the long valley, some too old to dance, some he had known as children and who even then were standing by his side; his eyes became dimmed and the rough texture of his grease-paint was furrowed by a hot tear. I think everyone present felt the solemnity of that beautiful moment. Impulsively the dancers kissed the old man with affection, then the male dancers lifted him shoulder-high and carried him to his dressing-room, where, with Madame Cecchetti beside him, he sank into a chair and wept.

What a reception old Cecchetti had and what a performance he gave! This was real miming, with every gesture, every step, timed to perfection. How few dancers of today appreciate the telling force of slow movement on the stage. I remember well his actions as the witch, Carabosse, in the second act. How casually he approached the fringe of bystanders watching the dancing of the Princess Aurora! How artfully he sidled nearer and nearer, allowing his cloak to open and reveal the spindle he carried beneath it! Then the ingratiating smile as he permitted another glimpse of the fatal instrument of his vengeance. And so on to the moment when, unable to resist the curiosity which the witch has so cunningly exploited, the Princess snatched the spindle from the stranger and pricked her finger. Then the witch's features became contorted with triumph, to change to a mocking malevolence when, just as the Princes were about to seize her, she vanished into the ground amid smoke and thunder.

When the curtain had fallen on the ballet, I and others of Cecchetti's friends went to escort him to the taxi waiting to take him home. He was pleased with this attention, but he would permit no one to help him carry his gifts, and, bent almost double from their weight, he staggered towards the taxi, his scroll sticking out of his coat pocket and a collection of silver articles under each arm, for all the world like a dealer leaving a sale of plate with his day's purchases.

After that famous evening the audiences commenced definitely to decline in increasing proportion. Diaghilev and his lieutenants began to look worried, and the atmosphere of the theatre which, until then, had seemed so assured and so triumphant, began to be charged with a feeling of unrest, all the more dramatic in contrast with Tchaikovsky's lively melodies. Discussing this matter one day with Barocchi, I ventured to suggest that the *Belle* should be given on alternate nights, the other three performances being composed of ballets from the regular repertory. I felt sure that this course would save the situation, and I have no doubt that a similar idea occurred to Diaghilev and his associates long before I mentioned it. But the plan was not adopted, for what reason I could never understand.[1] Years afterwards a chance remark

[1] I lately learned that when it was clear that the *"Belle"* was losing money, Stoll asked Diaghilev to vary the *"Belle"* with several ballets from his general repertory. Diaghilev, however, postponed his decision for over a fortnight. But when it came to his knowledge that Stoll not unnaturally resented the delay, Diaghilev decided to agree to the performances of the *"Belle"* being varied with a selection from six of his usual ballets. It was suggested to Diaghilev that it would perhaps restore good feeling if he himself called on Stoll. But a friend of Diaghilev's who had just entered the room announced that he had seen Sir Oswald having a shave in the barber's shop in the basement of the Alhambra. If Diaghilev went now he would meet Sir Oswald as he came out. Diaghilev agreed and went to the back of the

DIAGHILEV REPEATS CAMBRONNE'S MOT

suggested a clue. I believe Diaghilev, having formed the opinion that the *Belle* could not run for the six months essential to ensure a profit on the very high costs of production, was afraid to risk the settings and costumes of his general repertory, lest they might be seized for debt.

A few days later, Barocchi asked me to lunch with him at the "Isola Bella" in Frith Street. I suppose it was inevitable that we should talk about the *Belle*. I said how sorry I was that the houses had not been good, a situation which I found inexplicable, when the public were offered so wonderful an attraction. Barocchi, intending, no doubt, to create an impression of confidence, replied that all this would be changed in a day or two, for Diaghilev had in hand several schemes which would soon cause the house to be filled to capacity. Suddenly, above the quiet hum of conversation of the diners, came the French word *m——!* which assailed my ears like the vindictive slamming of a door. I turned in the direction of the sound and saw Diaghilev, seated a few tables away, glaring at us. We became silent. I have hesitated whether I should relate this incident, the only time I ever heard Diaghilev use remarks of such a nature, but I have done so because it proves conclusively how bitterly he felt the indifference of the public to support his cherished

Alhambra, and saw Stoll emerging as expected, but the latter turned aside and the meeting did not take place. The very next day Sir Oswald sent his manager to say that in view of the declining public interest he had decided to withdraw the *"Belle"*.

DIAGHILEV BALLET IN LONDON

Belle, in many respects the greatest of his many splendid productions.

January 17th marked the hundredth performance of the ballet, and, little more than a fortnight later, on February 4th, the *Belle* was given for the last time, the role of the Princess Aurora being taken by Lubov Egorova. In the rendering of the final mazurka, a member of the orchestra showed a strange sense of humour, by introducing some comical noises of his own composition. I saw Diaghilev flush with indignation at such an exhibition of downright bad taste.

Since then we have seen another revival of *La Belle au Bois Dormant,* by the Vic-Wells Ballet. But, although Petipa's choreography was again reconstructed by Nicholas Sergeyev, there was an immense difference in the manner of presentation of those two revivals. Is it not a strange comment on the vagaries of public taste that this latest revival should be patronized to capacity whenever it is given? The wonderful banquet prepared with such infinite care and exquisite taste by Diaghilev and his distinguished collaborators went unheeded and untasted by so many. The other dish is devoured. I seem to see a symbolic Carabosse wrinkling her lips over her toothless gums as she gives vent to a soundless scream of eldritch laughter—"Ho! Ho! Ho! Ha! Ha! Ha! Ha!—Times have changed indeed."

CHAPTER X

~ 1922—1925 ~

THE *Sleeping Princess* was Diaghilev's Moscow. Some days before the final performance he left for Paris, an embittered man, broken and dispirited by the burden of debts he had so recklessly contracted and which he had not the means to discharge, and still amazed by the inexplicable failure of the production, which had earned every right to be a triumphant success. Worse still, the harmonious relations which had previously existed between Sir Oswald Stoll and himself had been gravely disturbed, although the former had responded nobly to the demands made upon him, demands far in excess of the original estimates. The great adventure had failed, and the settings and costumes were seized and relegated to the storerooms; yet, even there, as we shall see, ill luck pursued the only salvage from the wreck.

Diaghilev was in neither mood nor condition to resume operations with the usual repertory, and the members of the company, left behind without resources, began to split up and fend for themselves. Massine, then in Paris, tried to form a small company of his own from certain of the scattered elements. His troupe consisted of 8 *danseuses* and 4 *danseurs*, including Lopokova, Savina, Sokolova, Ninette de Valois, Woizikowsky, Slavinsky, Addison, and himself. Their first engagement was at Covent Garden, London, on April 3rd (1922) in an entertainment composed partly of ballet and partly of films.

The items were "*Lesghinka*"; a revised version of the *pas de deux* from *Cimarosiana*, danced by Lopokova and Massine, the costumes a feeble imitation of those designed by Sert; a *pas seul*, "*Cupidon*", for de Valois; a "*Czardas*" by Sokolova, Moreton, and Woizikowsky; "*Ragtime*", a delicious parody rendered by Lopokova and Massine to Stravinsky's music of the same name; and *Fanatics of Pleasure*, a suite of dances to music by Johann Strauss. The last-named, an attempt to present a picture of Paris night-life during the Second Empire, was evidently inspired by the gay lithographs of Gavarni. Lopokova and Massine were attired *en débardeur*, Woizikowsky as an officer of the Lancers of the Imperial Guard, Slavinsky as a student out of Murger, while the ladies were in short crinolines. Here, one would imagine, were all the ingredients for a merry spectacle. Yet, apart from the slight excitement of the "*Diavolino*" danced by Lopokova and Massine, the whole was a very tame affair. The "*Valse*" and "*Polka*" were executed with the sugary good-humour of a family ball. There was little of the savage revel, the irrepressible gaiety demanded both by the title and the source of inspiration.

Certain members of the company also made a number of appearances at the Coliseum, the programme consisting of a short series of *divertissements*. First a

ACQUAINTANCE WITH FOKINE

combination consisting of Lopokova, Massine, Sokolova, and Woizikowsky; then Karsavina and Gavrilov; then Lopokova, Massine, Savina, Sokolova, and Woizikowsky. On October 9th, Lopokova, Sokolova, de Valois, Woizikowsky, Slavinsky, and company appeared in *The Masquerade*, a ballet by Vera Bowen, which was set in 18th century Venice and arranged to Mozart's *Serenade in G*.

In August 1923, I had the honour of a visit from Michel Fokine, with whom I had frequently corresponded, but never met, for he had not been in London since 1914, when he came to produce *La Légende de Joseph*.

Reandean were going to present on September 20th at His Majesty's Theatre, Flecker's beautiful and poetic play, *Hassan*, for which Delius had composed some equally beautiful songs and incidental music. Basil Dean, who was producing the play, had insisted that Fokine should be asked to arrange the dances, and the famous choreographer, having accepted the commission, had come to London accordingly.

Fokine, like most dancers, was short and slightly built. He was verging on baldness, dark, clean-shaven, with a small straight nose, small eyes, and small mouth. He had a frank, open countenance, and, although quiet and reserved in manner, radiated an unmistakable authority. He reminded me of Barrie, for, in his eyes and at the corners of his mouth, lurked a whimsical pawky humour which I found enchanting. In expressing his views on persons or things he spoke with a directness which was devastating.

DIAGHILEV BALLET IN LONDON

Despite the many years he had lived in America, he had never mastered the English language and spoke it with an attractive accent and phrasing which had a charm of their own. "You come see me at hotel, yes? I vait for you and ve have beeg conversation. I explain everything you veesh."

He was particularly pungent in his remarks on those he considered to have copied or plagiarized his choreographic compositions. When I asked him if he regarded X's production of an Oriental ballet—set to the same music by Rimsky-Korsakov—as an imitation of his own *Schéhérazade*, he said, "It ees same, vith vun beeg alteration. Vere I make Shah stand on right, he make Shah stand on left!"

Fokine was kind enough to invite me to some of the rehearsals of his dances for *Hassan*, which afforded me an excellent insight into his methods of composition. Unlike some choreographers, he seemed to have a definite image in his mind of what he wanted, and that image he always kept before him. He composed in the same way that an artist paints a picture. He would rough in a few details, such as a movement of the arm or leg, explain where the dancer was to be at a certain moment in the music, and, gradually, these apparently isolated movements and elements of poses would combine and form a whole.

When the members of his company were unknown to him, he would identify them by some physical characteristic or detail of practice dress, for instance—Beeg Boy, Small Boy, Blue Girl, Girl veeth Red Hair. He was an inspiring producer and always kept his artistes interested. He had a quiet but forceful way of correcting technical mistakes. I remember one girl who had her leg extended in a *développé à la 4me devant*, but with the toe turned upwards. Fokine asked her to hold the position, then requested the other dancers to look at the pose. The chosen dancer blushed with pride, but her fellow-artistes were puzzled by the prominence given to a technical fault. Then Fokine spoke:

"All, you see thees poss, ver' nice for Shinese dance, but *not* for classical ballet! You understan'. All right, ve continue."

Fokine expected his artistes to spare no pains and no effort to achieve the particular result he desired. He had no use for slackers; everyone, from the highest to the lowest, had to give their utmost. I remember going one morning to the St. Martin's Theatre—where the initial rehearsals were held—and finding the stairs leading to the stalls strewn with exhausted youths, whose panting, perspiring bodies showed that they had had a gruelling time. Presently, Fokine called them back to the stage and observed:

"You have right idee now, but I tink you shust valk it, yes? Now, pliss, you give me same dance *full strength! Fine!*"

The faces of the youths were a study.

In January of the following year (1924), Lopokova, de Valois, Massine, Woizikowsky, and Slavinsky, appeared in a series of *divertissements* introduced into a revue called *You'd Be Surprised*, given, of all places, at Covent Garden. All the dances were composed by Massine, and some of them, for instance, "*Togo; or*

DIAGHILEV BALLET IN LONDON

The Noble Savage", left a good deal to be desired. The best number was "*Rigaudon from Chinatown*", a pseudo-Chinese dance, at rare intervals slightly reminiscent of the Chinese Conjurer in *Parade*, but extremely original in conception, and distinguished by unusual rhythmic movements, which Massine executed with rare precision and artistry.

On March 31st, Lopokova, Idzikowsky, and a small *corps de ballet* appeared at the Coliseum in a short programme of *divertissements*: "*La Princesse Enchantée*", "*Valse*" (Chopin), and "*Soldier and Grisette*" (Lecocq).

On September 15th, Idzikowsky, Vera Savina, and *corps de ballet* appeared in a short ballet, *Les Roses*, arranged by Massine, and for which Laura Knight designed the costumes.

In October the Empire Theatre announced the unusual attraction of "The Principal Dancers of the Russian State Ballet", actually a little company of four —Alexandra Danilova, Tamara Sheversheyeva, George Balanchivadze, and Nicholas Efimov. They presented four numbers: "*Enigme*" (Arensky), danced by Sheversheyeva and Balanchivadze; "*Schön Rosmarin*" (Kreisler) by Danilova and Efimov; "*Egyptian Dance*" (Arensky) by Sheversheyeva; and "*Matelotte*", by Danilova, Balanchivadze, and Efimov.

At this distance of time I can recall only two things. First, that Sheversheyeva danced the Egyptian dance with her hair hanging down her back. Second, that "*Matelotte*" was brilliantly rendered and that I was greatly taken with the Matelotte herself—Danilova, a slim, vivacious, dark-haired young woman with laughing eyes, who was dressed, like her companions, in Russian sailor's costume.

At first sight these incidents may seem to have little connection with the subject of this book, but, indirectly, they are closely related to it. The performances given at the Coliseum and elsewhere by little groups of former members of the Diaghilev Ballet prove the straits to which they were reduced, while the little company of visitors at the Empire was shortly afterwards incorporated in the reconstituted Diaghilev Ballet, to provide it with a first-rate *ballerina* in Danilova, and a talented choreographer and character dancer in Balanchivadze, henceforth to be known as Balanchine.

In November, on the 24th, to be precise, the Diaghilev Ballet returned to the London Coliseum. But how, the reader may ask, had Diaghilev risen like a phœnix from the ashes? I have recorded his flight to Paris after the failure of the *Belle*. He was then so pushed for money that he could hardly find the price of a modest meal. But a friend, the Princesse Edmond de Polignac, came to his help, and, having placed a certain sum at his disposal, enabled him, bit by bit, to collect a company together again.

He arranged a short season at the Paris Opera, which was followed by occasional, but not very profitable, visits to the provinces and to Switzerland and Belgium. Then once more fortune smiled upon him and enabled him to conclude an agreement with the directorate of the Monte Carlo Theatre, by which he provided from his company the dancers needed for the ballets in their operas, a plan which still enabled him to give his own season in April in accordance with his usual practice.

This contract afforded Diaghilev a much needed base and enabled him to keep his company together. At the time of his return to the London Coliseum, the result of protracted negotiations most skilfully carried out on his behalf by his agent, Eric Wolheim, he had Nijinska for choreographer, Nemchinova as *ballerina*, and Anton Dolin—Patrikieff of the *Belle*, who had since made great progress under his teacher, Seraphina Astafieva—as *premier danseur classique*. Among the other members of the troupe were Tchernicheva, Sokolova, Schollar, Alice Nikitina, Vera Savina,[1] Nina Devalois (formerly Ninette de Valois), Dubrovska, Maikerska, Chamie, and Woizikowsky, Vilzak, Slavinsky, Zverev, Kremnev, Tcherkas, and Jazvinsky. There were also five promising young recruits: Lapitsky, Unger, the two Hoyers, and Lifar. And, before December was out, the troupe was reinforced by Danilova, Geverova (Sheversheyeva), Balanchine, and Efimov. The technical classes were taken by Tchernicheva, for in 1923 Cecchetti, having

[1] In 1924 Savina became separated from Massine. When Diaghilev arrived in London in November she wrote to him offering her services. He asked her to come and see him and agreed to take her into the company, but told her that he could not offer her the post of *ballerina*. Savina rejoined the company on the 24th of that month and was given many of her old parts. She danced the Brown Poodle in *Boutique* and the Street Dancer in *Petrouchka*, and appeared in the *pas de trois* and "Blue Bird" *pas de deux* from *Aurora's Wedding*, and the *pas de deux* from *Cimarosiana*.

LE TRAIN BLEU

been in indifferent health for some time, had accepted an invitation to return to his native Italy and take up the post of director of the School of Ballet at La Scala, Milan.

The season at the Coliseum opened with *Cimarosiana*, which comprised a new number, a *Pas de Quatre*, composed by Nijinska and danced by Devalois, Nikitina, Lifar, and Tcherkas. In the evening came the first performance in England of a new ballet, *Le Train Bleu*, which Diaghilev styled an *operette dansée*. The book was by Jean Cocteau, the music by Darius Milhaud, the costumes by Chanel, the setting by Laurens, and the choreography by Nijinska.

The ballet had originated from Cocteau's having watched Dolin trying out some acrobatic stunts, while exercising in the studio at Monte Carlo. These suggested to Cocteau the antics of sunburned youth disporting on the beach, and, with his flair for modernism, he conceived a ballet suggested by familiar sights on the *plage* of a fashionable seaside resort. It was the first ballet to be inspired by the new cult of the body beautiful.

The formalized setting, with its hint of cliffs, bathing-tents, and seascape, was effective, but the costumes —mostly woollen bathing-suits—were uninteresting. Nijinska had devised movements based on open air sports. There was a tennis number for herself, a golf number for Woizikowsky and Sokolova, and some group movements, suggested by swimming and beach games, for the *ensemble*, who represented flappers and their boy friends.

The ballet had a certain facile smartness, an atmosphere of the "very latest thing", but, as a whole, I found it dull, even boring. The one bright spot was Anton Dolin. The ballet had been built round him, and was produced to star him, and he made full use of the opportunity it afforded. This was a quite different Dolin from the mannered youth who, a few months previously, used to drop into my shop, his soft collared shirt always open to display his chest, while he was for ever taking out a pocket comb to tidy his thick dark hair, which he wore long and brushed back from his forehead.

On that night he danced like a man in ecstasy, like a man who suddenly felt possessed of a divine power of movement which raised him above mere mortals. His dancing was not pure classical ballet, but his sportive movements had that grace and beauty which come only from a thorough training in the technique of the classical ballet. Added to that he was personable and well made, and his fine figure gained still more from its complete sunburn make-up. All those complicated bounds, leaps, hand-stands, and back-bends, were, in essence, stunts, if you like, but they were done with such grace and such apparent ease, that it was only when you began to examine them, that you realized how dangerous they were. I say quite frankly that at any moment Dolin might have done himself serious injury and ruined his career, but he never faltered, and when the curtain fell he was accorded a well deserved ovation.

Unfortunately, his very success (and that of Sokolova as Perlouse, in the same ballet) was hailed and exploited by a certain section of the Press as a victory for two British dancers over their Russian colleagues. I quote the following from the *Star's* notice of *Le Train Bleu*:

"We confess that the cup of our satisfaction was not complete till this morning when we discovered from the detailed criticism of those very clever people, the critics who analyse for us the motions and emotions of Russian Ballet, that the two dancers who had most appealed to us were not Russians at all, but British. Antoine [*sic*] Dolin, the hero of the Bathing Beach, is a clever young Irishman, and the other principal and very charming bathing girl is the delightful little English *ballerina*, Mlle. Sokolova."

Diaghilev was infuriated by this article and threatened to dispense with even the few English dancers his company did contain.

There was another new production on December 1st, *The Faithful Shepherdess*, a ballet to music by the 18th century composer, Monteclair, arranged and orchestrated by H. Casadesus, with setting and costumes by Juan Gris, and choreography by Nijinska.

The principal roles were taken as follows: *The Shepherdess*, Vera Nemchinova; *the Shepherd*, Leon Woizikowsky; *the Marquis*, Thadeus Slavinsky; *Aphrodite*, Lubov Tchernicheva; *Hymen*, Anton Dolin; *the King*, Nicholas Singayevsky; *Courtiers*, Nicholas Zverev, Tcherkas, and Jean Jazvinsky.

The story was a simple one. It told of a shepherdess, in love with a shepherd, who remained faithful to him, despite the temptations of a rich Marquis. Her fidelity was rewarded by the appearance of Aphrodite and Hymen. Finally, the Roi Soleil himself appeared, to give his blessing to the union of the devoted lovers.

My principal recollection of this ballet is the formalized Watteau-like background, of a lovely pale grey, which made an admirable setting for the dancers in exquisitely matched pastel shades: courtiers in mauve, peasants in sap green, and the Marquis in pale blue and black.

There were some charming, if not too disciplined, *ensembles* in which the peasants danced with dainty baskets of flowers, but the chief moment was the *pas de deux* of Aphrodite and Hymen, in which Tchernicheva and Dolin, in simplified versions of 18th century ballet costumes in pink and silver, with the single bared shoulder characteristic of "gods and goddesses" at that period, danced with great feeling a number composed of elements of 18th century dance technique allied to a classical ballet foundation.

For some reason, however, the ballet did not take; perhaps it was too subtle a *pastiche* to appeal to the many, and it did not remain long in the repertory.

One night, I was sitting in the last row of the stalls at the Coliseum, watching the ballet, when I heard close to me a faint tapping and shuffling. I turned my head to see what this noise was and saw Diaghilev sitting in the gangway seat (the one he favoured at the Coliseum), while, standing behind him, was a handsome sunburned youth whose chief characteristics were an infectious smile and glowing dark eyes. I noticed that he responded to the music like a tuning-fork, unceasingly his feet softly beat time to the rhythm, while his head and shoulders dipped and swung in harmony.

I had never seen the young man before, and while I was wondering who he could be, Diaghilev leant towards me and said:

"This is my new protégé, Serge Lifar, of whom I have high hopes."

Lifar bowed, flashed his teeth in a smile, and, still smiling, allowed his body to respond again to the influence of the rhythm of the music.

A little later, I made the acquaintance of a new addition to Diaghilev's entourage, another Russian, a striking-looking, very dark, clean-shaven, young man, who had a trick of half-closing his eyes when talking, but who otherwise had an unusually keen and determined expression. His name was Boris Kochno and he had been appointed Diaghilev's secretary. Kochno was well versed in matters relating to the arts, and had a passion for the most advanced forms of expression. But he was both friend and secretary, and came to exert an increasing influence on the nature of Diaghilev's productions. Kochno had something of the outlook of Cocteau. He urged Diaghilev along the path of the chic and the "amusing"; he persuaded him to be always *le dernier cri*; unfortunately, few things stale more quickly than the sensation of a night or a week.

The final novelty of the season was *Aurora's Wedding*, presented on December 15th. When Diaghilev was preparing his 1922 season at the Paris Opera he found that the fame of the *Belle* had preceded him, and he was asked to revive *The Sleeping Princess*. Since, however, the scenery and costumes were held in London as security for debt, this was impossible. So he effected a compromise by contriving a one-act ballet, or rather a series of *divertissements*, composed of the best numbers from the *Belle*.

These were the *"Polonaise"* and the *"Pas de Sept of the Fairies and their Pages"* (styled on the programme *"Pas de Sept of the Maids of Honour and their Cavaliers"*) from Scene I; the *"Dance of the Duchesses"*, the *"Dance of the Marquesses"*, and the *"Farandole"* from Scene III; and the following numbers from the final scene—*"Florestan and his Sisters"*; *"Little Red Riding Hood"*; the *"Blue Bird"*; the *"Porcelain Princesses"*; the *"Three Ivans"* (*"Innocent Ivan and his Brothers"*); *"Grand Pas de Deux of Princess Aurora and Prince Charming"*; concluding with the *"Mazurka"*.

To dress the ballet, Diaghilev made use of the 17th century costumes designed by Benois for *Le Pavillon d'Armide*, which were still in good condition, moreover, as that ballet had not been given since the War, these even took on an air of novelty, while Goncharova was commissioned to design new costumes for the Fairy Tales. Her conceptions were good, but I preferred those of Bakst which had recaptured the spirit of those splendid 18th century designers—Jean Berain and Jean Baptiste Martin. *Aurora's Wedding* had an enthusiastic reception and became one of the most popular items in the repertory.

Diaghilev, having re-established good relations with Stoll, asked that Bakst's costumes and scenery for the *Belle* might be loaned for the production of *Aurora's Wedding* at the Coliseum. Stoll agreed, but when the costumes and scenes were taken from store and examined, they were found to be so perished that it was impossible to use them. The backcloth of the first scene, however, was in fairly good condition, and this was used as the setting for the ballet in its abbreviated form.

Aurora's Wedding gave the audience an opportunity of comparing different members of the company in the same roles. For instance, *"Florestan and his Two Sisters"* was danced alternately by Nikitina, Devalois, and Efimov; Nikitina, Devalois, and Zverev; and Danilova, Devalois, and Efimov. The *"Blue Bird"* was danced by Anton Dolin with either Dubrovska, Savina, or Nikitina. *"Little Red Riding Hood"* was danced by Antonova with Domansky or Tcherkas, or Geverova and Tcherkas. The *"Three Ivans"* was danced by Woizikowsky, Slavinsky, and either Kornetsky or Lapitsky. It was most interesting to observe how the same series of steps, executed with precision and style to the same phrase of music, played at the same *tempo*, could result in completely different impressions according to the artist or artists who danced them.

The season ended on January 10th (1925) with *Boutique* at the matinée and *Aurora's Wedding* in the evening. The season was definitely successful and Diaghilev was enabled to pay off a proportion of his debts on the *Belle*. The last night witnessed extraordinary scenes, to be compared only with the triumphs of pre-War days, for the audience cheered the ballet throughout its performance. When the curtain fell, the dancers were fêted with bouquets, laurel wreaths, and floral horseshoes. Presently, the orchestra struck up *Auld Lang Syne*, which was lustily sung by the audience. And when the principal dancers came to bow their final acknowledgments, the audience sang, *For They are Jolly Good Fellows*. The lights were then dimmed and the end of the show was proclaimed by the projection of a film—on the principles of good walking! But the audience did not cease from clapping and cheering, and it was not until an announcement was made from the stage to the effect that the company would return in May, that the spectators consented to go home.

CHAPTER XI

THE likeness of Diaghilev, known to every member of his company as Sergey Pavlovich, is so well known from the photographs reproduced during the last few years, that a description of him is almost superfluous, but some details may be of interest.

In his gay, carefree moods, he had a resemblance to the late King Manoel of Portugal. But when Diaghilev was annoyed and his nostrils dilated and quivered, and his lips curved in a hard bitter line, he had—if you imagine his head crowned with a wig—a striking resemblance to Rastrelli's bust of Tsar Peter the Great, and on occasion Diaghilev could be no less obstinate and ruthless.

You had only to meet him to realize at once that you were in the presence of a personality, for he radiated authority and determination. He was of medium height, broad-shouldered, and heavily built. It is his head and shoulders and hands that are most clearly pictured in my memory, possibly because you were so drawn to them that there was never any opportunity to consider his legs.

His head was broad-browed, square, and massive, and firmly set on a short and thick neck. His glossy black hair, parted at the side, had a highlight in the form of a white lock which early earned him the nickname of Chinchilla. He had a heavy jaw, full cheeks, thick and sensual lips, and eyebrows arched in a supercilious stare. His features were pale and clean shaven, except for a clipped moustache in the form of an inverted "v". The back of his head was curiously flat, and anyone sitting behind him and aware of this fact, could easily single him out. His well kept, unusually small hands were plump, white, and warm. He walked slowly and deliberately as though his body were heavy to bear.

He generally favoured dark clothes except in the height of summer, and in the evening he invariably wore dress clothes with either dinner jacket or "tails", unless he had been too busy with rehearsals and had had no time to change. His linen was immaculate, but his evening clothes sometimes showed signs of wear.

Diaghilev had the charming manners of the born aristocrat. As a general rule, he had a suave address, not unlike the bedside manner of a fashionable physician. His voice had a soft caressing tone, infinitely seductive. His *"mon cher ami"*, accompanied by an affectionate touch of his hand on your wrist or forearm, was irresistible. On the other hand, when cross, he could be brutally curt and arrogant, and no one could snub with more biting sarcasm. He always dressed his hair with a brilliantine perfumed with almond blossom—I believe he procured it from Paris —and if the fragrance of almonds were perceptible in a passage or room you might be sure that Diaghilev had passed by only a short while before.

He was a prodigious trencherman, for he had an appetite worthy of a Louis XVI, due, no doubt, to the diabetes from which he suffered, and he had a tacit understanding with the management of a well-known London restaurant not far from Cambridge Circus, that he should always receive a double portion of whatever dish he ordered, although he was only charged for one. He did not smoke, and he drank only a little light wine or an occasional vermouth.

Notwithstanding that Diaghilev had visited London many times and had numerous friends among the English aristocracy, he was often blissfully vague regarding matters of general knowledge. For instance, I recall an amusing anecdote related to me by Sacheverell Sitwell, who met Diaghilev in 1918. At this time Sitwell was serving in the Grenadier Guards, and, whenever he came to London to see the ballet, had to leave early in order to be back at Aldershot by midnight.

On several occasions, Sitwell, on taking leave of Diaghilev, had excused his early departure with the explanation :

"I am so sorry to go but I must get back to Aldershot by twelve."

One evening, a querulous Diaghilev, irritated and mystified by the mysterious and exacting Aldershot, enquired:

"*Qui est cet Aldershot qui insiste toujours que vous reveniez à minuit? Est-ce que c'est votre maîtresse?*"

DIAGHILEV BALLET IN LONDON

I had the good fortune to retain Diaghilev's friendship until his passing, and although I could not say that I ever knew him intimately—I imagine very few of his familiars even ever knew all the thoughts that filled that restless brain—I saw him many times and under various conditions of his artistic activities. I saw him in his workroom at the Savoy (where he always stayed), sitting at a piano piled with music, his plump white fingers evoking some Russian or Spanish melody, or perhaps he would be considering a number of designs for settings and costumes. I saw him at ballet rehearsals and at lighting rehearsals, and I sometimes sat beside him in his box or near his seat in the stalls. Over all those years he retained the same characteristics, except that he became a little stouter, a little slower in his walk, greyer, grimmer, while his lips took on a more bitter curl.

Atlas-like he bore the fortunes of the company on his own broad shoulders. He had to plan engagements well ahead to hold his troupe together, and yet keep his eyes and ears open for fresh talent. He was badgered by painters and musicians eager to be associated with his productions, well aware of the value of such a *cachet*. Diaghilev considered such suggestions, but he was a difficult man to please, and some of those whose offers were declined revenged themselves by decrying his productions.

He was possessed by four devils: his passion for physical beauty; his yearning for congenial companionship; his love for the pure classic ballet; and his passion for everything that was new.

DIAGHILEV'S DELIGHT IN THE HUMAN FORM

Diaghilev resembled the ancient Greeks in the genuinely aesthetic pleasure he derived from the contemplation of a beautiful human body, whether it were that of a male or a female.

He liked to surround himself with young men and women, although for companionship he preferred his own sex. Nothing pleased him so much as to discover some young dancer in whom he saw future possibilities as dancer or choreographer. He would mould his protégé *physically* by sending him to be trained by Maestro Cecchetti, and, *mentally*, by himself initiating him in the true appreciation of art and music, teaching him the importance of good design and good colour, from both aural and visual points of view, to which he gave practical illustration by taking him to concerts and exhibitions of painting. He was immensely gratified when his protégé achieved the success he had visualized, and no less deeply wounded when that protégé deserted him in the belief that he could achieve still greater glory by his own unaided efforts. Then followed angry scenes which left Diaghilev depressed and miserable; for all his blasé, cynical exterior, he was a sentimentalist at heart.

Diaghilev loved the great traditions of the classic school of ballet, and whenever he presented the famous works of Petipa or Ivanov, he took the greatest care that the original choreography should be reproduced both in the letter and the spirit. Yet, paradoxically enough, he always pined for novelty. He was not satisfied to be *in* the latest movement, he must always *anticipate* it. So he perpetually visited exhibitions and concerts, hurried to a private recital or to the studio of a still obscure painter, always listening and peering for the first indication of something new and important which could be adapted to his productions and afford them a new interest, a new surprise.

Of the many cities he visited in the course of his tours, he set Venice above them all. He regarded Venice as the most beautiful city in the world, and every season he never failed to make a pilgrimage there. He was also fond of Florence, with its statue of David by Michelangelo, and, nearby, that entrancing view of the valley of the Arno.

Diaghilev was good enough to be interested in my publications relative to the Dance, sometimes purchasing them, and sometimes giving me advice. He was particularly pleased with my reprint of that exciting book, Lambranzi's *New and Curious School of Theatrical Dancing*, originally issued in 1716, which I edited and published for the Imperial Society of Teachers of Dancing. He bought a copy each for Massine, Balanchine, and Lifar. The influence of that volume can be seen in certain of their ballets.

On one occasion, Diaghilev did not agree with my observations on one of his productions, and wrote me a letter of admonition, which I regarded as a compliment, for, as everyone knows, he thought letter-writing such a bore, that he would rather go a long journey to see someone, than set pen to paper.

He would sometimes call at my shop, which he dubbed the "Boutique Fantasque", when he thought I might have some material that he needed. He also had a nickname for me, though he never used it in my presence—Rizhka (the diminutive of the Russian for red, doubtless an allusion to the colour of my hair)—as my friend, Sacheverell Sitwell, confided to me. Diaghilev always arrived like Majesty honouring a subject with a visit, and, in the distance, like attentive equerries, hovered one or two immaculately groomed young men—dancers, secretaries, or friends. I noted one curious incident, that is, if I happened to be talking to a member of his company when Diaghilev called, he generally ignored him, not pointedly, but just as though he were not there at all.

There was something very Oriental about Diaghilev, and when he sat down in a chair, preoccupied, his eyes blinking through half-closed lids, he reminded you of one of those seated figures of Buddha, so typical of Japanese art. But those apparently sleepy eyes missed little. If it happened that he did not see me at the first performance of a new ballet, he did not fail to remind me of it. On one occasion he called on me just before eight in the evening, and, learning that I had not yet seen his latest production, insisted on my accompanying him forthwith and sharing his box. When I protested that I could hardly go to the theatre without first going home and changing, he waived the objection aside, quoting Pushkin's saying, *"Dans la nuit tous les chats sont gris!"*

With all his worldliness, Diaghilev was as full of superstitions as a peasant of the Middle Ages. He objected to being photographed; he was very alarmed if a visitor placed his hat on a table, which he interpreted as a certain loss of money, or on his bed, which forboded ill health; while the approach of a cat, even a black one, filled him with the most lively horror.

There is another name which can be found on every programme of the Diaghilev Company during its twenty years of existence, that of his *régisseur*, Grigoriev.

Serge Nikolayvich Grigoriev is probably the only man living who knows the history of the troupe from its first performance to its last, and who, except for the very few days when he was absent from illness, was present at every rehearsal and at every performance.

It is extremely unlikely that he will ever write his memoirs, first, because he looks on the intimate knowledge gained by him in his position as *régisseur* as a professional secret, and, secondly, because when it comes to discussing the company he is as dour and uncommunicative as a Scotsman.

When I first knew him he was tall, dark, and spare, with pale features and sad eyes. His hair, thin on the crown, was brushed straight back. He had a slight moustache which he later shaved off.

He was Diaghilev's right hand and, from what I have seen of him, I should say that no man was better served. His responsibilities were so vast and so all-embracing as to be almost illimitable. It may be said that short of actually composing the choreography of a ballet, he was responsible for the efficiency and smooth running of all future performances, once the details had been determined.

He watched all the rehearsals and knew at once when

SERGE GRIGORIEV: HIS RESPONSIBILITIES

a movement had been omitted or badly executed. He inspected the materials of which the costumes were made. He saw the lighting rehearsals, and, if the company appeared at a theatre where the lighting equipment was indifferent, he had to devise means to obtain the best results possible. He knew the music cues for the curtain to rise and fall, and those for the various dancers to make their entrance, and the *tempo* at which the different numbers should be played. He knew how each costume had to be worn and the type of make-up required. He knew how each scene had to be set. And when the season was over, he had to supervise the packing for transport of the immense quantity of material which the troupe had to carry with them. If any particular costumes or settings were not required, he had to arrange for their storage.

In consultation with Diaghilev he drew up the programmes and decided which artistes were best suited to understudy certain roles. He planned rehearsals to polish up ballets or numbers which did not accord with his own high standards of efficiency. He planned rehearsals for revivals of old ballets which had not been given for some time. And, in consultation with the choreographer, he planned rehearsals for the new productions in preparation. A sheet of paper pinned up on the notice-board at the entrance to the stage-door, set forth in his neat Russian script the time and place of rehearsal, ballets concerned, and artistes required.

He kept a watchful eye on the company's wardrobe, decided whether such and such a costume should be replaced or repaired, and to what extent, whether new embroidery or stage jewellery were to be purchased, or whether what was required could be adapted from a certain costume in store. He exercised a very strict economy upon all such expenditure and would not sanction the outlay of a shilling unless he deemed it necessary.

I remember just before a performance of *L'Après-Midi d'un Faune*, Mme. Chamie, who was one of the nymphs, approached Grigoriev with the entreaty that she might have a new costume.

"It is so ragged that I shall soon appear naked," she declared.

Grigoriev gave a swift glance at the costume and, turning away, observed:

"That will be charming, Madame."

He was always on the stage well in advance of the performance, ready to consider any of the innumerable requests that might arise—a plea to be excused a certain rehearsal, a request for an advance of salary, and so on. He quickly weighed up the matter and pronounced judgment.

His inseparable companion was a little pocket-book. Although he had a good memory, he always supplemented it. Everything that had to be done, every transaction that occurred, every decision, was methodically entered up in the famous pocket-book. And, as the various items were dealt with, so were they immediately crossed off.

A few moments before the performance was due to begin he was at his post in the prompt corner, his cold gaze directed on every phase of the performance. If he

HOW GRIGORIEV SUPERVISED THE PERFORMANCES

thought the ballet were well rehearsed he would cross the stage behind the back-cloth, slip through the pass door, and watch the ballet from the auditorium, noting the lighting and any omission on the part of the dancers. A little while before the curtain was due to fall, he would be back at his post to regulate the number of curtain calls to be given, and when the principals should make their final triumphant appearance before the now lowered curtain, the central fold of which would be drawn back for the dancers to pass through.

As soon as the ballet was over and the dancers were about to scamper to their dressing-rooms, Grigoriev would call out various names. The girls would come running towards him, when he would shout, with a great show of indignation, such phrases as, "You did not finish in such a pose on the last beat, why?" The culprits would look down. Out would come the pocket-book and their names would be entered for a fine, after which they would be dismissed with a curt wave of the hand.

Then Grigoriev had to be prepared for the possible illness of any of the soloists and have ready in his mind a suggestion for Diaghilev as to who might be entrusted to deputize for the dancer concerned. It required a deep knowledge of the company's varied talents to have such a choice ready to hand, and sometimes there might be special circumstances to be considered. For instance, a dancer might twist an ankle a few minutes before the ballet, so that a substitute had to be found at the shortest notice. Then the most suitable person might be passed over in favour of one who, though not so skilled technically, had a gift for quickly picking up a number or a phase of mime.

Grigoriev had many unusual qualities for a Russian. He was punctual and exacted punctuality from others, and the business of the company superseded all other claims. If a soloist were not at her post, he would go in search of her, and if he thought her dressing was delayed by the presence of a visitor, he would politely, but firmly, whisk that visitor out of the room, whatever her status.

It may be that from a personal point of view he liked some members of the company more than others, but he strove to be fair to all, and he maintained strict discipline because he never took advantage of his position—he claimed no *droits du régisseur*. In general, he was business-like and to the point, but, if annoyed, he could easily lose his temper, when he would shout, beat his brow, and shake his arms aloft with a flourish almost too reminiscent of the theatre to be genuinely intimidating.

Grigoriev was a splendid mime himself, his Shahriar in *Schéhérazade*, his Bibulous Merchant in *Petrouchka*, his Russian paterfamilias in *La Boutique Fantasque* will not easily be forgotten. But that did not mean that he forsook his duties as *régisseur*. Not at all, he was dressed for his role and at his post until it was time for him to go on the stage; and, no sooner had he played his part, than he was back in the prompt corner once more.

From first thing in the morning until long past midnight he was absorbed in his task. Imagine the nervous

GRIGORIEV'S INSATIABLE QUEST FOR KNOWLEDGE

energy poured out over those feverish years. And yet, if there was a day when he had an hour to spare, he would dash off to any other theatre where ballet might be given, to see if he could add something new to his boundless knowledge and experience.

CHAPTER XII

~ 1925 ~

TRUE to its promise the Diaghilev Ballet returned to the Coliseum on May 18th. Its composition was much the same as during the previous season, except that it had lost Vilzak, but had been reinforced by Idzikowsky and Vladimirov. Cecchetti's old place as technical adviser to the company was offered to, and accepted by, Nicholas Legat, his contemporary at the Imperial School of Ballet, St. Petersburg.

Two of Cecchetti's famous roles, the Marquis di Luca in *The Good Humoured Ladies* and the Shopkeeper in *La Boutique Fantasque* were taken by Zverev. There were also some additions to the *ensemble*, the most notable being another pupil of Astafieva—Alicia Markova—who in after years was to become the first English *ballerina* of rank, by virtue of her dancing the classic roles of Giselle in *Giselle* and Odette-Odile in *Le Lac des Cygnes*.

A special feature of the season was a new Russian Ballet drop-curtain, depicting a Russian St. George slaying the Dragon—did the dragon symbolize the vanquishing of the British Public?—which formed the basis of a fine decorative design by Vladimir Polunin,

THE HOUSE PARTY

the scenic artist who had realized so many conceptions of Diaghilev's collaborators.

It was intended to open with *Carnaval* in the afternoon; the evening to be devoted to the first performance in England of *Les Biches*, Englished as *The House Party*, which, in honour of the opening night, was to be preceded by *Carnaval*. Unfortunately, Woizikowsky, who danced an important part in the new ballet, sprained his ankle, and, at the eleventh hour, the new ballet was withdrawn and replaced by *Aurora's Wedding*.

The House Party was presented on May 25th. The music was by Francis Poulenc, the scenery and costumes by Marie Laurencin, and the choreography by Nijinska. The setting, in the palest of pastel shades, had an engaging simplicity and freshness. It represented a lounge in an expensive ultra-modern seaside villa. There were pale grey walls, a large window draped with a pinkish-blue curtain, and, beneath the window, a lavender-blue settee.

The ballet satirized the intimate type of house-party in a series of five *divertissements*, respectively entitled "*Chanson Dansée*" (Woizikowsky, Dolin, Zverev), "*Adagietto*" (Nemchinova), "*Jeu*" (Nemchinova, Woizikowsky, Dolin, Zverev, and *corps de ballet*), "*Rag Mazurka*" (Sokolova, Woizikowsky, Zverev), and "*Chanson Dansée*" (Tchernicheva, Danilova), which were framed in two *ensembles*—"*Rondeau*" and "*Finale*".

When the curtain rose you saw the room fill with guests, attractive young girls with their figures enhanced by summery frocks of pale pink, and bronzed young men in vests and shorts. There was also a very sophisticated young lady dressed in white tights and gloves, set off by a short close-fitting coat of blue velvet. Last, but by no means least, entered the hostess.

The ballet was built up on the reactions of the various groups—the girls who flirted with the youths; the youth who was attracted by the girl in blue velvet; two young men who seemed to find their own company all sufficient; two young girls who appeared to be very dear friends; and the wiles of the enterprising hostess. This artificial hothouse atmosphere provoked the strangest emotions, although they were masked by an affected and nervous air of frivolous gaiety. The hostess, pleased to see her guests amusing themselves and wishing to join in the fun, induced two young men to keep her company, for what guest could be so ungracious as to ignore the wishes of his hostess?

It was not a pleasant theme, and it was presented with an insight that could only be derived from an intimate knowledge of such occasions, but it was a genuine cross-section of a phase of contemporary life, a presentation rendered the more piquant by the very delicacy of its considerable imputations.

Notwithstanding that the ballet was all dancing, it contained only two important roles, those of the Hostess and of the Girl in Blue. The Hostess was admirably rendered by Sokolova in dancing that was also mimetic. It was so barbed a satire that I often wondered if Nijinska or Sokolova had fashioned the portrait from life. Sokolova presented a wealthy vulgar woman of uncertain age seeking to regain her lost youth by surrounding herself with young people and sharing in their amusements. Dressed with expensive simplicity, her soul was revealed in the jangling strings of pearls she wore about her neck and in the foot-long holder and cigarette at which she puffed without cease. She must even join in the latest dance—the *Rag Mazurka*—partnered by those inevitable young men.

The part of the Girl in Blue was the first important role to be created by Nemchinova, for in all her previous roles she had in the main been forced to follow the conceptions established by others. The Nemchinova of *The House Party* was a quite different Nemchinova from the dancer who had succeeded to Lopokova's Can-Can Dancer in the *Boutique*. Then she had been buxom, strong, over muscular, and often a little hard in her movements. Now she was even slender, her muscles were controlled and resilient, and she moved with a grace, sense of style, and feeling for line which commanded admiration. Her dark hair, parted in the centre, was dressed close to her head in a manner reminiscent of a mediaeval page. Nemchinova was groomed like a mannequin; she looked definitely chic. Something of this metamorphosis was due to Diaghilev, something to Nijinska, and not a little to Nemchinova's friend, Zverev, who was determined that her first creation should be a resounding success. He made her diet, supervised her practice, and encouraged her throughout; and perhaps he even fortified her for the ordeal with a course of those Tolstoyan ideals which ruled his own existence.

From a technical viewpoint, Nemchinova's *pas seul*, "*Adagietto*", was conceived on entirely new lines. The dancer travelled by means of steps based on the technique of the classical ballet, on a line parallel to the audience, the thighs well drawn up so that the legs, whatever their position, maintained a crisp tautness which conveyed an impression of elegance and sophistication. The shoulders were square to the audience in the manner of an early Egyptian bas-relief, and, in certain gliding movements, were dipped and raised in a wave-like rhythm, while the arms, either bent at the elbow or extended in the same plane, were disposed in angular positions, following the same line. Nemchinova's inspired performance placed her at one bound in the front rank of modern *ballerine*.

The ballet had a most enthusiastic reception and became a popular item in the repertory.

There was another new production on June 3rd, *Les Fâcheux*, a ballet by Kochno which was based on Molière's play. The music was by Georges Auric, the setting and costumes by George Braque, and the choreography by Nijinska. Unfortunately, my recollections of it are hazy, and the only thing that I can recall is that Dolin created an unusual precedent in it by dancing a short *pas seul sur les pointes* in soft ballet shoes.

June 29th saw the London *première* of another ballet by Kochno, who very soon became librettist-in-chief to the company. This ballet, called *Les Matelots*, contained five scenes and exactly five characters. The music was by Georges Auric, the setting and costumes by Pedro Pruna, and the choreography by Massine.

LES MATELOTS

The cast was as follows: *the Young Girl*, Vera Nemchinova; *her Friend*, Lydia Sokolova; *First Sailor*, Leon Woizikowsky; *Second Sailor*, Thadeus Slavinsky; *Third Sailor*, Serge Lifar.

The settings, with the exception of one scene, were conceived in the gay pastel shades fast becoming *de rigueur*, and suggested the quay and characteristic streets of a seaport town. An unusual feature of the setting was a large pinkish-brown cube, perhaps inspired by the *periaktoi* of the Graeco-Roman theatre, for each side was decorated with an appropriate design which could be turned to face the audience as occasion demanded. Thus one side was painted with a ship, which side was turned from view to indicate that the sailors had set out on a voyage; or the side was turned back to show that they were on their way home.

The plot itself was almost childish in its simplicity. Three sailors are on their way to rejoin their ship, one of whom is seen off by his sweetheart. The girl is sad at the absence of her lover. The sailors return and, disguising their features by means of false beards, in turn make love to the girl, but without success. The young girl has a friend of doubtful integrity who suggests meeting the sailors at a bar, but she refuses. The sailors return and take off their disguises. In real life, the lady would promptly return her engagement ring and the matter would end abruptly. Here, however, the lovers fall into each other's arms, while the sailors salute in admiration.

With this slight material and Auric's lively music—his *Fantasia on Circus Themes*—as inspiration, Massine contrived a lively little ballet which showed that he had studied the movements and habits of sailors to some purpose. Their rolling gait, their quick alert movements, their ability to retain their balance in almost every position, their susceptibility to women, and their passion for cards, were all admirably expressed in Massine's choreography, which filled the Coliseum with an authentic whiff of the sea. A number that particularly appealed to me was a card game played by the three sailors, each perched on the edge of a perilously balanced chair, as they leant over at odd angles and deftly slapped down their cards in turn. The poses and timing were exactly right.

Despite that the Young Girl and her Friend were played by Nemchinova and Sokolova, the sailors dominated the ballet throughout. But, although Woizikowsky and Slavinsky were in their element, it was Lifar, gay and debonair in his white vest and pale blue jacket and trousers, encircled with a red sash, who carried off the chief honours.

To give a further touch of local colour, Massine introduced into the "bar" scene a street musician familiar to frequenters of the Haymarket, an ex-bluejacket who entertained theatre queues by his dexterous manipulation of a pair of table-spoons. But, notwithstanding his skill, he did not really fit into the scheme, because the essence of ballet is suggestion rather than photographic reproduction, and the two did not blend.

The ballet evoked constant applause and the nautical atmosphere was retained to the end, when the sailors, on taking a call, were each presented with a lifebelt.

DOLIN LEAVES THE COMPANY

But the compliment seemed a little dubious in intent and certainly unjustified, for the success of *Les Matelots* was never in doubt.

The season ended on August 1st with *The Good Humoured Ladies* at the *matinée* and *Aurora's Wedding* in the evening.

The "Ballets Russes" returned to the Coliseum on October 26th, the programme consisting of *Boutique* in the afternoon and *Le Carnaval* and *Les Matelots* on the opening night.

The composition of the troupe was the same with the omission of Dolin. The English *premier danseur* had had a disagreement with Diaghilev during the early days of the Paris season which followed the summer engagement at the Coliseum, and, since his existing contract had just expired, he had declined to sign a new one.

Legat now became an active member of the company and took over certain of Cecchetti's roles, such as the Showman in *Petrouchka* and the Shopkeeper in *La Boutique Fantasque*. But although Legat was an excellent dancer and mime, I missed Cecchetti's rotund form, which invested his portraits with a certain mellowness and richness of humour denied to the tall soldierly figure of Legat.

The first new production was *Zephyr and Flora*, given on November 12th. The theme was by Boris Kochno, the music by Vladimir Dukelsky, the scenery and costumes by George Braque, the masks and symbols by Oliver Messel, and the choreography by Leonide Massine.

DIAGHILEV BALLET IN LONDON

The principal characters were *Flora*, Alice Nikitina; *Zephyr*, Constantin Tcherkas; *Boreas, Zephyr's Brother*, Serge Lifar. This was Lifar's first important role. The part of Zephyr had been originally created by Dolin early in the year at Monte Carlo.

The ballet was arranged in seven episodes. I will summarize the plot from the details given in the programme.

Flora and Zephyr are a happily married couple. Boreas, in love with Flora, invents the game of Blind Man's Buff to separate the lovers. Flora also takes part and falls into the arms of Zephyr. But jealous Boreas draws aside his brother who, being blindfold, mistakes him for Flora. Unseen by her, Boreas looses an arrow at Zephyr.

The Muses enter and dance with Flora, then depart. Boreas seizes the opportunity to pursue Flora, who repulses him. She falls into a swoon. Bearers carry in the wounded Zephyr, and Boreas takes to flight. Flora and the Muses lament the passing of Zephyr. But he recovers and dances. The Muses, overjoyed, bind the arms of the devoted couple that they may nevermore be parted. Zephyr and Flora depart, leaving Boreas to be punished by the Muses.

The costumes were fanciful. Nikitina wore a hat trimmed at the peak with flowers, short tunic, and tights which were decorated from the knee to the toe with a leaf design. Tcherkas wore a jockey's cap and a tunic sewn with large petals. Lifar's costume was composed of a helmet and gold trunks. The settings consisted of small back-cloths, framed in a false proscenium

BARABAU

and painted simply to suggest a landscape by means of several undulating masses of contrasting colour. I recall one particularly pleasant composition in varied tones of gold. As for the choreography I have a vague recollection of some fine leaps by Lifar, and that is all.

The only other new ballet given that season was *Barabau*, which had its first performance on any stage on December 11th. The story and music were by Vittorio Rieti, the scenery and costumes by Maurice Utrillo, and the choreography by George Balanchine.

The ballet was based on an old Italian nursery rhyme which has been rendered thus:

> *Barabau, Barabau, why did you die?*
> *You'd wine in your cellar, your bread was not dry.*
> *And salad you grew in your garden near by.*
> *Barabau, Barabau, why did you die?*

The scene represented a farm bounded by a typical Italian landscape. At one side of the scene was a short stretch of low wall, behind which stood a group of dingily clad men and women, who sang the doleful chorus at certain moments in the action.

The theme was slight. Barabau, a prosperous farmer, is entertaining his friends and relations, when his garden is invaded by a party of soldiers led by an officer. They requisition his vegetables, and, when Barabau objects, the officer strikes him with his sword and he expires.

The peasants were conceived as coarse buffoons, and to emphasize this quality they were given false noses and padded posteriors. Their movements, inspired by drunkenness and similar attributes of low comedy, were correspondingly gross and ugly. When the curtain rose there was a line of peasants, standing parallel to the footlights and with their backs to the audience, laboriously wriggling their buttocks. Perhaps the intention was to devise a ballet in a vein of robust peasant humour, a picture in the manner of a latter-day Breughel or Teniers. Actually the ballet was inclined to be merely vulgar and rather tedious.

As a whole, *Barabau* filled me with misgivings as to the wisdom of Diaghilev's choice of Balanchine as choreographer. There were, however, two interesting moments. First, when Lifar, as the officer, rendered his solo, a classical number with a military accent, which he danced with all the forcefulness and elasticity of a steel spring. Second, Woizikowsky's contortions as the dying Barabau. Lying down on his back, he succeeded, by the exertion of some rare muscular control, in repeatedly flinging himself slightly off the ground, a most difficult feat in a prone position.

The season ended on December 19th, with *Aurora's Wedding* at both afternoon and evening performances.

CHAPTER XIII

~ 1926 ~

THE month of June witnessed the return of the "Ballets Russes", but this time they were housed in the more congenial surroundings of His Majesty's Theatre, while the season was honoured by the patronage of H.R.H. the Duke of Connaught.

The company was much the same as at the end of 1925, the principal loss being Vera Nemchinova, who, from April 29th, had been appearing with Massine at the Pavilion in *Cochran's Revue* (1926), for which Massine had devised two ballets: *The Tub*, based on the story of Giannello Sirignario in Boccaccio's *Decameron*, and set to the music of Haydn; and *Gigue*, arranged to a selection of airs by Bach, Handel, and Scarlatti. The scenery for *Gigue* was designed by Derain.

But, if Nemchinova were absent, the season was graced by the appearances from time to time of Thamar Karsavina, Lydia Lopokova, and Vera Trefilova.

The programme for the opening night, June 14th, was *Le Carnaval*, *Les Noces*, and *Les Matelots*, the second ballet being presented in London for the first time. *Noces*, originally produced in Paris as long ago as 1923, had never been shown in London, because

DIAGHILEV BALLET IN LONDON

Diaghilev had always felt doubtful as to the reception that would be accorded so iconoclastic a work.

It was a series of choreographic episodes grouped into four scenes, with words and music by Igor Stravinsky, scenery and costumes by Natalia Goncharova, and choreography by Bronislava Nijinska.

The ballet was an attempt to give expressive form to the inner spirit of the semi-pagan rites and century-old ceremonies associated with a marriage of peasants in provincial Russia. The score was unusual in that it required for its interpretation an orchestra, two double grand pianos, four solo singers, and a chorus.

To bare the soul, so to speak, the scenery and costumes were reduced to the simplest terms. The setting consisted of little more than a drab back-cloth, a narrow rostrum set against it, and a few benches. The costumes were stylized peasant dresses in black and white.

The main characteristic of *Noces* was its novel choreographic conception, the dancers being used as material with which to construct human pyramids and groups, most impressive in their austere dignity and deep emotional content.

But the spectators generally were baffled or irritated by this entirely new form of ballet, in which dancers were grouped and even made to lean one upon the other to form sculptural masses in which arms and legs, and even heads played a vital part in the general design. Whatever the merits of the ballet as a whole, there can be no doubt that certain episodes radiated a genuine spirituality.

LES NOCES

The two double pianos were set on either side of the stage in full view of the audience. They were played by Georges Auric, Vladimir Dukelsky, Francis Poulenc, and Vittorio Rieti.

It was interesting to look from the wings towards the auditorium. I could clearly see, faintly luminous above the shadowy orchestra pit, the pale precise features of Eugene Goossens, tense with the strain of directing the difficult score. I also had an excellent view of the two sets of pianists. They, too, felt the responsibility of their role, and kept glancing anxiously from conductor to music and back again, awaiting their cue to play. I can still visualize their serious preoccupied faces, glistening from concentration and exertion.

Les Noces was an experience rather than an entertainment, and the success of its appeal depended very largely on the mental attitude of the spectator, from whom it required an unprejudiced approach, a willingness to understand, and a mood of reverence attuned to the significance of the episodes presented.

For such reasons as these, or perhaps from the very novelty of its choreography and the austerity of its presentation, the ballet did not find favour either with the general public or with the Press. One stalwart, Mr. H. G. Wells, not previously suspected of being an enthusiast for ballet, wrote a letter to *The Times* in which he stoutly championed the cause of *Les Noces*, but even his trenchant pen failed to stem the tide of adverse opinion, and, although the ballet was revived from time to time, it was generally regarded as a curiosity rather than the work of art it really was.

DIAGHILEV BALLET IN LONDON

There was a new production on June 21st: *Romeo and Juliet*, in ballet form. It was styled—a rehearsal, without scenery, in two parts. The music was by Constant Lambert, the first Englishman to compose a ballet for Diaghilev; the "painting" by Max Ernst and Joan Miro, and the choreography by Bronislava Nijinska. The choreography of the entr'acte was by George Balanchine.

When Diaghilev had agreed to produce Lambert's ballet, the composer particularly requested that the settings and costumes might be entrusted to his friend, Christopher Wood, and it was always a sore point with Lambert that the director ignored this suggestion. The so-called "painting" by Ernst and Miro contributed little to the ballet, whereas Wood's collaboration, to judge by his easel pictures, might have achieved a great deal.

The principal characters were *Juliet*, Thamar Karsavina; *Romeo*, Serge Lifar; *Nurse*, Tatiana Chamie; *Peter, Servant to Capulet*, Richard Domansky; and *the Maestro, who also plays Tybalt*, Thadeus Slavinsky.

I remember very little about this ballet either musically or choreographically. The first part permitted the audience a view of the company at class, practising their daily exercises under the eye of the maestro. The class is momentarily interrupted by the late arrival of Karsavina and Lifar, who quickly change into practice dress, and take their places.

Later, the maestro teaches them a *pas de deux*, to which, however, they pay scant attention, being engrossed with their love for each other. But the lovers are separated by their indignant fellow-artistes and carried off to rehearsal.

Then came a curious entr'acte, without music, in which the curtain was raised a few inches off the ground to reveal the feet of many dancers describing a series of *ronds de jambe à terre*.

The second scene showed a rehearsal of five episodes (expressed in choreographic terms) from *Romeo and Juliet*—Romeo meeting Juliet at the ball; the duel between Romeo and Tybalt; the balcony scene; the entry of Paris, accompanied by Musicians, searching for Juliet; the death of Juliet.

The ballet ended, I think, with Juliet's coming to life and the lovers gliding from the room and returning in flying kit, in readiness to elope. Their departure in an aeroplane was conveyed by Lifar's making his exit, carrying Karsavina poised horizontally on his shoulder.

I have retained so few memories of this ballet that I am forced to conclude that the work made no lasting impression upon me.

June 28th saw the first London production of *La Pastorale*, another ballet by Boris Kochno, with music by Georges Auric, scenery and costumes by Pedro Pruna, and choreography by George Balanchine.

This was another attempt to be amusing which, however, only succeeded in being very dull. The music was thin. The setting and costumes were undistinguished; few would have recognized the lively and inventive Pruna of *Les Matelots* in the decorator of *La Pastorale*.

The principal characters were: *the Star*, Felia Dubrovska; *a Young Lady,* Alexandra Danilova; *Telegraph Boy,* Serge Lifar; *Producer,* Leon Woizikowsky; *First Actor,* Constantin Tcherkas; *Second Actor,* Nicholas Efimov.

The ballet dealt in a trite manner with the adventures of a telegraph boy, riding a bicycle, who, instead of delivering his telegrams, plays truant, and goes for a bathe. While he is in the water some young ladies arrive, one of whom runs off with his wallet of telegrams. The boy returns and falls asleep behind a rock.

The members of a film company arrive to "shoot a scene". The operators set up their cameras and the producer indicates what is to be done. The Star and two actors go through a scene. She receives a letter and sends away the two actors. Alone, she tears up the letter.

The telegraph boy awakes and is amazed to find himself alone with the Star. They fall in love and stroll away. The producer and his staff begin an agitated search for the Star. The young lady of the first episode appears and, seeing the boy returning arm-in-arm with the Star, puts her to flight; the boy disappears. The members of the film company depart. Presently the boy returns, stealthily mounts his bicycle and rides away, but the young lady leaps to his side and the couple go off together.

There was very little dancing in this production except for a solo rendered by Dubrovska, whose exotic features and abnormally long and supple arms and legs made her well suited to the role of a glamorous film star.

DIAGHILEV'S QUEST FOR AN ENGLISH THEME

As a whole the ballet impressed me unfavourably. Weak in design, feeble in action, slight in dance invention, it had very little to recommend it, and was accorded a deservedly lukewarm reception.

On July 5th there was a *Festival Erik Satie* in honour of the composer who had died the previous year. The programme consisted of *Cimarosiana*; a revival of *Parade*, with Sokolova as the American Girl and Woizikowsky as the Chinese Conjurer; a new short ballet of three dances, called *Jack in the Box*, the music for which, written for piano, had been found among Satie's papers—after his death, it was scored for orchestra by Darius Milhaud; and *Les Matelots*. During the interval, the French pianist, Marcelle Meyer, played a group of works by Satie, and Stravinsky's latest composition *La Sérénade*.

Jack in the Box was not a work expressly produced for Diaghilev; it had been acquired from the Comte de Beaumont, who had originally produced it in Paris. The costumes were by Derain; the choreography by Massine. The dancers were Danilova and Idzikowsky. Unfortunately, I never saw this work and therefore am unable to describe it.

During the last month of the season, Diaghilev was preoccupied with the desire to produce a ballet on an English theme, and perhaps also linked with an English composer, as an expression of gratitude to the country which had supported him so faithfully and so generously. Since he was little versed in English music, he imparted his project to Sacheverell Sitwell who, it need hardly be said, was full of interesting and unusual suggestions; but to play the role of mentor to Diaghilev was a difficult and even a thankless task, for he was seeking for something which he was still unable to visualize.

At first he toyed with the idea of a ballet dealing with the Elizabethan period and suggested to Sitwell that *The Merry Wives of Windsor* or *As You Like It* might be adapted to that purpose. Then came the question as to what music could be used. To this end Sitwell enlisted the co-operation of Mrs. Gordon Woodhouse, who played for Diaghilev the music of certain Elizabethan composers such as John Bull. Diaghilev was interested, but commented that the music was too old.

Sitwell then proposed that Rowlandson's drawings might make a good basis for a ballet, and that suitable music might be found in the works of William Boyce or of Thomas Roseingrave, Domenico Scarlatti's bosom friend and pupil. If, however, Diaghilev preferred a modern composer, Sitwell suggested William Walton, for he knew that the director was fond of that composer's *Portsmouth Point*—also inspired by a Rowlandson drawing—which Diaghilev had included in his series of musical interludes for performance during the intervals between the ballets. Diaghilev listened to typical works of the composers mentioned, but seemed unable to arrive at any definite conclusion. Perhaps Roseingrave interested him the most, but primarily, I think, because the composer is said to have suffered from a mental affliction which was reflected in the strange construction of his chords.

At this point Lord Berners appeared on the scene

DIAGHILEV INTRODUCED TO THE JUVENILE DRAMA

with some dance pieces he had recently composed and which greatly appealed to Diaghilev, who told Sitwell that if he could devise a suitable synopsis he would produce a ballet with music by Berners.

Sitwell then asked Diaghilev what artist he had in mind to design the settings and costumes, for he thought that this might influence the style of the scenario. Diaghilev said he had no particular artist in mind, but thought he would prefer a modern painter. Sitwell suggested that it would be interesting to have an English painter for designer. To this Diaghilev retorted:

"Are there any English painters? I have only heard of X—, and, curiously enough, he has only one eye!"

Sitwell replied by taking Diaghilev to see paintings by William Roberts, by Edward Wadsworth, and by Wyndham Lewis; but Diaghilev did not reciprocate Sitwell's enthusiasm.

Sitwell then thought that a "book" in the style of the English pantomimes of the early 19th century might offer good possibilities for expression in ballet form. Moreover, it occurred to him that it would be something of a novelty to present such a ballet with settings and costumes in the manner of the Juvenile Drama.

Diaghilev was definitely interested in this project, although naturally he could not envisage the possibilities of the mysterious Juvenile Drama. So one day Sitwell took him to see the last surviving priests of the cult of the "penny plain and twopence coloured":

Benjamin Pollock in Hoxton, and H. J. Webb in Old Street. The two rivals each assumed surprise on hearing of the existence of the other.

Thus Pollock, who had once been visited by R.L.S., now received a call from Diaghilev. The director was enchanted by the quaint appearance of the shop with its model theatres flanked by gaily coloured sheets of "scenes and characters". Pollock invited Diaghilev into his inner sanctum, where the colouring was carried out. Amazed at this unexpected store of rich material, the director could only murmur delightedly: *"C'est inouï!"*

He purchased a selection of prints from both Pollock and Webb and returned to his hotel to brood over their possibilities, both publishers having accorded him full permission to adapt the prints as he thought fit. He was greatly intrigued by the names of the artists responsible for the drawings and would completely baffle gossip-writers with the information (absolutely confidential, of course) that the settings for his new English ballet were to be by George and Robert Cruikshank, Tofts, Honigold, and Webb.

The season ended on July 23rd, the programme being *La Boutique Fantasque*, with Lopokova; *Romeo and Juliet*, with Karsavina; and *Aurora's Wedding*, with Vera Trefilova, who had first appeared as a guest artist this season in the same ballet on July 19th.

Soon afterwards, Diaghilev left for Florence, where he was later joined by Sitwell, who brought him the script of his ballet-pantomime-harlequinade, entitled *The Triumph of Neptune*.

NEW SETTINGS FOR L'OISEAU DE FEU

Towards the end of the year, the company returned to London for a four weeks' season at the Lyceum Theatre, an innovation which found great favour with the majority of the ballet-going public, because of the popular prices and the excellent view of the stage from all parts of the house. But Diaghilev, unacquainted with the glorious traditions of that theatre, and knowing it only as the home of melodrama, felt his presence there marked a decline in his status. Perhaps the old days of the Châtelet seemed very far away.

There were some changes in the troupe which now lacked Karsavina, Dubrovska, and Nikitina; Nemchinova, too, was still absent. Conversely there was an addition to the soloists in the person of Vera Petrova.

The winter season opened on November 13th with *Petrouchka*, the parts of Petrouchka, the Moor, and the Ballerina being taken respectively by Woizikowsky, Sokolova, and Slavinsky; *The Swan Lake* (*Le Lac des Cygnes*) with Danilova and Idzikowsky; and *The House Party* (*Les Biches*), with Petrova as the Girl in Blue Velvet.

On the 25th, *L'Oiseau de Feu*, now called *The Fire Bird*, was re-staged with new settings and costumes by Goncharova. For this revival Lopokova returned to take the title-role. The scene of the enchanted forest, with its low trees, first shrouded in mist and later seen against a greenish-gold background, was beautiful, but it lacked the fantastic glowing colour and fairy-like atmosphere achieved by the original setting. The second scene was a formalized rendering of a Russian city—a medley of towers and spires massed in tiers, in the manner of a mediaeval representation of a walled town, to form a richly decorative pattern.

The new costumes were striking and effective, but inclined to be too bizarre for my taste; for instance, Kostchei was attired in black fleshings painted with a white design suggestive of a skeleton. Balanchine, who took the part, also made up his face in a manner more suited to a representation of a ceremonial mask worn by an African witch-doctor than a Russian enchanter; he also wore gloves with long gleaming metal nails.

At last came the principal event of the season, *The Triumph of Neptune*, with book by Sacheverell Sitwell, music by Lord Berners, and choreography by George Balanchine, which had its first performance on any stage on December 3rd.

The more the ballet progressed, the more interested Diaghilev became in it. One day he went with Sitwell to May's, the famous costumiers in Garrick Street, where they discovered two early 19th century foil-stone tunics, such as used to be worn by the principals when walking on in the final transformation scene which was so essential a feature of pantomimes of that period. The tunics were made of innumerable small squares or discs of glass, backed with coloured foil, and sewn to a foundation garment. Diaghilev purchased the two for £30. One was worn by Sokolova when dancing her hornpipe in front of the act-drop, the other adorned Neptune in the final scene.

When it came to the final rehearsals Diaghilev sat up two whole nights, without going to bed, settling the lighting to his satisfaction. He also insisted on contributing to the successful effect of the transformation scene by himself helping in the application of tinsel to the columns of Neptune's palace.

The Triumph of Neptune, with its dozen scenes and host of characters,[1] was in marked contrast to the solitary scene typical of the modernist ballets. The theme itself was bewildering in its rapid change of scene, its varied and sensational incident, its fantastic and inconsequent plot.

The ballet was a real pantomime mixture which Sitwell had compounded in accordance with the well tried recipes of Dibdin and Planché. The only difference was that it was mimed and danced, in place of being mimed, spoken, and sung. Nothing was missing: the hero, an honest Jack Tar setting out on a voyage fraught with peril; the villain in fine clothes courting the hero's wife in his absence; the fairy queen; the sportive negro servant—to say nothing of police, ogres, harlequins, and clowns—with a happy ending in which the hero, now changed into a fairy prince, marries the sea-king's daughter amid the glories of a glittering transformation scene, and brings down the curtain with a rousing hornpipe which he dances with his bride.

The music was witty and danceable, and contained many attractive numbers with engaging rhythms. In construction and orchestration it sometimes resorted to the quips and quirks of the continental modernist school, yet retained a sense of period and was infused with a robust and occasionally mordant humour.

The settings, skilfully adapted from selected prints,

[1] See Appendix F for full cast.

were most effective in colour and design, and radiated a refreshing and ingenuous charm. So far from being old-fashioned, the scenes might have been designed specially for the production.

For this ballet Balanchine had temporarily discarded his modernist experiments and devised a straightforward choreography which maintained a nice balance between the humorous and the sentimental. The dances, always simple and effective, included classical compositions which were most poetical in their graceful lines and chaste beauty.

I am thinking in particular of the scenes called "Cloudland" and "The Frozen Wood," which gave opportunities for dances in the tradition of the pure academic ballet. Danilova as the Fairy Queen, and Tchernicheva and Petrova as Fairies, were captivating in their well-fitting wine-coloured bodices and white skirts, although it must be stated that some of their movements were marred as a result of the introduction of certain jerky and angular movements more suited to the animation of Coppelia; it is possible, however, that these were suggested to Balanchine by the faulty fifth positions *en haut* shown in some of the prints representing fairies.

In the Frozen Wood—known to facetious stagehands as Wigan by Night—there was a flying ballet, in which skilled dancers, linked together with floral garlands held in their hands and now indifferent to the laws of gravity, traversed the air to form lovely and ever-changing designs contrived of misty sylphs and loops and knots of garlands.

NOTABLE PERFORMANCES IN NEPTUNE

Two of the scenes failed in their appeal. First, the episode of the Shipwreck, in which the sailor hero was seen clinging to a rock while subjected to the loud thunder of percussion instruments and the screaming gale of a lustily turned wind-machine. The other incident was the "Ogres' Cavern", sprung from nowhere, which our hero and a friend attempt to enter with supposedly horrifying results. Unfortunately, the ogres who inhabited it, like those of the ill-fated *Dieu Bleu*, failed to produce a shudder and only succeeded in looking clumsy and stupid.

There were three outstanding numbers.

First, the remarkable solo by Balanchine as the negro, Snowball; a dance full of subtly contrasted rhythms, strutting walks, mincing steps, and surging backward bendings of the body, borrowed from the cake-walk, the whole invested with a delicious humour derived from the mood of the dance, a paradoxical blend of pretended nervous apprehension and blustering confidence.

Next, the hornpipe danced by Sokolova in front of the act-drop, in which she wore a glengarry, kilt, and, for some inexplicable reason, one of the foil-stone tunics, moreover, the heavier of the two. Few members of the audience can have realized the intolerable conditions under which Sokolova had to render her number, for she danced with the utmost liveliness and apparent ease. Only when she had made her exit did she reveal something of the strain she had undergone. The first time I watched *Neptune* from the wings I saw her come off, panting and streaming with perspiration, and sit on a bench. She unfastened the tunic and, handing it to me, said:

"My God, you ought to feel the weight of this thing!"

I did and I expressed my sympathy and amazement that it was possible to move at all under such a burden.

Lastly, there was the lilting, rollicking hornpipe *pas de deux* danced by Danilova and Lifar in the final scene. What a gallant and sprightly pair they made, in their fanciful sailors' costumes! The sparkle and gaiety and fire of their dancing were communicated to the audience, whose enthusiastic approval was expressed in rapturous applause.

When the curtain fell there were shouts of "author", and Sitwell received a whole call to himself. Alas, being short-sighted, he added one more joy to the many diversions of the evening by making his entrance with his back to the audience and attempting to pass through the act-drop, to what he imagined was the auditorium. But this mishap was speedily rectified and he turned round and faced the audience with unruffled calm to receive a well-earned tribute to his resource and ingenuity. He had hinted in his synopsis at "a slightly unexpected ending", but even he had not foreseen that it would be provided by himself.

In subsequent performances the scene with the ogres was cut, while, at a later date, there was an addition in the form of a new solo, danced by Idzikowsky. It was inspired by a second visit to May's, which houses a remarkable collection of tinsel pictures, one of which, a representation of John Reeve as

ORIGIN OF CUPID'S DANCE IN NEPTUNE

Cupid, so took Diaghilev's fancy, that he copied the dress and invited Berners to write the music for a fantastic Cupid's dance, which was then arranged by Balanchine.

The costume was certainly unusual, for Cupid wore a headband with alternate red and silver roses, a pink tunic with a pair of wings at the back and blue shoulder-knots on the shoulders, blue breeches, and white stockings; he carried a bow in one hand and a large arrow in the other.

The season ended on December 11th, the programme consisting of *The Fire Bird*, *The Triumph of Neptune*, and *Aurora's Wedding*.

CHAPTER XIV

~ 1927 ~

IN 1927 the Diaghilev Company visited London once only, during June, for a season of some six weeks at the Prince's Theatre. The troupe, in the main the same as at the end of the previous year, was strengthened by the return of Alice Nikitina and Leonide Massine, the latter acting in the dual capacity of dancer and choreographer.

The first performance was given on the 13th, and the original programme, as announced, consisted of *Petrouchka*, *The Cat* (*La Chatte*), and *La Boutique Fantasque*, the second ballet having its London *première*. Unfortunately, owing to some hitch in the Customs' formalities, it was found impossible to get the scenery of *The Cat* to London in time, so the presentation of the new ballet had to be postponed.

The Cat was eventually presented on the 14th. It was another ballet by Boris Kochno, who on this occasion, for some obscure reason, styled himself Sobeka. It was an adaptation of one of Aesop's fables. The music was by Henri Sauguet, the setting and costumes by Gabo and Pevsner, and the choreography by George Balanchine.

UNUSUAL SETTING FOR THE CAT

When the curtain had fallen on *Petrouchka*, I went behind to watch the stage being set for the new ballet. The setting was designed in the constructivist manner and consisted of a number of straight and curved sections of talc—a decorative material new to ballet—which had to be built up into various structures. The multiform units suggested a constructional game for the child of an architect of the modernist school, or, better still, "parts of a —— greenhouse," as one of the stage-hands commented.

The back-cloth and stage-cloth were of shiny black American-cloth, which set off the talc shapes to perfection. The various units were each provided with pins and sockets, and the structures were erected by fitting the pin belonging to one unit into the appropriate socket of the unit below.

The process sounds purely mechanical and uninteresting. Actually, on this first night at least, it was a most diverting spectacle. Imagine, for instance, a burly stage-hand gingerly climbing a tall ladder, balancing himself on a selected rung, and bending down to receive from his mate a unit which he then held out at arm's length, swaying perilously backwards and forwards as he endeavoured to drop the pin of it into the socket of the preceding unit, a most delicate and exasperating operation, for, when the pin was at last home, he very often jerked it out as he took his hands away. As the work proceeded, tempers became high and language grew heated.

In one corner of the wings I observed a silent watcher, a dapper little man wearing a squat bowler hat, who appeared to be suffering agonies during the setting of the scene. Could this have been Gabo or Pevsner? From time to time he sought to assist by mutely pointing to the various units stacked at one side of the stage and indicating which came next. But the carpenter preferred to keep to his official plan, and ignored the help so kindly meant. Exasperated and irritated by the temporary hitches that occurred in the work of construction, the little man vented his outraged feelings by clapping his hands over his eyes, as if to shut out a revolting sight, or else seized his bowler "fore and aft" and gave it a vicious half-turn so that the back was now the front, or *vice versa*.

At this point Diaghilev walked on to the stage, leaning heavily on a walking-stick. I noticed that he had developed a curious habit of moving his jaws with a circular motion, as though he were chewing something. He examined the work in progress and expressed dissatisfaction with the dusty stage-cloth, directing that it should be thoroughly swept and cleaned. He then went towards the dressing-rooms to see Lifar, a splendid figure of athletic manhood, who was putting the final touches to his appearance by affixing a silver sequin to each upper eyelid with the aid of spirit-gum, a device which gave him a flashing eye which matched the gleaming talc.

Diaghilev returned to the stage where Nikitina was rehearsing a few poses. In her simple hat and short skirt of flexible talc, she looked like a scientifically clad woman from a Wellsian world to come. Grigoriev emerged from the shadows and, seeing the dancers

INCIDENTS AT LONDON PREMIÈRE OF THE CAT

standing ready in the wings, flashed the "stand by!" and "go!" to the conductor. The curtain swung up to reveal the fantastic-looking edifice with its gleaming floor. I admired the way in which the dusty cloth had been drawn tight and made to shine like Chinese lacquer.

Lifar darted on to the stage, but, hardly had he taken a few steps, when he was swept along as though carried on a moving conveyor belt. As soon as he had reached the other side, he ran round behind the back-cloth and complained bitterly to Grigoriev that the stage was like glass. Grigoriev made instant enquiry and learned that one bright member of the stage staff had rubbed the cloth with salad oil! For the rest of the performance, Grigoriev tried to counter this disadvantage by flinging handfuls of sand from the fire buckets on to the cloth, each time the dancers passed on to the stage.

What was the story of the ballet? A youth (Serge Lifar), in love with a cat (Alice Nikitina), prays to Aphrodite to change the animal into a girl. The Goddess assents, the cat becomes a girl, and the youth succeeds in winning her affection.

But, during their love-making, Aphrodite puts the girl's constancy to the test, by tempting her with a mouse which scampers across the bridal chamber. The girl immediately forsakes her lover to pursue it. Then Aphrodite changes the girl back into a cat, to the great grief of her lover, who dies.

Kochno's story was actually a direct contradiction of Æsop's fable, in which it is the cat, who, for love of a handsome young man, prays to Aphrodite to change her into a woman. The temptation of the mouse introduced by the Goddess into the bridal chamber, is appropriate to the moral of the fable, but meaningless in the adaptation.

The setting for *The Cat* was, as I have said, an arrangement of talc shapes, with the exception of a black box-like edifice with two rounded windows, in one of which could be seen the head and fore-paws of the cat. Above this structure was a rhomboidal figure of talc symbolizing Aphrodite. The cat at the window was a dummy figure which vanished and reappeared as required by the progress of the action. The mouse was actually a clockwork one, which proved so unreliable and so unmanageable that eventually it had to be left to the imagination.

The theme, rendered by the unusual cast of seven men and one woman, was, like that of so many modernist ballets, the feeblest excuse for a series of dances. The chief merit of *The Cat*, paradoxical as it may seem in so advanced a production, was its power to convey much more forcefully than ballets directly inspired by classical mythology, something of that ideal of physical beauty which was the dominant motive in the dance festivals of the ancient Greeks.

There was something intensely refreshing and exhilarating in the sight of those trained, well formed, lissom brown bodies, worthy of a Grecian frieze, leaping, bending, twirling, finally to mass into an impressive group. Those figures were further enhanced and almost deified whenever the talc in their costumes caught the light and reflected it back in a myriad flashes.

SERGE LIFAR IN THE CAT

There was one memorable moment when Lifar made his entrance carried in a triumphal car formed from his companions. Three youths stood in line abreast, the outer two bending forward, so that Lifar could set one knee on each back; the centre youth rested his elbows on the backs of his companions and locked his forearm about each of Lifar's knees. Three more youths stood in front, the centre one holding his rear arm upright for Lifar to grasp, his other arm being held horizontally forward, and grasped at the wrist by the youth on either side of him. The whole group was held together by the two outer youths in the back row gripping the belts of those immediately in front of them. Lifar, borne on high in this fantastic car, and seen in the very flower of his beauty, seemed to symbolize the Triumph of Youth.

These gymnastic episodes were relieved by the love passages between Nikitina and Lifar, which *pas de deux* included some pleasing and unusual poses. The ballet ended with Lifar's dying of grief and being carried away by his sorrowing companions.

The Cat, with its tuneful and attractive music, unusually classical in its inspiration, was enthusiastically acclaimed and became one of the most popular of the later ballets.

Les Fâcheux, with new choreography by Massine was revived on the 20th, but of this I have no memory. This same night the musical entr'actes included Rieti's *Concerto for Piano and Orchestra*, with the composer as soloist.

The 27th was a special Stravinsky night, the programme consisting of *Petrouchka*, *Pulcinella*, and *The Fire Bird*, conducted by the composer.

The next new production was *Le Pas d'Acier*, which had its London *première* on July 4th. This was a ballet in 2 scenes by Serge Prokofiev and George Jakulov, with music by S. Prokofiev, constructions and scenes by G. Jakulov, and choreography by Leonide Massine.

The ballet seemed to be intended to express the spirit of Soviet Russia in its two main aspects: the life in the fields, and the life in the factory. Here again the setting was inspired by constructivist theories, the main features being a series of platforms of varying heights over which the dancers moved. In the second scene, signal discs, wheels, and pulleys were introduced.

Unfamiliar with the rest period diversions of the local workers on a communal farm, I could make little of the dances of the first part. There were men, presumably soldiers, in long coats coloured brown or a dull greyish green. There were women in equally drab and utilitarian costumes. There were quasi-military movements and gestures, and much hearty fraternizing between the soldiers and the women-folk. Towards the end Danilova and Massine danced a character *pas de deux* and the first part ended with an *ensemble*. There was a great deal of activity accompanied by considerable noise, but it all appeared rather meaningless.

The second part, however, gave a masterly impression of the rhythmic power and beauty of machines. There was hardly any melody, for no sooner did the suggestion of one appear than it was engulfed in the

LE PAS D'ACIER

mighty whirlpool of rhythm. The music hummed and throbbed and hammered with ever-increasing intensity to which the dancers gave visual form and emphasis.

There were isolated movements which gradually built up into one huge machine, now of this type, now of that. Arms weaved, swung, and revolved; feet pounded the floor; even bodies took part in the movement, swinging from the waist in different arcs and at varying angles. The dancers massed, divided, strung out into line, and, with arms outstretched sideways, sharply turned their hands up and down, flat to the audience, which action ingeniously suggested a flashing lamp; this flashing, arranged in changing patterns, was most effective. So the rhythmic force ceaselessly grew in intensity until there appeared on a central platform two figures bearing giant hammers, which they swung and wielded more and more strongly until, at the height of the tumult, the climax was reached with the constructivist elements adding their quota—signal discs snapping on and off, and wheels spinning faster and faster. At this point the curtain fell to the accompaniment of a frenzied outburst of applause.

The second part of this ballet made a considerable impression on me and renewed my admiration for Massine's rare ability to contrive movements appropriate both to the theme of the piece and to the rhythm of the music, and then to combine the component parts into one vast orchestration of sound and expressive action, ever increasing in intensity until the conclusion was attained.

It is rather extraordinary that the second part of *Le Pas d'Acier* has never been revived, for not only is it complete in itself, but it is certainly the best example of what might be termed the "machine ballet" that I have so far seen.

On July 7th there was a Gala Performance in honour of H.M. King Fuad of Egypt, the programme being *Le Carnaval*, *The Triumph of Neptune*, and *Aurora's Wedding*, the first ballet being conducted by Sir Thomas Beecham, the second by Eugene Goossens, and the third by Dr. Malcolm Sargent.

The 11th saw the London *première* of *Mercury* (*Mercure*), styled "a series of *poses plastiques*," with music by Erik Satie, scenery and costumes by Pablo Picasso, and choreography by Leonide Massine. That same evening Rimsky-Korsakov's *Concerto* was given as a musical entr'acte, the pianist being Nicholas Kopeikine.

Mercury, which was to be given for one performance only, was a revival of a piece which had been originally presented some three years before at a private party in Paris; it also formed part of the repertory of a season of choreographic and dramatic works known as *Soirées de Paris* and presented there from May to June, 1925, by the Comte de Beaumont.

All I can remember of this production is that it contained some male dancers, crudely attired to represent women, who wore crude wigs with thick plaits dangling over their shoulders, and were provided with enormous imitation breasts. There were also strange contraptions in iron wire—designed by Picasso—

REVIVAL OF LE ROSSIGNOL

which were carried on the stage. The whole thing appeared incredibly stupid, vulgar, and pointless.

Diaghilev's allowance of one performance was justified, the marvel is that he should have permitted such a work to be shown at all in association with his company. Yet those who had not been able to see *Mercure* on that unique occasion were curious and clamoured for a second performance, which, in response to their appeals, was given on the 19th.

There was another Gala Performance on the 15th, this time in honour of H.M. King Alfonso of Spain. The programme consisted of *Les Sylphides*, *The Triumph of Neptune*, *The Cat*, and the *Polovtsian Dances from "Prince Igor"*. Lopokova, who had often danced before the King when the company was in Spain, reappeared for this single and special occasion.

On the 18th, Stravinsky's *Le Rossignol*, now called *The Song of the Nightingale*, was revived with entirely new choreography by George Balanchine. I have no recollection of this production and must therefore content myself by merely mentioning it.

The season ended on the 23rd, with *Children's Tales*, *L'Après-Midi d'un Faune*, *The Cat*, and *Aurora's Wedding*.

CHAPTER XV

~ 1928 ~

THE Diaghilev Company returned to London in June for a four weeks' season at His Majesty's Theatre. There were some changes in the constitution of the troupe, Vera Petrova, Lydia Sokolova, and Nina Gevergeva being absent, while Felia Dubrovska and Nina Devalois had returned.

The season opened on the 25th with *Cimarosiana*, *Apollo Musagetes*, and *L'Oiseau de Feu*, the second ballet having its London *première*.

Apollo Musagetes was a ballet in two scenes with music by Igor Stravinsky, scenery and costumes by A. Bauchant, and choreography by G. Balanchine.

The characters were: *Apollo Musagetes*, Serge Lifar; *Terpsichore*, Alice Nikitina; *Calliope*, Lubov Tchernicheva; *Polymnia*, Felia Dubrovska; *Two Goddesses*: Dora Vadimova, Henrietta Maikerska; *Leto*, Sophie Orlova.

Apollo Musagetes was not so much a ballet as a series of *variations* introduced by a short prologue. The setting showed a cave, from the interior of which Apollo emerged. He was met by two goddesses who invested him with a white tunic and a golden girdle.

The scene changed to a mountain, set against a

turquoise-blue sky. Fair-haired Apollo, wearing a pink tunic, gold shoes cross-gartered to the knee, and bearing a gold lyre, danced a solo. Then entered the three muses—Calliope, Polymnia, and Terpsichore, who, each receiving from Apollo an appropriate symbol, became the respective representatives of Poetry, Mime, and Dancing. Each muse danced in turn a *variation* expressive of her particular art. Then followed a *pas de deux* between Apollo and Terpsichore, who afterwards induced Calliope and Polymnia to join them in a dance. The ballet ended with an apotheosis showing Apollo conducting the muses to Parnassus.

Such, in brief, was the basic structure of the ballet. The music was quite unlike the novel forms and harmonies associated with Stravinsky's works, for, in this instance, the composer had most unexpectedly sought inspiration from purely classical sources.

Balanchine had again set aside his modernist experiments and planned a ballet which, while based on academic technique, had a certain novelty in its choreographic conception. One of the most successful dances was a *pas de quatre*, at one point in which there was a lovely dance formation in which Apollo, charioteer-like, seemed to be driving three fleet-footed nymphs; such was the impression conveyed by their positions and linked arms. Balanchine made great play with this "diamond" figure, a muse set at each of three angles, with Apollo at the remaining apex. As the dancers glided, posed, or leaped, their arms and raised legs were woven into a variety of unusual patterns, full of poetry and a certain sculptural charm.

DIAGHILEV BALLET IN LONDON

The apotheosis with which the ballet concluded must still linger in the memories of those who saw it. I refer to that simple but inspiring prospect of the three muses, their outstretched hands resting on each other's shoulders, as they climbed in single file slowly up the mountain-side, led by Apollo, now poised on its very summit, with his arms raised in greeting towards the many-horsed chariot, which, in the manner of an 18th century *gloire*, slowly descended from the skies to bear him and his companions to Parnassus.

The next new production was *Las Meninas*, to music by Gabriel Fauré, with scenery by Prince A. Schervachidze, costumes by J. M. Sert, and choreography by Leonide Massine.

This composition, which had its London *première* on July 2nd, was really a revival of a single number from a work originally known as *Les Jardins d'Aranjuez*, a suite of three dances originally produced in Madrid many years before, but for some reason never given out of Spain. I believe Polunin told me that the back-cloth of Socrate's setting for *Les Sylphides* was painted on the back-cloth of the Spanish ballet.

The cast consisted of: *Maids of Honour*, Lubov Tchernicheva, Felia Dubrovska; *Gentlemen*, Leon Woizikowsky, Serge Lifar; *the Dwarf*, Natalia Miklachevska.

The music was Fauré's well-known *Pavane*. The setting showed a Spanish garden, a balustrade overhung with foliage. The men, dressed in rich doublet and hose, and the women, in exaggerated versions of the hooped costumes worn by the Infantas in the paintings of Velasquez, danced a formal measure, varied with changes of partners and punctuated with courtly bows and stately curtsies. The dwarf introduced a grotesque element appropriate to the period. The choreography was a charming *pastiche*, partly inspired perhaps by the illustrations in Caroso's *Il Ballerino*.

On July 9th, the strangest of all the Diaghilev productions had its London *première*. This was *Ode*,[1] a Spectacle in Two Acts, with theme by Boris Kochno, music by Nicholas Nabokov, decorative contributions by Pavel Tchelichev in collaboration with Pierre Charbonnier, and choreography by Leonide Massine.

This ballet, certainly the most extraordinary of a host of unusual works, was a philosophical treatise expressed in terms of light, line, and movement.

I was told that Nabokov had been working on the composition of *Ode* many years before he had come into contact with Diaghilev. This musical conception was inspired by a poetical work written by Lomonosov, a well-known author in the 18th century, a minor Russian Goethe, who meditated upon the marvels of Nature and their relation to Man. The work in question was entitled, *Ode: Meditation on the Majesty of God on the Occasion of an Apparition of the Aurora Borealis*. Nabokov, looking for an opportunity to have his work performed, made the acquaintance of Diaghilev, who agreed to present it as the musical basis of a ballet, to which the composer consented, although not without reluctance.

[1] See Appendix G for full cast.

DIAGHILEV BALLET IN LONDON

Not a little of the artistic success of *Ode* was due to the collaboration of Tchelichev, who devised some quite new decorative effects based on the use of light and shadow, and of plastic materials appropriate to the development of linear designs; materials such as cord, string net, and gauze.

The focal point of his setting was a structure resembling the base of a signal mast; other white cords, knotted together or crossing each other in the form of a geometrical pattern, hung from the flies and joined the main structure. Immediately above, and parallel to, the two outer braces holding the mast, stretched a taut wire, supporting a row of dolls, dressed in tight bodices and wide crinolines of silver cloth; these dolls were graduated in size—the largest being nearest the audience—to convey a sense of perspective. In one scene masked women in similar dresses danced before the mast, the dolls providing an ideal background, a suggestion of the multiplication of the dancers through reflection in a series of mirrors.

There were other dancers dressed in fleshings with even their necks covered and gloves on their hands, while on their heads they wore light cloth helmets with gauze masks, reminiscent of those worn by fencers. These dancers danced with the cords which they held in their hands, pulling them in various directions to form interesting lines and geometrical designs. These strange figures, rendered impersonal by their masks, appeared like beings from another sphere, and gave a mystic Blake-like character to their sinuous movements and sculpturesque groupings.

GEOMETRICAL BEAUTIES OF ODE

Massine displayed the greatest invention and originality in the composition of his ever-changing groups, which were never symmetrical and yet always harmonious. The actual movements were in the manner of the classical ballet whose linear beauty was here given its full value by reason of the bodies being, for all practical purposes, unclothed. But the lines had an unusually austere and chaste quality, a geometrical rather than an emotional beauty.

There were other scenes in which light was the dominant factor. For instance, strange forms were projected on to a deep blue scene in front of which a dancer leaped in the myriad shafts of light reflected from a rotating crystal sphere. In another episode the stage lighting was dimmed and the three-dimensional figures that previously had been dancing suddenly dematerialized into whirling specks of light.

In the final episode there was a suite of four dances presented against a background of grouped figures. The dancers of the suite wore white fleshings and close-fitting caps, but with their faces visible. One of these numbers was almost acrobatic in the intricacy and difficulty of its movements.

Another number might be likened to an elegy. I am thinking of a *pas de deux* in which the dancers jointly upheld, each with one upraised hand, a slender, horizontal pole, from the first and last third of which was suspended a length of gauze, a little higher than a man and about twice the breadth of his body. This device was like two straight curtains with a gap between them equal to the width of one. A number of

DIAGHILEV BALLET IN LONDON

beautiful effects were achieved when the dancers danced behind the gauze, which invested them with an ectoplastic quality, or else appeared alternately in the open space, so that a solid form danced with a shadowy one; sometimes their arms alone curved and crossed in the intervening space.

It is not easy to convey the mystical character, the strange celestial beauty, and the unusual intellectual appeal of *Ode*. Those extraordinary designs, formed of ever-changing lines and triangles of cord, suggested animations of the diagrams illustrating Euclid's propositions; and yet always in and out of those corded mazes moved, crouched, leaped, and glided those beautiful unknown forms. To me they suggested a kind of visual "laying bare" of the intelligence at work, in which thoughts and ideas were drawn this way and that by all the fears and doubts to which Man is heir.

Ode could never have become a popular ballet—I use the term for convenience' sake—yet this stark conception attempted the boldest flight of all—it sought to attain the infinite, and, more wonderful still, came at times to reach it.

It was during this period that I planned a book of drawings representing Serge Lifar in his best known roles. I entrusted this work to Eileen Mayo, and, in order that the drawings should be as accurate as possible, I asked Lifar if he would co-operate by posing in the various characters. I arranged a number of sittings and one afternoon I took Eileen Mayo to His Majesty's Theatre to begin the first drawing.

SERGE LIFAR: HIS APPEARANCE

When we arrived we found not only Lifar, in high good humour and eager to pose, but also the omnipotent Diaghilev and the cynical Kochno. This was an unexpected audience, not calculated to help our enterprise. Eileen Mayo asked if she might remove her cloak, to which Diaghilev replied:

"Please take everything off if you wish."

Diaghilev could be lighthearted on occasion.

At subsequent sittings we were left to ourselves, which, in some ways, was a blessing, because certain of Lifar's poses were most difficult to hold and I had to improvise various means of support based on the use of chairs, the waste-paper basket, and anything else to hand. Now and again, when I was kneeling on the floor supporting Lifar's raised leg, the door of the room would silently open a few inches and Diaghilev's great head would peer in. Sometimes the director looked startled at the unorthodox proceedings, but, apparently reassured, he withdrew his head and softly closed the door.

I looked forward with great pleasure to these sittings which gave me an excellent opportunity of studying Lifar at close range. There was something very charming about his infectious high spirits, his evident delight in being alive, his almost boyish eagerness to earn the affection of the public.

His dark eyes, thick lips, and golden-brown skin gave him an exotic, almost oriental appearance. There was a strain of the wild in him, a suggestion of kinship with woodland folk. His head and torso, with its broad shoulders, rippling muscles, and narrow hips, reminded one of a faun of classical mythology, or of the head and shoulders of a fabled centaur. His movements, too, had the same lithe, sinuous quality associated with a wild animal.

One afternoon, as I went through the stage-door entrance, I found several members of the *corps de ballet* standing in the doorway, or sitting about while waiting the moment for their entrance in *Ode*. Dressed in fleshings and with small square boxes strapped to their backs, from which boxes emerged various wires, they resembled those fantastic beings only to be encountered in the pages of scientific romances by such writers as Jules Verne and H. G. Wells.

The final new production of the season was *The Gods go a-Begging*, which had its world *première* on the 16th. The theme was by Sobeka, the music by Handel, arranged by Sir Thomas Beecham, and the choreography by George Balanchine.

The principal characters were: *the Serving Maid*, Alexandra Danilova; *the Shepherd*, Leon Woizikowsky; *two Ladies*, Lubov Tchernicheva, Felia Dubrovska; *a Nobleman*, Constantin Tcherkas.

I do not know how this ballet came into being. It was clearly produced mainly as a tribute to Sir Thomas Beecham, and its success depended largely on the music and choreography, for Bakst's opening scene for *Daphnis et Chloé* provided the setting, while—with two exceptions—the costumes worn in *The Faithful Shepherdess* were pressed into service to dress the new ballet. The theme was a pastoral, typical of the scenes depicted in the paintings of Fragonard, Lancret or Watteau.

THE GODS GO A-BEGGING

A serving-maid, assisted by several lackeys, spreads a cloth on the grass and sets out refreshments in readiness for an elaborate picnic. The noble host and his guests arrive and among them strays a shepherd.

Two of the ladies find amusement in enticing the shepherd to dance with them. But he suddenly espies the serving-maid, whom he prefers. They take delight in a dance which is expressive of their mutual affection.

The noblemen are highly indignant at this rebuff to the ladies, and are minded to chastise the shepherd, when the two lowly persons doff their rags and prove themselves to be two divinities, who have descended upon earth in humble guise.

The selection and arrangement of airs by Handel—ten numbers in all—was admirable, both for the quality of their music and its danceability. The choreography was once more in Balachine's classical manner and contained few modernist innovations. One of the outstanding numbers was the *pas de deux* (*Gavotte*) between the shepherd and the serving-maid, which I regard as one of the most poetic and most successful of Balanchine's dance compositions. It fitted the music like a glove and admirably conveyed in terms of dancing the tender emotions of first love.

The ballet was conducted by Sir Thomas Beecham who shared in the ovation awarded the ballet at the fall of the curtain, his own considerable contribution being marked by the presentation of a large laurel wreath.

The season ended on the 28th, the programme consisting of *Cimarosiana*, *The Cat*, *The Gods go a-Begging*, and *Aurora's Wedding*.

CHAPTER XVI

~ 1929 ~

THE end of June saw the Diaghilev Company back in London for a four weeks' season at the Royal Opera, Covent Garden, beginning on the 29th, the opening performance consisting of *Cimarosiana*, *Petrouchka*, and *The Three Cornered Hat*.

The troupe had suffered several serious losses in the absence of Nikitina, Massine, Idzikowsky, and Kremnev, but had regained Petrova and Dolin.

The first new production, which had its London *première* on July 1st, was *The Prodigal Son*, a ballet in three scenes by Boris Kochno, with music by Serge Prokofiev, scenery and costumes by Georges Rouault, and choreography by George Balanchine.

The principal characters were: *the Prodigal Son*, Serge Lifar; *the Father*, Michel Fedorov; *the Siren*, Felia Dubrovska; *the Servants*, Eleanora Marra, Natalia Branitska; *Friends of the Prodigal Son*, Leon Woizikowsky, Anton Dolin.

The theme closely followed the well-known parable. The first scene showed the Prodigal Son quarrelling with his father and leaving in the company of his two

THE PRODIGAL SON

false friends. The second scene was concerned with the carousal, at which the Prodigal Son was stupefied with wine and then stripped of his possessions. The third scene dealt with the Prodigal's return home and his father's forgiveness.

From beginning to end the ballet impressed me with its sombre grandeur, the more marked in contrast with the flippant character of certain of the preceding modernist works. There was something elemental and archaic about Rouault's stark and gloomy landscape, relieved with faint flushes of deep green and blue.

Perhaps the second episode was the most unusual. Here the lighting, though still subdued, was brighter. The principal change was the introduction of a long narrow table flanked with jars of wine in preparation for the carousal. Grouped about the table were a number of the Prodigal Son's friends, their shaven heads at once suggesting the early Egyptians.

They contrived that the Prodigal Son should be plied with wine and tempted by a Siren who glided in *sur les pointes*. She wore a short tunic and tights painted with an appropriate web-like design, while from her shoulders hung a long narrow purple cloak which writhed in the breeze of her movements.

The long table, tilted high up at one end, became the semblance of a boat, with the woman as figurehead. The Prodigal Son leaped on this improvised barque and strode to its prow, while his companions played pipes and danced, and incited him to still greater excesses.

At last, dazed and exhausted, he sank on his knees and fell into a stupor. Quickly the Siren and his false friends fell on their prey. Some took the rings from his fingers, others filched his gold pieces, still others fought for his clothes. Plundered and stripped, he was left to sleep off the effects of the wine.

The dance movements were unusual. There were some elements of classical ballet technique in the dance for Dubrovska, but the men's movements had an element of acrobacy, as though inspired by gymnastics or the circus. In fact, they suggested tumblers rather than dancers.

But, interesting as certain episodes were, the whole ballet was dominated by Lifar. He presented a vivid picture of a young man's headstrong disregard of parental counsel, and his reckless determination to seek his own pleasure. Then followed the moment of bitter illusion when, ruined and forsaken, he came too late to see the error of his ways and resolved to repent and seek his father's forgiveness.

Lifar gave an intensely moving performance as he approached his old home, where his father stood hoping against hope for his son's return. The Prodigal Son, his fine garments replaced by a torn black tunic, seemed determined to neglect no humiliation of the body in endeavour to atone for his fault. I remember well how Lifar, with the help of his two hands resting on a stave, dragged himself slowly and painfully along through the dust, his shins scraping the ground, until he reached his father, a silent grey-haired patriarch.

LIFAR'S TRIUMPH IN THE PRODIGAL SON

The Prodigal Son, now at his father's feet, gradually stretched out his hands until they reached and clasped his father's arms, when, stricken with shame and remorse, he slowly raised his head and gazed imploringly into that calm face for a sign of mercy. The stern father, filled with pity, put his arms about his son with a beautiful gesture, drew the youth to his breast and allowed his wide cloak to fall and envelop him in its protective folds.

Lifar's role in this ballet was mime rather than dancing, and he revealed himself a fine exponent of that difficult art. His actions seemed to come straight from the heart, as though he felt the moving story in every fibre of his being. When the ballet ended I felt conscious of having witnessed one of those rare performances that constitute a landmark in one's memories, something to be treasured and relived.

The ballet was enthusiastically received and Lifar achieved a great personal triumph in the title-role. Fedorov, too, was highly praised for his dignified portrait of the father.

But Diaghilev, although delighted with the excellent reception accorded both to the new ballet and to his protégé, resented the increasing charges that his new productions were becoming more and more imbued with the ideals of gymnastics and acrobatics. Perhaps these observations irritated him the more in the knowledge that his next novelty, *Renard*, was to be more acrobatic still and therefore likely to provoke further censure. In endeavour to offset this opinion and to prepare both critics and public for *Le Renard*, he wrote a long letter to *The Times*[1] which appeared in the issue of July 13th.

On the 8th and 15th respectively, two new ballets were produced—*The Ball* (*Le Bal*) and *Le Renard*. For some reason I had to go out of town and so I missed the London *première* of both these ballets. Worse still, I did not have a second opportunity of seeing *The Ball*, another ballet by Boris Kochno, with music by Vittorio Rieti, costumes by Giorgio di Chirico, and choreography by George Balanchine.

Nevertheless, I did see the dress rehearsal of *Renard*, for which Diaghilev sent me a formal invitation, which event took place on the 15th at 12 noon. The guests were received *en grand seigneur* by Diaghilev, who stood at the head of the short flight of stairs leading to the stalls. The guests filled some two rows of seats. This was the first time I had seen Diaghilev during the season and I was shocked by the change in his appearance since the year before. His cheeks were of a strange leaden pallor and he appeared to be a very sick man. The cynical glance, the familiar curl of the lip, were still there, but he seemed to be unusually reserved and uncommunicative.

Le Renard has a special interest in that it was Lifar's first completed essay in choreography. The music was by Igor Stravinsky and the setting and costumes by Michel Larionov.

The principal characters were: *the Fox*, Leon Woizikowsky; *the Cock*, Nicholas Efimov, Louis Agustino;

[1] See Appendix H.

LE RENARD

the Goat, Boris Lissanevich, Bernado Agustino; *the Cat*, Jean Hoyer, Adolf Hierlinger.

The music was rendered by a small orchestra, which included a cymbalum, which was accorded a prominent role. The action was sung by singers in the orchestra-pit.

The setting, partly constructivist in conception, showed the interior of a Russian logwood hut, open at the back to reveal a forest landscape in winter, dark gaunt trees with their boughs lightly coated with snow. The stage was bare save for a white post about 7 foot high supporting a small rectangular platform.

There were two casts, one in which the characters were taken by dancers, the other by professional acrobats. They wore white or sober-coloured fleshings, their identity being established by the addition of such simple details as a little cap with ears in the case of the Cat, or a beard and horns for the Goat. As a final means of quelling any doubt, the name of the character was painted in block letters on the chest of each artiste.

This is the story according to the programme.

"Renard, disguised in religious manner, succeeds in seizing the cock, but is put to flight by the cat and the goat. They dance with joy.

"Renard reappears disguised as a beggar. He offers to the cock some dainties and succeeds in seizing him afresh. The cock is unfeathered. But the cat and the goat come to save the cock again. They choke and hang his executioner, and leave the stage together, completely happy in their triumph."

I have a vague memory of seeing agile forms leap on

to the platform and thence to the ground; of other figures whirling in somersaults and cart-wheels; of dancers succeeded by acrobats, and *vice versa*; of acrobats performing on a trapeze.

It was an interesting experiment in the possibilities of combination of various kinds of movement, but I felt that it would have been best to have confined it to the studio, and not to present it as a stage production. It seemed to me to express little or nothing, and to get nowhere. A few days later I saw *Renard* again, but my first impression remained unchanged.

In regard to the general repertory there were some notable performances of the company's condensed version of *Le Lac des Cygnes*, for which Olga Spessiva came to London specially to give her flawless performance as Odette; she was admirably partnered by Lifar.

The season ended on July 26th, the programme being *The Ball*, *The Prodigal Son*, and *Aurora's Wedding*.

When I took leave of my friends in the company, and lightly discussed plans for when they returned in the autumn, I never suspected for a moment that the Diaghilev Company had appeared for the last time.

Diaghilev went off to the Lido to recuperate, and, although obviously far from well, I had every hope that the rest and change of air would restore him to health.

On Monday, August 19th, I was walking down Charing Cross Road when I caught sight of a newspaper poster bearing the inscription, "Death of Famous Producer". I did not attach any particular

DEATH AND FUNERAL OF DIAGHILEV

significance to that news, it was only when I opened the evening paper that I learned it was Diaghilev who had passed away that very morning, at the Lido, near water, just as a fortune-teller had long ago foretold he would.

A few days later the illustrated dailies reproduced photographs of Diaghilev's funeral, that last fantastic journey on a state barge which bore him over the lagoons to the island cemetery of San Michele at Venice, where he sleeps amid the tall guardian cypresses.

Diaghilev was so familiar a figure in the London artistic world, and the visits of his company so much a part of any year's activities in the theatre that a season without him seemed inconceivable.

As the full implications of that grave loss began to take shape, speculation and rumour were rife. What would happen to the company? Would Lifar take charge? Would Grigoriev form a new directorate, in which a composite Diaghilev might be formed from the brains and talents of several persons?

Attempts were made to devise means for carrying on the company. But the responsibilities appeared too great, there were endless doubts and fears. All these projects resulted in the conclusion—*aut Cæsar aut nihil*. Diaghilev, the great dictator in the Theatre, had laid down his mantle and none dared to assume it.

The Diaghilev Company, like the genius who had given it birth, and sustained it through so many years of experiment and endeavour and travail, years in which so many beautiful things had been given to the world, suddenly ceased to exist, to pass into imperishable legend.

But something of the spirit of that great artistic enterprise; of the director who guided it; of the choreographers, dancers, composers, and painters who were part of it; and of the high standards they set; has by various means been preserved to posterity. That rich and exciting material must surely give perennial interest and inspiration to all those who work or take delight in the Theatre, especially in its particular manifestation known as Ballet.

APPENDIX

A. "If Pavlova had never Danced." (*The Times, July 18th,* 1910).
B. "The Russian Ballet." (*The Times, June 24th,* 1911).
C. A Typical Contract for a Member of the Corps de Ballet, 1918.
D. Cast of "La Boutique Fantasque", Alhambra Theatre, June 5th, 1919.
E. Cast of "The Sleeping Princess", Alhambra Theatre, November 2nd, 1921.
F. Cast of "The Triumph of Neptune", Lyceum Theatre, December 3rd, 1926.
G. Cast of "Ode", His Majesty's Theatre, July 9th, 1928.
H. Letter from Serge Diaghilev to "The Times", July 13th, 1929.
I. Serge Diaghilev's "Ballets Russes", London, 1911-1929. Details of Repertory, Soloists, and Conductors for each Season.

A: IF PAVLOVA HAD NEVER DANCED
Article in The Times, July 18th, 1910

"... If Pavlova had never danced ... the public stock of harmless pleasure during the past theatrical season would certainly have been diminished. Nothing like it has been seen before in the London of our time. There was, to be sure, the delightful Genée, with her gaiety and brilliance, and there was the seductive posturing of Isadora Duncan and Maud Allan. But Pavlova and the Russian dancers of the present moment (including not only those of Pavlova's own troop, but the beautiful Lydia Kyasht of the Empire—a rival who runs, or rather dances, her very close—and others at the Coliseum and the Hippodrome) have given us Londoners something really new: an extraordinary technical accomplishment, an unfailing sense of rhythm, an unerring feeling for the elegant in fantasy, and what Hazlitt would have called a "gusto", a passionate enjoyment. The dancing of Anna Pavlova is a thing of perfect beauty. This is no case of Mr. Pepys and his "best legs that ever I saw". In the presence of art of this stamp one's pleasure is purely æsthetic. Indeed, the sex-element (though of course necessarily somewhere in the sub-consciousness) counts for very little; for a man the dancing of

M. Mordkin is *almost* as pleasure-giving as that of Mlle. Pavlova. The combination of the two, above all in their Bacchanalian dance, is an even choicer thing than their *pas seuls*. Quite as much of a novelty to Londoners is the dancing of the troop. The freedom and swing of their limbs in the Mazurka almost lures you from your seat to "shake a leg" with them; but you sit quite still while they are alternately quickening up and slowing down in the *tempo rubato* of the "Rhapsodie Hongroise", seeing clearly that here is something you couldn't do to save your life. This is a very different thing from the ballet to which Londoners used once upon a time to be mercilessly subjected—rank after rank and file after file of honest breadwinners from Camberwell and Peckham Rye performing mechanical manœuvres with the dogged perseverance of a company of Boy Scouts. When people tell you, as they sometimes will, that ballet dancing is a bore, you recognize the trail of the honest British bread-winners. Once they have seen the Russian dancers they will hardly again be guilty of that *bêtise*.

B: THE RUSSIAN BALLET

Article in The Times, June 24th, 1911

Having easily come to the conclusion that the Russian Ballet provides us with a new and enchanting pleasure, it is worth while to examine a little into the sources and method of the pleasure. In that way we shall be able to enjoy it with greater security of judgment, to persuade others to enjoy it too, and perhaps

APPENDIX

in time even to arrive at some imitation of it on our own stage. We have had ballet-dancing in England ever since we can remember; but here we are face to face with something which, if not new in kind, is at any rate so different in degree that it needs to be put in a fresh category. The arrival of a whole *corps de ballet*, and the devotion of whole evenings at a time to it, under the splendid conditions provided at Covent Garden, give us an opportunity at last to deepen an analysis which has hitherto been forced to keep rather on the surface.

What then are the essential characters which differentiate the art of the Russian Ballet from that which we have hitherto known in England? That they dance better—the simplest explanation—is one of the most misleading, for the elusive differentia does not lie in technique. Certainly their technique is exquisite; all of them can do the most wonderful things with no appearance of effort, and they can do many sorts of wonderful things. But technique is no more the source of the highest pleasure in dancing than it is in painting, in music, or any other of the arts. It is a channel of communication; it is the means by which the artistic idea comes from the mind of the creator to the senses of the spectator. The Russians, in fact, have so long since brought their technique of dancing, their command of their limbs and bodies, their instinct for balance, for energy without exertion, to the highest point that they have been able to develop the art for which that technique exists—namely, the conveyance of choreographic ideas. Russian ballet-dancing never for one moment escapes from its subjection to ideas—and, moreover, to artistic ideas, ideas, that is, conceived at a high pitch of emotional intelligence.

Of course, every ballet is subject to some sort of design. If only for the sake of discipline there must be some order in the movements. But this has never been treated in England as the be-all and end-all of ballet-dancing, to which all executional allurements must be sacrificed; nor have the ideas expressed been pushed upwards, as the Russian ideas have, into the adventurous realms of artistic experiment. Our ballet-designing has always been a democratic art, so far as it can be reckoned among the arts at all. Our dancing has been to please the people without calling for any mental exertion on their part. It has been an essential principle in this, as in all democratic arts, not to divert any of the spectators' imaginative energy to the central inward idea, but to save it all for the enjoyment of the expression; to use only themes, such as coquetry, pursuit, evasion, the simplicity and familiarity of which would recommend them at once to the least cultivated spectator. In Russia, on the other hand, the ballet has been essentially an aristocratic institution, maintained by an autocratic Government for the use of the cultivated classes. It has not depended for its existence on giving immediate pleasure (the bane of all democratic art), but has been able to follow its own bent. It has not had to husband the imaginative energies of the spectators, but, on the contrary, has been able to pursue the proper aim of all arts—to trouble and exert their imagination.

APPENDIX

Our English ballets have had so little concern with the imagination that even the most pitiful little crumbs of imaginative food, the evolution of recent English choreographic impressionists and mysterious orientals from Montmartre, have caused something of a flutter among us. And now that we have suddenly set before us the abundant fare supplied by the inventive genius of a Benois and a Fokine, inheritors of a great tradition that has been gradually developing, all unknown to us, beyond the Baltic, and the interpretative genius of a Nijinsky, a Karsavina, an Elsa Will, is it to be wondered at that we fall to so greedily? For here we are introduced to a whole range of ideas such as we have never met before.

It is, in fact, not in the technical skill of the dancing, but in the variety and imaginative quality of those ideas which the dancing succeeds in expressing that the true differentia of the Russian Ballet is to be found. Take, for example, the dances from *Prince Igor*—in itself a rather tedious opera, founded on a turgid ballad that was foisted on Russian literature by an eighteenth-century forger and has been allowed to stay there to avoid a scandal. How excellently every means that the theatre offers has been made use of to produce the desired effect; the menace of the coming cloud of barbarians that is to lie for centuries on the desolate face of Russia (for we are in the camp of the Polovtsians, forerunners of the great invasion); not the loud blustering of Tamburlaine the Great, but the awful quiet vigour, half melancholy, half playful, of a tribe that is itself but a little unit in the swarm; the

DIAGHILEV BALLET IN LONDON

infinite horizons of the steppe, with the line of the burial *tumuli* stretching away to endless times and places, down the centuries, into Siberia; the long-drawn, resigned, ego-less music (Borodin drew his themes from real Tartar-Mongol sources); the women that crouch, unconscious of themselves, or rise and stretch lazy limbs, and in the end fling themselves prone when their dance is over; the savage-joyful panther-leaping of the men; the stamping feet and quick nerve-racking beat of the drum; and, more threatening than all, the gambolling of the boys, like kittens unwittingly preparing themselves for the future chase.

In *Carnaval* is a whole new range of ideas again. The *Igor* dances express a literary or historical idea. *Carnaval* expresses a series of purely musical ideas, literary or dramatic, it is true, in general scheme, for Schumann himself provided the main verbal notions, Carnaval, Pierrot, Columbine, Eusebius, Florestan; but the inspiration of the details is drawn from music, and certain movements and gestures of the dancers, certain trippings and stridings—such as Harlequin's and Estrella's [*sic*] in "Reconnaissance" and Pierrot's exquisite exit at the end of "Coquette"—convey humorous ideas which can be conveyed only by music and dancing and which cannot be put into words. This is pure choreography (as also is the dancing of the clowns at Armida's Court), musical comment, abstracted from all drama or mimesis.

How much of the work of a ballet-master suffers from being given piece-meal may be seen by comparing

APPENDIX

the effect of the detached "turns" of Pavlova and her company at the Palace Theatre before an irrelevant purely "decorative" back-cloth, with the effect of *Carnaval* in its entirety at Covent Garden. *Carnaval* is an exquisitely delicate artistic whole, from the first coy scamperings and hidings of Chiarina and Estrella to the good-natured *grand rond* in chase of the Philistines; and not a detail of it could be spared; least of all the black dado with the giant golden tulips and the two little roguish Pierrots of sofas, crouching against the wainscot, which make one alert from the beginning for the airy mockery of the whole intention. It is the sum of all these details which leaves us in the end with a quite new and brilliant vision of Schumann's work, purged of all possible suspicion of any Germanic seriousness of purpose.

Of course it is a dangerous matter handling musical themes in this way. Music often expresses emotional generalizations of the very widest content, and there is a danger that the choreographic commentary may limit, instead of enhancing the musical conception. Take, for instance, the illustration of a Chopin Nocturne given by the Russians at the Palace Theatre. We are ready to suppose a very wide sentimental significance in the music, embracing all sorts of emotional worlds; and the interpretation sought to be given to it by a series of graceful groupings of attractive young women in rose-coloured light seems not only restrictive, but positively unfriendly and irrelevant. Why not ugly women? Why not men? Why not clouds and mountains and a lake?

DIAGHILEV BALLET IN LONDON

Of pure mimesis, the imitation of actual material movements, there is but little in the Russian Ballet. Still less of convention: that mysterious language of gesture—comparable only to the means by which omnibus-conductors communicate with each other in the hubbub of Oxford-street—with which ballet-dancers are wont to darken the mind of the spectator, seems to have been entirely banished from their stage. Neither do they seek to entertain us by the mere portrayal of such simple matters as love, invitation, refusal, indignation, and forgiveness. There has to be some differentia in the emotion, some *callida junctura* which gives it a new significance, to make it worthy of their reproduction. Pavlova does not so much imitate the movement of a butterfly as the emotional quality of a butterfly-flight, the sense raised in our minds by watching it; and then it is not an ordinary butterfly, not a plain lepidopteron, but a Grimm butterfly, a dream butterfly, a butterfly multiplied many times by itself, raised as it were to the Pavlova-th power.

When for the moment they are confined to mere mimesis—the representation, for instance, of the joy of youth—they catch immensely expressive gestures which have eluded our home-impressionists, such as that wholly child-like bold swinging of the arms, as if they were pinned on at the shoulders, that we see in "L'Automne Bacchanal" and the Polovtsian dances. In all ballet-dancing there is a dim attempt to represent the spiritual and the fantastic by means of the material; the tip-toeing and the lifting-up of the women

APPENDIX

is a suggestion of the ethereal; but the perfect ease and grace of the Russians enable them to carry this to a far higher point, so that in their suggestion of things flying, things swimming, things poised, or blown by the wind, the sense of the material passes altogether away. The dancers are able in their turn to create the art of the ballet-master for him by offering him new possibilities, such as Karsavina's instinctive plant-like correlations of balanced extremities, and the contrary movements of head and limbs with which Nijinsky is able to create the grotesquest abstract, half-mathematical sensations.

In the general disposition, too, of the crowd on the stage, they have evolved new harmonies of grouping and of movement, avoiding symmetry, that bugbear of all design; there is always a certain natural asymmetry in the disposition of colours, in the entries and movements of the figures. And, above all, in everything there is restraint, which is the *sine qua non* not only of art but of all effective movement (as golfers know). There is restraint in the proportion of contrary or subsidiary movements, as in the excellently-judged waving of the feather-fans by the black slaves in the Armida Palace dances; restraint in stationary grouping, in the subjection of human masses to the scale of the scenery, a rule never observed at all in the designing of English ballet, which seeks rather to stun and overwhelm the judgment by multitudes.

And above all there is restraint of emotion. For this is one of the first principles of the art of expressive dancing, that nothing must be taken too seriously.

DIAGHILEV BALLET IN LONDON

There is a delightful lesson on this theme in one of the dances at the Palace Theatre. Two young women wrangle rhythmically, to the most mischievously ironical of Chopin's waltzes, for the possession of a nosegay, the trophy of some amourette; and when you think one has triumphed and the other is in despair, they throw it on the ground and run away with mocking laughter, leaving you ashamed of having minded. A Coquette dancing with two roses at the Carnival shows the graces of the early Victorian period at their daintiest, but all the time you guess that she is making fun of them and of the absurd people who believe in her. Eusebius, her lover, the character that Schumann invented to represent the serious side of his nature, takes himself with immense gravity; but we must never do the same, any more than we must believe in the warlike intentions of the beaver-hatted Davidsbündler, romping after the discomfited Philistines. No need to shed tears for young ladies who languish forlorn on the tips of their toes, or for poor gentlemen who die of love for such elfin creatures. Remember that this is an aristocratic tradition, with something of Boucher and Beaumarchais clinging to it, arch, mischievous, *gouailleur*. It is immensely serious as Art, but never for a moment serious as Life.

APPENDIX

C: A TYPICAL CONTRACT FOR A MEMBER OF THE CORPS DE BALLET, 1918

Memorandum of Agreement between the undersigned:

Monsieur Serge de Diaghilev, Director of the Russian Ballet, of the one part,

and Miss —— ——

the other part.

It has been agreed that:

1. M. de Diaghilev engages
Miss —— —— who accepts the engagement to join M. de Diaghilev's ballet troupe for the performances which he is to give from September 2nd to October 16th, 1918.

2. For this engagement M. de Diaghilev will pay to Miss —— —— the sum of £4 per week, London; £5 per week, provinces; and £28 (Twenty-Eight Pounds) per month Continent respectively. The salary will be paid in money of the country in which the performances take place. Railway fares on journeys necessitated by the performances will be paid for by M. de Diaghilev at second class rates for rail and boat fares.

3. Miss —— —— undertakes to attend the course of choreography and dancing given by the teachers attached to the Management.

4. In the event of this contract being broken the party breaking the contract will pay to the other party the sum of £25 (Twenty Five Pounds) as indemnification for losses sustained in consequence of the breach of contract.

5. In case of illness the performer will notify the Management immediately, and furnish a medical certificate within twenty-four hours after the notification.

6. The performer is not to leave the town in which the performances are taking place without the permission of the Management or its authorized representative.

7. The Management is not prepared to entertain any objections raised by the performer to the part allotted in the production.

8. Performers are to accept any change made in the piece performed.

9. The Management has the right to fine any performer who is late at rehearsals or performances, and the fines will be deducted from the performer's salary.

10. After the second fine the Management has the right to consider this contract as broken.

11. The performer undertakes to comply with the regulations in force at the theatres where the performances or rehearsals take place, and to obey them strictly, the said regulations constituting a clause in this contract.

12. The performer undertakes to attend regularly the rehearsals and performances and to follow strictly the instructions of the Management or its authorized representative concerning the obligations undertaken under this contract.

13. Costumes, wigs, and shoes for classical or character dances will be supplied by the Management. On the other hand, performers are to provide themselves with dancing tights.

APPENDIX

14. At all public and private rehearsals performers are to appear in costume and made up as requested by the Management.

15. M. de Diaghilev is entitled to give performances at theatres, concert-halls, or private houses.

16. M. de Diaghilev will pay the performer twice monthly in equal parts.

17. The performer has the right, without incurring a forfeit, to refuse to carry out this agreement in the event of the Management neglecting to pay the performer's salary on request within three days of the stipulated date.

18. In each case of illness the performer will receive the visit of the doctor employed by the Management. If the performer is prevented by illness or other unavoidable cause from fulfilling this engagement for a period exceeding twenty-eight days, the Management is entitled to terminate this agreement without indemnifying the performer.

19. From the date of the signature of this agreement until its termination, and in the event of its being extended or renewed, until the termination of such extension or renewal, the performer undertakes not to dance or otherwise engage in professional services either in public or in private, with or without payment, under any other management or in any other theatre or building than those indicated by M. de Diaghilev, unless the written consent of M. de Diaghilev has been previously obtained.

20. During the same period the performer is not entitled to dance for any person, company, or syndi-

cate, engaged in cinema work or other mechanical reproduction of dancing performances.

21. Any infraction of this agreement, whether completed or begun, will entitle M. de Diaghilev, apart from any claim that may arise for damages, to apply to a competent Court, without notifying the performer, in order to obtain an injunction prohibiting the infraction, or intended infraction, of this agreement.

22. On arrival in a town the performer must immediately furnish his address to the Management, and, in the event of a change of address, notify the same immediately to the Management.

23. If the performer arrives late or is absent at a rehearsal, a fine will be incurred of 5s. (Five Shillings), and if the performer arrives late or is absent at a performance a fine will be incurred of 10s. (Ten Shillings), such fines to be deducted from the salary.

24. The number and duration of rehearsals are fixed by M. de Diaghilev.

25. In the style of costume and make-up the performer will strictly carry out the instructions of the Management or of the producer.

26. It is agreed that in the event of the theatre at which performances are to take place being destroyed, M. de Diaghilev is not under an obligation to give performances, and in such case the performer will not be entitled to payment for the performances that cannot be given. M. de Diaghilev will in that event do his utmost to secure the resumption of performances as quickly as possible. M. de Diaghilev will also have

APPENDIX

the right to terminate this contract in the event of an epidemic, or of a closure of theatres by the authorities, or in consequence of raids, or if the events of the war render it impossible for him to continue the performances.

27. Certification of this contract will be effected at the expense of whichever party renders it necessary.

28. M. de Diaghilev has the option to extend this agreement from month to month to the full duration of a year, that is to say, until September 1st, 1919. During a period of two-and-a-half months within the said year, when there will be only rehearsals and no performances, the performer will be paid half salary.

D: CAST OF "LA BOUTIQUE FANTASQUE"

As first performed at the Alhambra Theatre, June 5th, 1919

CHARACTERS

The Shopkeeper	M. ENRICO CECCHETTI
His Assistant	M. ALEXANDER GAVRILOV
Two Porters	MM. PAVLOV & KOVALSKY
A Thief	M. OKHIMOVSKY
An English Old Maid	MLLE. KLEMENTOWICZ
Her Friend	MME. MIKULINA
An American	M. JAZVINSKY
His Wife	MME. ALLANOVA
Their Son	M. BOURMAN
Their Daughter	MME. EVINA
A Russian Merchant	M. SERGE GRIGORIEV

His Wife - - -	MME. JOSEPHINE CECCHETTI
Their Son - -	M. LUKINE
Their Four Daughters	MMES. NEMCHINOVA, ZALEVSKA, POTAPOVICH, MASCAGNO
DOLLS—	{ MME. LYDIA SOKOLOVA
Tarantella Dancers	{ M. LEON WOIZIKOWSKY
Mazurka:—	
The Queen of Clubs	MME. LUBOV TCHERNICHEVA
The Queen of Hearts	MME. VERA NEMCHINOVA
The King of Spades	M. STATKIEWICZ
The King of Diamonds - -	M. NOVAK
The Snob - -	M. STANISLAS IDZIKOWSKY
The Melon Hawker	M. KOSTETSKY
A Cossack Chief -	M. NICHOLAS ZVEREV
Five Cossacks -	MM. KOSTROVSKY, KEGLER, OKHIMOVSKY, RIBAS, MASCAGNO
A Cossack Girl -	MME. ISTOMINA
Dancing Poodles -	{ MME. VERA CLARK { M. NICHOLAS KREMNEV
Can-Can Dancers -	{ MME. LYDIA LOPOKOVA { M. LEONIDE MASSINE
Twelve of their Friends	MMES. KLEMENTOWICZ, VERA NEMCHINOVA, KOSTROVSKA, SLAVISKA, ISTOMINA, WASSILEVSKA, RADINA, GRANTZEVA, OLKHINA, PETIPA, PAVLOVSKA, MIKULINA

APPENDIX

E: CAST OF "THE SLEEPING PRINCESS"
As revised and presented by Serge Diaghilev, Alhambra Theatre, November 2nd, 1921

King Florestan XXIV	M. LEONARD TREER
The Queen	MME. VERA SUDEIKINA
Cantalbutte, Master of the Ceremonies	M. JEAN JAZVINSKY
The Fairy of the Pine Woods	MME. FELIA DUBROVSKA
Her Page	M. ERROL ADDISON
The Cherry Blossom Fairy	MME. LYDIA SOKOLOVA
Her Page	M. LEON WOIZIKOVSKY
The Fairy of the Humming-Birds	MME. NIJINSKA
Her Page	M. NICHOLAS ZVEREV
The Fairy of the Song-Birds	MME. LUBOV EGOROVA
Her Page	M. NICHOLAS KREMNEV
The Carnation Fairy	MME. VERA NEMCHINOVA
Her Page	M. THADEUS SLAVINSKY
The Fairy of the Mountain Ash	MME. LUBOV TCHERNICHEVA
Her Page	M. ANATOL VILZAK
The Lilac Fairy	MME. LYDIA LOPOKOVA
Her Page	M. STANISLAS IDZIKOWSKY
Carabosse, the wicked fairy	MME. CARLOTTA BRIANZA
Her Two Pages	MM. FEDOROV AND WINTER

DIAGHILEV BALLET IN LONDON

Her Four Rats	- -	MM. Savitzki, Kornetsky, Yalmuzhinsky, Lukine
Royal Nurses	- -	Mmes. Allanova, Krassovska, Majcherska, Komarova
Ministers of State	-	MM. Semenov, Singaievsky C. Stepanov
Royal Pages	- -	MM. Mikolaichik, Bourman, Okhimovsky, Patrikieff
The King's Herald	-	M. Kosiarsky
The Royal Physician	-	M. Pavlov
Maids-of-Honour	-	Mmes. Klementowicz, Bewicke, Moreton, Sumarokova
The Princess Aurora	-	Mlle. Olga Spessiva
The Spanish Prince	-	M. Anatol Vilzak
The Indian Prince	-	M. Leon Woizikowsky
The Italian Prince	-	M. Thadeus Slavinsky
The English Prince	-	M. Errol Addison
Countess	- - -	Mme. Lubov Tchernicheva
Prince Charming	-	M. Pierre Vladimirov
Pierrette	- - -	Mme. Nijinska
Columbine	- - -	Mme. Vera Nemchinova
Pierrot	- - -	M. Nicholas Zverev
Harlequin	- - -	M. Anatol Vilzak
Puss-in-Boots	-	M. Errol Addison
The White Cat	-	Mme. Ludmilla Schollar
The Blue Bird	-	M. Stanislas Idzikowsky
The Enchanted Princess		Mme. Lydia Lopokova

APPENDIX

Red Riding Hood	Mme. Lydia Sokolova
The Wolf	M. Mikolaichik
Bluebeard	M. Fedorov
Ariana	Mme. Lubov Tchernicheva
Sister Anne	Mme. Felia Dubrovska
Schéhérazade	Mme. Maria Dalbaicin
The Shah	M. Pavlov
His Brother	M. Singaievsky
The Porcelain Princesses	Mmes. Bewicke, Moreton
The Mandarin	M. Nicholas Kremnev
Innocent Ivan and his Brothers	MM. Leon Woizikowsky, Thadeus Slavinsky, Kornetsky

Ladies-in-Waiting, Lords, Pages, Negro Lackeys, Village Maidens, Village Youths, Duchesses, Dukes, Baronesses, Marchionesses, Marquises, Huntsmen, Nymphs, Beaters, Servants, Princess Aurora's Friends, Ladies of the Court, Dignitaries of the Court, etc.

F: CAST OF "THE TRIUMPH OF NEPTUNE"

As first performed at the Lyceum Theatre, December 3rd, 1926

The Fairy Queen	Mlle. Alexandra Danilova
Tom Tug, a sailor	M. Serge Lifar
W. Brown, a journalist	M. Michel Fedorov
Goddess	Mme. Lydia Sokolova

Emerald } Fairies Ruby	-	{ Mme. Lubov Tchernicheva { Mme. Vera Petrova
Sylphs - -	-	{ Mme. Lubov Tchernicheva { Mme. Vera Petrova
Street Dancer -	-	Mlle. Tatiana Chamie
The Sailor's Wife	-	Mlle. Barasch
The Sailor's Mother	-	Mlle. Fedorova
Snowball, a black man	-	M. George Balanchine
Dandy - -	-	M. Constantin Tcherkas
Journalists - -	-	MM. Jazvinsky, Winter
Policemen - -	-	MM. Hoyer, Cieplinsky
Cab Driver -	-	M. Pavlov
Telescope Keepers	-	MM. Borovsky, Petrakevich
Waiter - -	-	M. Lissanevich
Beggar - -	-	M. George Balanchine
Street Hawkers -	-	MM. Romov, Ladre
Workmen - -	-	MM. Strechnev, Ignatov, Hoyer II
Newsvendors -	-	MM. Jazvinsky, Winter
Newspaper Boys	-	MM. Strechnev, Hoyer II, Ignatov
Officer - -	-	M. Domansky
Chimney Sweep -	-	M. Gaubier
King of the Ogres	-	M. Pavlov
Clowns - -	-	MM. Petrakevich, Ladre

Fairies, Harlequins, Pages, Ogres, Attendants on Neptune.

APPENDIX

G: CAST OF "ODE"

As presented at His Majesty's Theatre, July 9th, 1928

Nature   Miss ORIEL ROSS
The Pupil   M. SERGE LIFAR

Nature descends from her pedestal, answers her pupil's questions and shows him:

The Constellations—MM. NICHOLAS EFIMOV, TCHERKAS, DOMANSKY, BOROVSKY, LISSANEVICH, KOCHANOVSKY, LADRE, PETRAKEVICH, HOYER II.

The River—MMES. MARRA, SUMAROKOVA, FEDOROVA, SLAVINSKA, MIKLACHEVSKA, ZARINA, OBIDENNAIA, CHULGHINE.

MM. JAZVINSKY, FEDOROV, PAVLOV, WINTER, HOYER, IGNATOV, M. SERGE LIFAR.

Flowers and Mankind   Projections
The Light Fleck   M. SERGE LIFAR

Not satisfied with what he has seen, the pupil begs Nature to show him her Festival:

MMES. VADIMOVA, MAIKERSKA, MARRA, SUMAROKOVA, CHAMIE, FEDOROVA, ORLOVA, PAVLOVA, ZARINA, KLEMETSKA, OBIDENNAIA, SLAVINSKA, CHULGHINE.

MM. KREMNEV, JAZVINSKY, FEDOROV, PAVLOV, WINTER, HOYER, LISSANEVICH, KOCHANOVSKY, PETRAKEVICH, LADRE, HOYER II, IGNATOV, KATCHUROVSKY.

The Dancers—

1. MLLE. ALEXANDRA DANILOVA, M. LEONIDE MASINE.

2. Mlle. Nathalie Branitska, MM. Nicholas Efimov, Constantin Tcherkas.
3. Mme. Felia Dubrovska.
4. MM. Leon Woizikowsky, Richard Domansky, Mezeslav Borovsky.

The Aurora Borealis   Projections and Lights

Captivated by the beauty of the Festival, the pupil darts forward, enters it and destroys by his presence the vision of the Aurora Borealis. Nature becomes again a Statue.

H: LETTER FROM SERGE DIAGHILEV TO "THE TIMES," JULY 13TH, 1929

To the Editor of "The Times".

Sir—The longer the globe revolves, the less movement we will find on it! Peoples may fight world wars, empires may tumble, a colossal Utopia may be given birth to, but the inborn traditions of humanity remain the same. Social revolutions upset political statuses, but they do not touch that side of the human spirit which leads to beauty. On the contrary, in such moments one has not got the time to busy oneself with æsthetic problems. In a period of this description we find ourselves at the present moment, when individual talent and human genius, always alive, enter like a microbe into the human system, but then it is refused any support.

Our century, without halting, interests itself with new "Mouvements mécaniques", but whenever new "Mouvements artistiques" occur people seem to be more frightened of being run over by them than by a

APPENDIX

motor-car in the street. For 25 years I have endeavoured to find a new "Mouvement" in the theatre. Society will have to recognize that my experiments, which appear dangerous to-day, become indispensable to-morrow. The misfortune of art is that everybody thinks he is entitled to his own judgment. When a scientist invents an electrical machine it is only experts who assume the right to be competent to criticize, but when I invent my artistic machine, everybody, without ceremony, puts his finger into the most delicate parts of the machine and likes to run it his own way.

But let us come to the events of to-day!

The new appreciation of my "Spectacles" of to-day is a series of exclamations: What an "Etrange", "Extravagant", "Repellent" show, and the new definition of the choreography are "Athletics" and "Acrobatics". The show, before anything, must be "Etrange". I can picture to myself the bewilderment of the people who saw the first electric lamp, who heard the first word on the telephone. My first electric bell for the British public was the presentation of the Polovtsian dances of *Prince Igor*. The small audience could not then tolerate this eccentric and acrobatic savagery, and they fled. And this only happened in 1911, at Covent Garden. At the very same theatre in 1929 the critics announced that my dancers had transformed themselves into "athletes" and my choreographic parts were "Pure acrobatics".

I have no reason here to discuss this grave question in detail, but, in a few words: "The classical dance has never been and is not to-day the Russian Ballet.

DIAGHILEV BALLET IN LONDON

Its birthplace was France; it grew up in Italy, and has only been conserved in Russia. Side by side with the classical dance there always existed the national or character dance, which has given the evolution of the Russian Ballet. I do not know of a single classical movement which was born of the Russian folk-dance. Why have we got to take our inspiration from the minuet of the French Court and not from the Russian village festival? That which appears to you acrobatic is a dilettantic terminology for our national dance step. The mistake really, in fact, goes much deeper, because it is undoubtedly the Italian classical school which has introduced into the dance the acrobatic elements. The coarsest acrobatic tricks are the toe-dancing, the "Doubles tours en l'air", next to the classical "Pirouettes en dehors", and the hateful 32 "Fouettés", that is where acrobatics should be attacked. In the plastic efforts of Balanchine, in *The Prodigal Son*, there are far less acrobatics than in the final classical *Pas de deux* of *Aurora's Wedding*.

Monday next I am presenting to the public two new items. Lifar is, for the first time, in charge of the dancers; he is the inventor of the choreography of the *Renard*, and it is there where really one has the first opportunity to talk of acrobatic ballet. It is not all Lifar's principle, but just because he could not see any other form to express the acrobatic music of Stravinsky. Stravinsky is, without doubt, the acrobat of sound, as Picasso is the acrobat of outline. Several constructive elements have introduced themselves into the field of acrobatics, and "Constructivisme" in

APPENDIX

painting, *décor*, music, and choreography is the craze of to-day.

The forms change. In painting and in scenery this craze is finishing. But in music, where we were full of impressionism and neo-sentimentalism, and in choreography, where we paid reverence to the classical dance, "constructivisme" acquired an extraordinary strength. In Paris we have just passed through a scandalous period in music. It was the period of cynical sentimental simplicity. It began with the cult of Gounod, Tchaikovsky, and Donizetti. It ended with the Pastiches of Goddard and Lecocq. Melody without any choice was imposed as an inevitable principle, and the poor music sank to such banality, even surpassing the ladies' ballads of the end of the 19th century. That is why I welcome everything that can help us to forget the fatal errors of the "Paris international market". My young countryman, Igor Markevitch, will play for the first time his piano concerto. He is 16 years old. His music is dear to me, because I see in it the very birth of that new generation which can protest against the Paris orgies of the past few years. Evidently Markevitch and people who think like him fall into another extreme; all sentimentalism of melody is absent. Markevitch begins with an extreme dryness of composition; he tolerates no compromise. The insistence of his dynamic rhythm is particularly surprising, in view of his age, and all his themes are well hidden in contrapuntic valises. His music is next door to pleasure.

Lifar has the same sense of construction and the

same dread of compromise. On the outside cover of the score of the *Renard* Stravinsky has written: "This ballet must be executed by buffoons, acrobats, or dancers." Lifar has taken dancers and real acrobats of the circus, and the task of the choreographist has been to combine the plastic of the circus and dance tricks, while Stravinsky compels the bass to sing with a female falsetto voice and expresses the sentimentality of the fox by the sounds of the cymbalum of the restaurant. The public and the critics will probably be annoyed with my two young friends, but they are both "débutants", and they are not afraid of it.

The more the globe revolves, the less movement we will find on it.

I am, etc.,

SERGE DIAGHILEFF

I: SERGE DIAGHILEV'S "BALLETS RUSSES", LONDON, 1911-1929

Details of Repertory, Soloists, and Conductors for each Season

NOTE.—The date in brackets after the name of a ballet is that of the London *première*. The initial "E" implies first performance in London, and "W" world *première*, or first performance on any stage.

1911

Royal Opera, Covent Garden, June 21st-July 31st.

Repertory. Le Pavillon d'Armide (E. June 21st), Le Carnaval (E. June 21st), Polovtsian Dances from "Prince Igor" (E. June 21st), Le Spectre de la Rose

APPENDIX

(E. June 24th), Les Sylphides (E. June 27th), Cléopâtre (E. July 7th), Schéhérazade (E. July 20th).

Company.[1] Thamar Karsavina, Vera Fokina, Ludmilla Schollar, Elsa Will, Sophie Fedorova, Nijinska, Astafieva, Wassilievska.

Vaslav Nijinsky, Adolph Bolm, Kussov, Leontiev, Orlov, Semenov, Maestro Enrico Cecchetti.

And Corps de Ballet.

Régisseur. Serge Grigoriev.

Conductors. Nicholas Tcherepnine, Thomas Beecham.

Royal Opera, Covent Garden, October 16th-December 9th.

Repertory. Giselle (E. October 16th), Schéhérazade, Le Pavillon d'Armide (2nd act only), Le Carnaval, Les Sylphides, Le Spectre de la Rose, Cléopâtre, "L'Oiseau d'Or"—*pas de deux* (E. November 3rd), Polovtsian Dances from "Prince Igor", "Aurore et le Prince"—*pas de deux* (E. November 14th), Le Lac des Cygnes (E. November 30th).

Company. Matilda Kshesinskaya, Anna Pavlova, Thamar Karsavina, Sophie Fedorova, Piltz, Nijinska, Schollar, Astafieva, Roshanara, Gachewska, Wassilievska.

Vaslav Nijinsky, Adolph Bolm, Kussov, Leontiev, Orlov, Sergeyev, Semenov, Frohman, Maestro Enrico Cecchetti.

And Corps de Ballet.

Régisseur. Serge Grigoriev.

Conductor. Pierre Monteux.

[1] The term "company" applies to the artistes actually appearing in the ballets.

DIAGHILEV BALLET IN LONDON

1912

Royal Opera, Covent Garden, June 12th-August 1st.

Repertory. Le Carnaval, Thamar (E. June 12th), L'Oiseau de Feu (E. June 18th), Les Sylphides, Le Spectre de la Rose, Polovtsian Dances from "Prince Igor", Schéhérazade, Le Pavillon d'Armide, Narcisse (E. July 9th), Le Lac des Cygnes.

Company. Thamar Karsavina, Piltz, Baranovich, Nijinska.

Vaslav Nijinsky, Adolph Bolm, Sergeyev, Semenov, Maestro Enrico Cecchetti.

And Corps de Ballet.

Régisseur. Serge Grigoriev.

Conductors. Nicholas Tcherepnine, Rhené-Baton, Thomas Beecham.

1913

Royal Opera, Covent Garden, February 4th-March 7th.

Repertory. Thamar, Les Sylphides, Petrouchka (E. February 4th), Polovtsian Dances from "Prince Igor", Le Spectre de la Rose, Thamar, "L'Oiseau et le Prince" (*pas de deux*), Le Carnaval, L'Après-Midi d'un Faune (E. February 17th), Le Dieu Bleu (E. February 27th), Cléopâtre, Narcisse.

Company. Thamar Karsavina, Sophie Fedorova, Piltz, Nijinska, Astafieva, Wassilievska, Nelidova.

Vaslav Nijinsky, Adolph Bolm, Alexander Kotchetovsky, Sergeyev, Semenov, Maestro Enrico Cecchetti.

And Corps de Ballet.

Régisseur. Serge Grigoriev.

Conductors. Michel Steimann, Pierre Monteux.

APPENDIX

Theatre Royal, Drury Lane, June 25th-July 25th.

Repertory. Le Pavillon d'Armide, Jeux (E. June 25th), Schéhérazade, Prélude à l'Après-Midi d'un Faune, Les Sylphides, Petrouchka, La Tragédie de Salomé (E. June 30th), Polovtsian Dances from "Prince Igor", Thamar, Schéhérazade, Narcisse, Le Carnaval, L'Oiseau de Feu, Le Sacre du Printemps (E. July 11th), Le Spectre de la Rose, Le Lac des Cygnes.

Company. Thamar Karsavina, Ludmilla Schollar, Sophie Fedorova, Marie Piltz, Nijinska, Wassilievska, Nelidova.

Vaslav Nijinsky, Adolph Bolm, Alexander Kotchetovsky, Semenov, Maestro Enrico Cecchetti.

And Corps de Ballet.

Regisseur. Serge Grigoriev.

Conductor. Michel Steimann, Rhené-Baton, Pierre Monteux.

1914

Theatre Royal, Drury Lane, June 8th-July 25th.

Repertory. Prince Igor (opera with ballet), Daphnis et Chloé (E. June 9th), Thamar, Schéhérazade, Papillons (E. June 11th), Petrouchka, Le Coq d'Or —opera with ballet (E. June 15th), L'Oiseau de Feu, Le Carnaval, Le Rossignol—opera with ballet (E. June 18th), Midas (E. June 18th), La Légende de Joseph (E. June 23rd), Cléopâtre, Nuit de Mai—opera with ballet (E. June 26th), Les Sylphides, Le Lac des Cygnes, Narcisse.

Company. Thamar Karsavina, Vera Fokina, Lubov Tchernicheva, Ludmilla Schollar, Wassilevska, Klementowicz, Munings, Pflanz.

Michel Fokine, Adolph Bolm, Fedorov, Maestro Enrico Cecchetti.

And Corps de Ballet.

Régisseur. Serge Grigoriev.

Conductors. Pierre Monteux, Emile Cooper, Dr. Richard Strauss.

1918

Coliseum Theatre, September 5th-March 29th (1919).

Repertory. Cléopâtre, The Good Humoured Ladies (E. September 5th), Le Carnaval, Polovtsian Dances from "Prince Igor", "The Enchanted Princess" (*pas de deux*), Papillons, Schéhérazade, Sadko—with new choreography by Bolm (E. October 31st), The Midnight Sun (E. November 21st), Children's Tales—Contes Russes (E. December 23rd), Les Sylphides, Thamar.

Company. Lydia Lopokova, Lubov Tchernicheva, Lydia Sokolova, Josephine Cecchetti, Felia Radina, Alexandra Wassilievska, Marie Zalevska.

Leonide Massine, Alexander Gavrilov, Stanislas Idzikowsky, Leon Woizikowsky, Jean Jazvinsky, Nicholas Kremnev, Maestro Enrico Cecchetti.

And Corps de Ballet.

Régisseur. Serge Grigoriev.

Conductor. Henry Defosse.

1919

Alhambra Theatre, April 30th-July 30th.

Repertory. The Good Humoured Ladies, Petrouchka, Les Sylphides, Papillons, Schéhérazade, Le Carnaval, Polovtsian Dances from "Prince Igor", L'Oiseau de Feu (The Firebird), Petrouchka, Children's Tales,

APPENDIX

Narcisse, Cléopâtre, La Boutique Fantasque (W. June 5th), The Midnight Sun, Thamar, The Three Cornered Hat—Le Tricorne (W. July 22nd).

Company. Thamar Karsavina, Lydia Lopokova, Lydia Kyasht, Lubov Tchernicheva, Lydia Sokolova, Josephine Cecchetti, Alexandra Wassilevska, Felia Radina, Vera Nemchinova, Leokadia Klementowicz.

Leonide Massine, Alexander Gavrilov, Stanislas Idzikowsky, Nicholas Kremnev, Nicholas Zverev, Leon Woizikowsky, Jean Jazvinsky, Maestro Enrico Cecchetti.

And Corps de Ballet.

Régisseur. Serge Grigoriev.

Conductors. Ernest Ansermet, Henry Defosse.

Symphonic Interludes[1] *played during Season.* Glinka, Jota Aragonesa; Balakirev, Overture on Russian Themes; Borodine, Scherzo; Mussorgsky, Overture to "The Fair at Sorochinsk"; Mussorgsky, Scherzo in B; Mussorgsky, Intermezzo in C; Rimsky-Korsakov, Chanson Russe; Rimsky-Korsakov, Overture on Russian Themes; Liadov, Mazurka, Près de la Guinguette; Stravinsky, Scherzo from "Symphony in E flat"; Debussy, Clair de Lune; Ravel, Le Rouet; Ravel, Alborada del Gracioso; Florent Schmitt, Rhapsody Valse; Albert Roussel, La Ville Rose; Déodat de Severac, Fête des Vendanges; Louis Aubert, Suite Brève; Arnold Bax, In a Vodka Shop; Eugene Goossens, Four Conceits; Lord Berners, Three Pieces; Herbert Howells, Scherzo and Mazurka from "The B's"; Elgar, Pomp and Circumstance; Borodine,

[1] Introduced for the first time during this season.

March of the Polovtsi; Chabrier, Valses Romantiques; Chabrier, Menuet Pompeux.

Empire Theatre, September 29th-December 20th.

Repertory. Children's Tales, The Three Cornered Hat, Polovtsian Dances from "Prince Igor"; Le Carnaval, Petrouchka, Schéhérazade, Les Sylphides, La Boutique Fantasque, Cléopâtre, The Good Humoured Ladies, The Midnight Sun, Thamar, Papillons, Parade (E. November 14th).

Company. Thamar Karsavina, Lubov Tchernicheva, Lydia Sokolova, Josephine Cecchetti, Alexandra Wassilevska, Felia Radina, Vera Nemchinova, Leokadia Klementowicz.

Leonide Massine, Veceslas Svoboda, Stanislas Idzikowsky, Nicholas Kremnev, Leon Woizikowsky, Nicholas Zverev, Jean Jazvinsky, Maestro Enrico Cecchetti.

And Corps de Ballet.

Régisseur. Serge Grigoriev.

Conductors. Ernest Ansermet, Adrian C. Boult, Edward Clark.

Symphonic Interludes played during Season. Balakirev, Finale from First Symphony; Borodine, Intermezzo and Mazurka; Liadov, Scherzo; Glazunov, Allegro from Second Symphony; Chabrier, Suite Pastorale; Debussy, Marche Ecossaise sur un thème populaire; Arnold Bax, In a Vodka Shop; Goossens, Tam-o'-Shanter; Dargomijsky, Baba-Yaga; Balakirev, Islamey; Borodine, Unfinished Symphony; Rimsky-Korsakov, A Fairy Tale; Rimsky-Korsakov, Suite "The Maid of Pskov",

APPENDIX

Zolotarev, Fête Villageoise; Florent Schmitt, Danse Désuète; Albert Roussel, Suite "Le Festin de l'Araignée"; Satie, Gymnopédies; Roger-Ducasse, Course aux Flambeaux; Albeniz, Triana; Albeniz, El Puerto.

1920

Royal Opera, Covent Garden, June 10th-July 30th.

Repertory. Contes Russes, Pulcinella (E. June 10th), Les Sylphides, Le Carnaval, Polovtsian Dances from "Prince Igor", La Boutique Fantasque, Papillons, Le Astuzie Femminili—opera-ballet (E. June 22nd), The Good Humoured Ladies, Schéhérazade, The Midnight Sun, The Three Cornered Hat, Le Rossignol—ballet with new choreography by Massine (E. July 16th), Thamar.

Company. Thamar Karsavina, Vera Nemchinova, Lubov Tchernicheva, Lydia Sokolova.

Leonide Massine, Stanislas Idzikowsky, Leon Woizikowsky, Nicholas Kremnev, Maestro Enrico Cecchetti.

And Corps de Ballet.

Régisseur. Serge Grigoriev.

Conductors. Ernest Ansermet, Henri Morin.

1921

Princes Theatre, May 26th-July 30th.

Repertory. Children's Tales, Les Sylphides, The Good Humoured Ladies, Le Carnaval, Cléopâtre, Schéhérazade, Polovtsian Dances from "Prince Igor", The Three Cornered Hat, Papillons, Chout (E. June 9th), Petrouchka, The Midnight Sun, Thamar, Le Sacre du Printemps—with new choreography by Massine (E.

June 27th), Pulcinella, L'Oiseau de Feu, "La Princesse Enchantée" (*pas de deux*).

Company. Lydia Lopokova, Lubov Tchernicheva, Vera Nemchinova, Catherine Devillière, Lydia Sokolova, Josephine Cecchetti, Leokadia Klementowicz, Hilda Bewicke.

Pierre Vladimirov, Stanislas Idzikowsky, Leon Woizikowsky, Nicholas Kremnev, Nicholas Zverev, Jean Jazvinsky, Thadeus Slavinsky, Sigismund Novak, Maestro Enrico Cecchetti.

And Corps de Ballet.

Régisseur. Serge Grigoriev.

Conductor. Ernest Ansermet.

Symphonic Interludes played during Season. Stravinsky, Symphonie à la Mémoire de Debussy; Stravinsky, Scherzo Fantastique; Prokofiev, Symphonie Classique; Satie, Trois Pièces Montées; Satie, Deux Gymnopédies; Poulenc, Rhapsodie Nègre; Poulenc, Ouverture; Poulenc, Suite du Gendarme Incompris; Honegger, Pastorale d'Eté; Auric, Ouverture pour Les Fâcheux; Auric, Adieu à New York, Fox Trot; Darius Milhaud, Printemps; Darius Milhaud, Sandades do Brazil; H. Gibson, Veil Dance; Goossens, Tam o' Shanter; Lord Berners, Spanish Fantasy; Bliss, Rout; Bax, Irish Suite; Quilter, Children's Overture; Ravel, Alborada del Gracioso; Chabrier, Menuet Pompeux; Debussy, Marche Ecossaise; Borodine, Finale of "Mlada"; Rimsky-Korsakov, Sadko; Rimsky-Korsakov, Overture to "Ivan the Terrible"; Rimsky-Korsakov, Intro. and Gopak from "The Fair at Sorochinsk"; Rimsky-Korsakov, Russian Song; Bala-

APPENDIX

kirev, Islamey; Mussorgsky, Intro. and March from "Le Coq d'Or".

Alhambra Theatre, November 2nd-February 4th (1922).

Special Production. The Sleeping Princess (La Belle au Bois Dormant).
Company. Augmented. For cast see pp. 319-321.
Régisseur. Serge Grigoriev.
Conductors. Gregor Fittelberg, Eugene Goossens.

1924

Coliseum Theatre, November 24th-January 10th (1925).

Repertory. Cimarosiana[1], Le Train Bleu (E. November 24th), The Faithful Shepherdess (E. December 1st), Children's Tales, Polovtsian Dances from "Prince Igor", Aurora's Wedding (Arrangement of Dances from "La Belle au Bois Dormant"—"The Sleeping Princess" (E. December 15th), La Boutique Fantasque, The Midnight Sun, Les Sylphides, The Three Cornered Hat.

Company. Bronislava Nijinska, Vera Nemchinova, Lubov Tchernicheva, Lydia Sokolova, Felia Dubrovska, Ludmilla Schollar, Alice Nikitina, Alexandra Danilova, Thamar Geverova, Vera Savina, Ninette de Valois, Maikerska, Coxon.

Leon Woizikowsky, Anatol Vilzak, Anton Dolin, Thadeus Slavinsky, Nicholas Zverev, Nicholas Kremnev, Jean Jazvinsky, Michel Fedorov, Lifar, Tcherkas.

[1] The last act—the one devoted to ballet—of *Le Astuzie Femminili*. Its first English performance in this form was on November 24th.

And Corps de Ballet.
Régisseur. Serge Grigoriev.
Conductor. Edouard Flament.

1925
Coliseum Theatre, May 18th-August 1st.

Repertory. Le Carnaval, The House Party—Les Biches (E. May 25th), Aurora's Wedding, Narcisse, Les Fâcheux—choreography by Nijinska (E. June 3rd), The Three Cornered Hat, Cimarosiana, La Boutique Fantasque, Les Matelots (E. June 29th), Polovtsian Dances from "Prince Igor", Les Sylphides, Tchaikovsky Divertissement (July 10th).

Company. Vera Nemchinova, Lubov Tchernicheva, Lydia Sokolova, Alice Nikitina, Felia Dubrovska, Alexandra Danilova, Thamar Gevergeva,[1] Vera Savina, Ninette de Valois,[2] Markova, Maikerska, Coxon.

Leon Woizikowsky, Stanislas Idzikowsky, Anton Dolin, Thadeus Slavinsky, Nicholas Zverev, Serge Lifar, Nicholas Kremnev, Jean Jazvinsky, Michel Fedorov, Constantin Tcherkas.

And Corps de Ballet.
Régisseur. Serge Grigoriev.
Conductor. Eugene Goossens.

Coliseum Theatre, October 26th-December 19th.

Repertory. La Boutique Fantasque, Le Carnaval, Les Matelots, Polovtsian Dances from "Prince Igor", Petrouchka, The House Party, The Three Cornered Hat, Zephyr and Flora (E. November 12th), The Good

---

[1] Geverova.   [2] Originally spelt Nina Devalois.

APPENDIX

Humoured Ladies, Aurora's Wedding, Cimarosiana, Barabau (W. December 11th).

Company. Lydia Lopokova, Vera Nemchinova, Lubov Tchernicheva, Lydia Sokolova, Alice Nikitina, Alexandra Danilova, Felia Dubrovska, Nadejda Nicolayeva, Thamar Gevergeva, Vera Savina, Alicia Markova, Maikerska.

Leon Woizikowsky, Stanislas Idzikowsky, Thadeus Slavinsky, Nicholas Zverev, Serge Lifar, George Balanchine, Nicholas Kremnev, Nicholas Efimov, Constantin Tcherkas, Jean Jazvinsky, Michel Fedorov, Nicholas Legat.

And Corps de Ballet.

Régisseur. Serge Grigoriev.

Conductor. Roger Desormière.

1926

His Majesty's Theatre, June 14th-July 23rd.

Repertory. Le Carnaval, Les Noces (E. June 14th), Les Matelots, Pulcinella, La Boutique Fantasque, Polovtsian Dances from "Prince Igor", Cimarosiana, The Three Cornered Hat, Barabau, Romeo and Juliet (E. June 21st), Les Sylphides, La Pastorale (E. June 28th), The House Party, Petrouchka, Jack in the Box (E. July 5th), Parade, Thamar, Zephyr and Flora, The Good Humoured Ladies.

Company. Thamar Karsavina, Lydia Lopokova, Lubov Tchernicheva, Lydia Sokolova, Alice Nikitina, Alexandra Danilova, Felia Dubrovska, Thamar Gevergeva, Nina Devalois, Vera Savina, Maikerska, Sumarokova.

Leon Woizikowsky, Stanislas Idzikowsky, Pierre Vladimirov, Thadeus Slavinsky, Serge Lifar, George Balanchine, Constantin Tcherkas, Nicholas Kremnev, Richard Domansky, Jean Jazvinsky, Michel Fedorov, Michel Pavlov.

And Corps de Ballet.

Régisseur. Serge Grigoriev.

Conductor. Eugene Goossens.

Symphonic Interludes played during Season. Gounod, Petite Symphonie; Chabrier, Menuet Pompeux; Satie, Trois Pièces Montées; Stravinsky, La Sérénade; Lord Berners, Fugue; Rimsky-Korsakov, Kershenetz; Chabrier, Suite Pastorale; Lord Berners, Spanish Fantasy; Chabrier, Fête Polonaise; Bizet, Jeux d'Enfants; Bliss, Polonaise; Goossens, Fantasy Nonet; Prokofiev, March from "The Love of the Three Oranges"; Rimsky-Korsakov, "The Flight of the Bumble Bee" from "The Legend of the Tsar Saltan"; Walton, Portsmouth Point; Mozart, Ein Musikalischer Spass.

Lyceum Theatre, November 13th-December 11th.

Repertory. Petrouchka, The Swan Lake, The House Party, Children's Tales, L'Après-Midi d'un Faune, Polovtsian Dances from "Prince Igor", Les Matelots, La Boutique Fantasque, Le Carnaval, L'Oiseau de Feu (The Firebird), The Three Cornered Hat, Cimarosiana, Aurora's Wedding, The Triumph of Neptune (W. December 3rd).

Company. Vera Petrova, Lubov Tchernicheva, Alexandra Danilova, Lydia Sokolova, Vera Savina, Maikerska, Sumarokova, Markova, Istomina, Vadimova.

APPENDIX

Leon Woizikowsky, Serge Lifar, George Balanchine, Nicholas Kremnev, Jean Jazvinsky, Constantin Tcherkas, Michel Fedorov, Nicholas Efimov, Richard Domansky.

And Corps de Ballet.

Régisseur. Serge Grigoriev.

Conductor. Henry Defosse.

Symphonic Interludes played during Season. Rossini, Sinfonia dal "Signor Bruschino"; Debussy, L'Isle Joyeuse; Chabrier, L'Education Manquée; Borodine, Scherzo; Borodine, Unfinished Symphony; Chabrier, Valses Romantiques; Glinka, Polka Primitive; Dargomijsky, Tarantelle Slave; Gemignani, Largo; Tailleferre, Les Jeux en Plein Air; Glinka, Suite from "Russlan and Ludmilla"; Walton, Suite from "Façade".

1927

Princes Theatre, June 13th-July 23rd.

Repertory. Petrouchka, La Boutique Fantasque, Cimarosiana, The Cat (E. June 14th), The Three Cornered Hat, The House Party, The Triumph of Neptune, Polovtsian Dances from "Prince Igor", L'Oiseau de Feu (The Firebird); Les Fâcheux—with new choreography by Massine (E. June 20th), Romeo and Juliet, Le Carnaval, Pulcinella, L'Après-Midi d'un Faune, Le Pas d'Acier (E. July 4th), Les Matelots, Aurora's Wedding, Mercury (E. July 11th), The Swan Lake, Les Sylphides, The Song of the Nightingale—with new choreography by Balanchine (E. July 18th), Children's Tales.

Company. Alice Nikitina, Lubov Tchernicheva, Vera

Petrova, Alexandra Danilova, Lydia Sokolova, Thamar Gevergeva, Vera Savina, Maikerska, Sumarokova, Markova, Vadimova, Chamie.

Leonide Massine, Leon Woizikowsky, Serge Lifar, George Balanchine, Nicholas Kremnev, Theodore Slavinsky, Jean Jazvinsky, Constantin Tcherkas, Nicholas Efimov, Richard Domansky, Michel Fedorov.

Régisseur. Serge Grigoriev.

Conductors. Eugene Goossens, Dr. Malcolm Sargent (after June 21st), Sir Thomas Beecham (July 7th only), Roger Desormière (from July 15th).

Symphonic Interludes played during Season. Mozart, Allegro and Rondo from Eine Kleine Nachtmusik; Chabrier, Menuet Pompeux; Prokofiev, March from "The Love of the Three Oranges"; Rimsky-Korsakov, Scherzo "The Flight of the Bumble Bee" from "The Legend of the Tsar Saltan"; Chabrier, Valses Romantiques; Weber, Overture to "Turandot"; Goossens, Rhythmic Dance; Rieti, Concerto; Rimsky-Korsakov, Concerto in C sharp minor; Glinka, Overture to "Russlan and Ludmilla"; Tchaikovsky, Piano Concerto.

1928

His Majesty's Theatre, June 25th-July 28th.

Repertory. Cimarosiana, Apollo Musagetes (E. June 25th), L'Oiseau de Feu, Les Biches, La Boutique Fantasque, Les Sylphides, The Three Cornered Hat, L'Après-Midi d'un Faune, Polovtsian Dances from "Prince Igor", The Triumph of Neptune, Le Carnaval, The Cat, Las Meninas (E. July 2nd), Aurora's

APPENDIX

Wedding, Le Pas d'Acier, The Midnight Sun, Pulcinella, Ode (E. July 9th), Les Noces, Barabau, Les Matelots, The Gods go a-Begging (W. July 16th), Le Lac des Cygnes.

Company. Alice Nikitina, Lubov Tchernicheva, Alexandra Danilova, Felia Dubrovska, Vera Savina, Nina Devalois, Natalie Maikerska, Lubov Sumarokova, Alicia Markova, Doris Vadimova, Tatiana Chamie.

Leonide Massine, Stanislas Idzikowsky, Leon Woizikowsky, Serge Lifar, George Balanchine, Nicholas Kremnev, Jean Jazvinsky, Constantin Tcherkas, Nicholas Efimov, Richard Domansky, Michel Fedorov.

And Corps de Ballet.

Régisseur. Serge Grigoriev.

Conductors. Sir Thomas Beecham, Dr. Malcolm Sargent, Roger Desormière.

Symphonic Interludes played during Season. Rieti, Madrigal Suite; Walton, Façade; Méhul, Ouverture Burlesque; Méhul, Overture to "Euphrosine et Coradin, ou le Tyran corrigé"; Bizet, Jeux d'Enfants; Bizet, Sérénade and Danse Bohémienne from "The Fair Maid of Perth"; Rimsky-Korsakov, Scherzo, "The Flight of the Bumble Bee" from "The Legend of Tsar Saltan"; Walton, Portsmouth Point.

1929

Royal Opera, Covent Garden, June 29th-July 26th.

Repertory. Cimarosiana, Petrouchka, The Three Cornered Hat, The Gods go a-Begging, The Prodigal Son (E. July 1st), Aurora's Wedding, Les Sylphides,

DIAGHILEV BALLET IN LONDON

Apollo Musagetes, La Boutique Fantasque, Las Meninas, Polovtsian Dances from "Prince Igor", Pastorale, Les Matelots, Le Bal (E. July 8th), The Cat, Le Carnaval, L'Après-Midi d'un Faune, Le Renard (E. July 15th), Le Lac des Cygnes, Baba Yaga—scene from Children's Tales, Les Fâcheux, Le Sacre du Printemps—choreography by Massine.

Company. Olga Spessiva, Alexandra Danilova, Lubov Tchernicheva, Vera Petrova, Lydia Sokolova, Felia Dubrovska, Vera Savina, Natalie Maikerska, Lubov Sumarokova, Alicia Markova, Doris Vadimova, Tatiana Chamie.

Serge Lifar, Leon Woizikowsky, Anton Dolin, George Balanchine, Jean Jazvinsky, Constantin Tcherkas, Nicholas Efimov, Richard Domansky, Michel Fedorov, Jean Hoyer.

And Corps de Ballet.

Régisseur. Serge Grigoriev.

Conductor. Roger Desormière.

Symphonic Interludes played during Season. Rieti, Noah's Ark; Markevich, Piano Concerto; Lambert, Music for Orchestra.

INDEX

Note. Names of artists in casts are not included.
References to ballets and divertissements, and to theatres, are grouped together.

Ache, Caran d', 142*n*.
Addison, Errol, 159, 191, 204, 216
Aesop, 272, 275
Aladdin and the Wonderful Lamp, 198
Alfonso, King of Spain, 104, 281
Allanova, Mlle., 127, 137
Allinson, Adrian, 123, 142, 142*n*.
Andersen, Hans, 97
Anisfeld, Boris, 78, 120
Ansermet, Ernest, 133
Antar, 119
Antonova, Mlle., 229
Arensky, 60, 220
Art of Léon Bakst, The, 70
Art of Nijinsky, The, 82
As You Like It, 262
Astafieva, Seraphina, 61, 110, 222, 244
Auric, Georges, 248, 249, 257, 259

Bach, J. S., 255
Bakst, Léon, 7, 9, 18, 21, 24, 26, 33, 37, 51, 57, 58, 60, 68, 70, 71, 85, 88, 97, 98, 108-111, 114, 118, 129, 192-194, 196, 197, 200, 210, 228, 229, 290

Bakst, Léon, *The Art of*, 70
Léon, *L'Œuvre de, pour la Belle au Bois Dormant*, 200
Balakirev, 9
Balanchine, George, 157, 220-222, 236, 253, 254, 258, 259, 266, 268, 269, 271, 272, 281, 282, 283, 290-292, 296
Balanchivadze, George, *see* Balanchine, George
Baldina, Mlle., 4
Ballarino, Il, 285
Ballets and Divertissements—
Amarilla, 7
Apollo Musagetes, 282
Après-Midi d'un Faune, L', 8, 51, 70, 240, 281
Astuzie Femminili, Le, 161, 163, 166
Aurora's Wedding, 222*n*., 227, 228, 229, 245, 251, 254, 264, 271, 280, 281, 291, 298
"*Bacchanale*", 111
Bal, Le, see *Ball, The*
Ball, The, 296, 298
Barabau, 253, 254
Belle au Bois Dormant, La, 51, 114, 191, see also *Sleeping Princess, The*

345

INDEX

Ballets and Divertissements—
ctd.
Biches, Les, see House Party, The
"Blue Bird" (pas de deux), see "Oiseau Bleu, L'"
Boutique Fantasque, La, 100, 128, 132, 134, 135, 139, 140, 141, 153, 155, 183, 184, 191, 200, 222n., 229, 242, 244, 247, 251, 264, 272
Carnaval, Le, 6, 20, 21, 27, 38, 41, 83, 89, 90, 111, 112, 134, 145, 168, 245, 251, 255, 280
Cat, The, 272, 276, 277, 281, 291
Chatte, La, see Cat, The
Children's Tales, 123, 145, 159, 183, 188, 281
Chout, 187, 188
Cimarosiana, 166, 216, 222n., 223, 261, 282, 291, 292
Cléopâtre, 6, 34, 60, 105, 107, 109, 111, 146, 147
Contes Russes, see Children's Tales
Coq d'Or, Le, 93, 94, 99
"Cupidon", 216
"Danse Grecque", 83
"Danse Orientale", 78, 79, 82, 83
"Danse Polovtsienne", 82
Daphnis et Chloé, 84, 84n., 85, 86, 87, 128, 290
Dieu Bleu, Le, 8, 57, 58, 110, 269
"Egyptian Dance", 220
"Enchanted Princess, The," see "Oiseau Bleu, L'"
"Enigme", 220
Fâcheux, Les [Massine], 277
 [Nijinska], 248

Ballets and Divertissements—
ctd.
Faithful Shepherdess, The, 225, 290
Fanatics of Pleasure, 216
Fils Prodigue, Le, see Prodigal Son, The
Fire Bird, The, see Oiseau de Feu, L'
Gardens of Aranjuez, The, 128, 284
Gigue, 255
Giselle or la Sylphide, 4
Giselle ou les Wilis, 4, 7, 244
Gods go a-Begging, The, 290, 291
Good Humoured Ladies, The, 107, 129, 160, 191, 244, 251
House Party, The, 245, 247, 265
Jack in the Box, 261
Jardins d'Aranjuez, Les, see Gardens of Aranjuez, The
Jeux, 68, 69, 70, 76
Lac des Cygnes, Le, 4, 7, 30, 31, 154, 244, 265
Légende de Joseph, La, 98, 99–101, 104, 217
"Lesghinka", 216
Masquerade, The, 217
Matelots, Les, 248, 251, 255, 259, 261
"Matelotte", 220
Meninas, Las, 284
Mercure, see Mercury
Mercury, 280, 281
Midas, 97
Midnight Sun, The, 121, 123, 168, 188
Narcisse, 31, 37, 128, 134
Noces, Les, 255, 256, 257
Nuit d'Egypte, Une, 60
Ode, 285, 286, 288, 290

346

INDEX

Ballets and Divertissements—ctd.
"*Oiseau Bleu, L'*," 7, 50, 51, 83, 114, 119, 173, 191, 220, 222*n*.
Oiseau de Feu, L', 9, 17, 41, 128, 129, 134, 150, 154, 190, 265, 271, 278, 282
"*Oiseau d'Or, L'*," see "*Oiseau Bleu, L'*"
"*Oiseau et le Prince, L'*," see "*Oiseau Bleu, L'*"
Papillons, 88, 89, 90, 101, 123, 144, 154, 168
Parade, 128, 149, 220, 261
Pas d'Acier, Le, 278, 280
Pastorale, 259
Pavillon d'Armide, Le, 6, 31, 56, 68, 83, 228
Petrouchka, 17, 42, 43, 52, 73, 99, 101, 128, 129, 134, 151, 167, 222*n*., 242, 251, 265, 272, 273, 278, 292
"*Prince Igor*", Polovtsian Dances from, 6, 25, 29, 38, 41, 42, 84*n*., 113, 114, 123, 134, 137, 139, 191, 281
Prodigal Son, The, 292, 298
Pulcinella, 100, 159, 163, 278
Puppenfee, 134
"*Ragtime*", 216
Renard, Le, 295, 296, 298
"*Rigaudon from Chinatown*", 220
Romeo and Juliet, 258, 264
Roses, Les, 220
Rossignol, Le (ballet by Balanchine), 281
Rossignol, Le (ballet by Massine), 172
Rossignol, Le (opera), 97
Sacre du Printemps, Le, [Nijinsky], 72, 73, 74

Ballets and Divertissements—ctd.
Sadko [Bolm], 119, 123 [Fokine], 120
Schéhérazade, 6, 31, 33, 34, 41, 58, 68, 76, 84, 119, 127, 134, 150, 218, 242
"*Schön Rosmarin*", 220
Sleeping Princess, The, 197, 199*n*., 200, 204, 205, 207, 212, 212*n*., 213, 213*n*., 214, 215, 221, 228, 229, see also *Belle au Bois Dormant, La*
"*Soldier and Grisette*", 220
Song of the Nightingale, The [Balanchine], 281
Spectre de la Rose, Le, 6, 25, 26, 27, 28, 29, 38, 41, 76, 77, 78, 80, 81, 83
Swan Lake, The, see *Lac des Cygnes, Le*
Sylphide, La, 90
Sylphides, Les, 6, 9, 13, 14, 16, 17, 27, 38, 42, 77, 78, 79, 81, 126, 127, 129, 150, 154, 159, 166, 167, 184, 281, 284
Thamar, 9, 10, 13, 14, 17, 34, 38, 42, 84, 126
Three Cornered Hat, The, 100, 128, 143, 145, 152, 155, 187, 292
"*Togo: or The Noble Savage*", 219
Tragédie de Salomé, La, 71, 76
Train Bleu, Le, 223
Tricorne, Le, see *Three Cornered Hat, The*
Triumph of Neptune, The, 264, 266, 267, 269, 271, 280, 281
Tub, The, 255
Zephyr and Flora, 251

347

INDEX

Bal Mabille, 138
Barbier, George, 66
Barocchi, Randolfo, vii, 114–117, 125, 130, 131, 135, 136, 140, 188, 191, 192, 212, 213
Barrie, J. M., 217
Basil, Col. de, x
Bauchant, H., 282
Beardsley, Aubrey, 71
Beaumont, Comte Etienne de, 261, 280
Beecham, Sir Joseph, 68, 83, 101
Beecham, Sir Thomas, 41, 280, 290, 291
Beer, Gustave de, 55, 56, 71, 77, 82, 102
Beggar's Opera, The, 197
Belle Edition, La, 66
Benois, Alexandre, 13, 42, 78, 97, 126, 228
Berain, Jean, 200, 228
Berlioz, Hector, 25
Berners, Lord, 262, 263, 266, 271
Bernouard, François, 66, 67
Bewicke, Hilda, 193
Bibiena family, 200
Blake, William, 147, 286
Blanche, Jacques Emile, 79, 83
Blasis, Carlo, 15
Blum, René, x
Boccaccio, Giovanni, 255
Bolm, Adolph, 4, 11–13, 19–21, 29, 49, 57, 70, 85, 87, 95, 96, 101, 104, 107, 112, 114, 120, 126
Bonni, Mlle., 78, 79
Boris Godunov, 70
Borodine, 29
Botticelli, 87
Bourman, Anatol, 128, 137
Bowen, Vera, 217

Boyce, William, 262
Braque, George, 248, 251
Breughel, Pieter, 254
Brianza, Carlotta, 193
Bruce, Henry, 93
Brunoff, Maurice de, 63–66, 70, 200
Buddha, 237
Buenos Aires, 77
Bulgakov, Alexis, 95
Bull, John, 262
Butt, Sir Alfred, 78, 81, 83, 145

Canaletto, 108
Carlin, 160
Caroso, F., 285
Casadesus, H., 225
Cecchetti, Enrico, vii, 20, 24, 25, 36, 49, 50, 104, 107, 137, 156, 159, 168, 171, 173–182, 209–211, 222, 235, 244, 251
   Josephine, 104, 137, 179, 211
Chamie, Tatiana, 222, 240
Chanel, 223
Charbonnier, Pierre, 285
Chirico, Giorgio di, 296
Chopin, Frédéric, 78, 220
Clark, Vera, 105, 127, 137, 138, 162, 165. *See also* Savina, Vera
Cochran, Charles B., 183
Cochran's Revue [1926], 255
Cocteau, Jean, 57, 149, 223, 227
Comœdia Illustré, 63, 64, 65
Concerto [Rimsky-Korsakov), 280
Concerto for Piano and Orchestra [Rieti], 279
Coxon, Dorothy, 193

348

INDEX

Cruikshank, George, 264
            Robert, 264
Cuadro Flamenco, 184

Dalbaicin, Maria, 185, 186, 187
Dalcroze, Jacques Emile, 70
Danilova, Alexandra, 220–222, 229, 261, 265, 268, 270, 278
Darinska, Mlle., 78
Dean, Basil, 217
Deburau, 21, 22
Debussy, Claude, 51, 52, 68
Decameron, 255
Defosse, Henry, 133, 135, 136
Delaunay, Robert, 109
        Sophie, 110
Delius, Frederick, 217
Derain, André, 132, 134, 135, 136, 255, 261
Devalois, Nina, *see* Valois, Ninette de
Diaghilev, Serge, x, 6, 27, 38, 39, 41, 45, 54, 72, 77, 84, 84*n*., 85, 86, 100, 101, 102, 103, 105, 113, 114, 117, 118, 125, 130–134, 138, 148, 165–167, 184, 187, 191–193, 195, 197–200, 202, 203, 208, 212–215, 222, 222*n*., 223, 226–229, 231–239, 241, 245, 247, 251, 254, 256, 258, 261–266, 271, 274, 281, 285, 289, 295, 296, 298, 299
Dibdin, Thomas, 267
Dobuzhinsky, Mitislav, 88, 97, 98
Dolin, Anton, 193, 222–226, 229, 248, 251, 252, 292
Domansky, Richard, 229
Dubrovska, Felia, 222, 229, 259, 260, 265, 282, 294
Duke of Connaught, 255
Duke of York, 207

Dukelsky, Vladimir, 251, 257
Dumas, Alexandre, 201

Efimov, Nicholas, 220, 222, 229
Egorova, Lubov, 193, 208, 214
Ernst, Max, 258
Euclid, 288
Evans, Edwin, 72
Evina, Wanda, 127, 137, 146, 147

Falla, Manuel de, 143, 144
Fantasia on Circus Themes, 249
Fauré, Gabriel, 284
Fedorov, Michael, 295
Fedorova, Sophie, 41, 61–63, 70, 84, 104, 110
Finck, Herman, 81
Fine Art Society, 70, 83
Flecker, J. E., 217
Fokina, Vera, 84, 85, 104, 112
Fokine, Michel, 20, 26, 30, 37, 42, 52, 57, 59, 60, 79, 84, 84*n*., 87, 88, 93, 95, 97, 104, 111, 157, 217, 218, 219
Forbes, Vivian, 143
Fouquet, Jean, 200
Fragonard, Jean Honoré, 290
Fraser, Mrs. Claud Lovat, 196
Fuad, King of Egypt, 280
Fuller, Loie, 71

Gabo, 272, 274
Garrick, David, 160
Gautier, Théophile, 14, 25, 115
Gavarni, Paul, 216
Gavrilov, Alexander, 104, 126, 129, 137
Gay, John, 197
George V, King, 207
Geverova, *see* Sheversheyeva
Gillot, Claude, 162

349

INDEX

Glazunov, Alexander, 60
Glinka, Michael, 60
Goethe, 285
Goldoni, Carlo, 108
Golovine, A., 30, 129
Goncharova, Natalia, 93, 94, 120, 228, 256, 265
Goossens, Eugene, 257, 280
Goya, Francisco, 185
Grigoriev, Serge, vii, 118, 131, 133, 137, 147, 152, 156, 197, 205, 238–243, 274, 275, 299
Gris, Juan, 225
Gross, Valentine, 82
Guardi, Francesco, 108

Hahn, Reynaldo, 57
Handel, George Frederick, 255, 290, 291
Hassan, 217, 218
Haydn, Franz Josef, 255
Hélène de Sparte, 70
Henri IV, King of France, 178, 198
Hofmannsthal, Hugo von, 98
Honigold, 264
Hoppé, E. O., 70
Hoyer, Brothers, 222

Idzikowsky, Stanislas, 104, 112, 114, 125, 137, 146-148, 162, 163, 165, 169–171, 184, 204, 220, 244, 261, 265, 270, 292
Imperial School of Ballet, St. Petersburg, 17, 63, 91, 128, 244
Imperial Society of Teachers of Dancing, The, 236
Impressions of the Russian Ballet, 123, 141, 204
Invitation à la Danse, L' [Weber], 25
Iribe, Paul, 67

Irving, Sir Henry, 40
Istomina, Mlle., 105, 127
Ivanov, Leo, 198, 237

Jakowlewa, Mlle., 78
Jakulov, G., 278
Jazvinsky, Jean, 104, 137, 222
Juvenile Drama, 13, 263
Jwanowa, Mlle., 78, 79

Karsavina, Thamar, 4, 6, 9, 10, 13, 14, 17–20, 23, 26, 28, 32, 35, 37, 40, 48–50, 56, 60, 70, 71, 84, 87, 90, 91, 94, 96, 100, 104, 107, 108, 112, 119, 128, 130, 134, 141, 142*n*., 144, 146, 148, 159, 162–165, 174, 191, 217, 255, 258, 259, 264, 265
Kessler, Count Harry, 98
Kiaksht, George, 4, 4*n*.
Klementowicz, Leokadia, 127, 128
Knight, Dame Laura, 116, 220
Kochno, Boris, 227, 248, 251, 259, 272, 275, 289, 290, 292, 296
Komishov, 153, 201
Kopeikine, Nicholas, 280
Kornetsky, 229
Korovine, C., 30, 129
Koslov, Alexis, 4
Kotchetovsky, Alexander, 41, 49, 78–80, 84
Krasnitska, Mlle., 78
Kremnev, Nicholas, 104, 125, 137, 292
Kshesinskaya, Matilda, 112
Kyasht, Lydia, 4, 4*n*., 128, 129, 210

Lambert, Constant, 258
Lambranzi, J. G., 236

INDEX

Lancret, Nicholas, 290
Lanfranchi, Rachel, 105
Lapitsky, 222, 229
Larionov, Michel, 121, 124, 187, 188–190, 296
Larionowa, Mlle., 78
Lascelles, Lord, 207
Laurencin, Marie, 245
Laurens, H., 223
Le Brun, Charles, 197, 201
Lecocq, 220
Legat, Nicholas, 244, 251
Le Nôtre, André, 32
Levinson, André, 107, 200
Lewis, Wyndham, 263
Liadov, Anatole, 123
Lifar, Serge, 222, 223, 227, 236, 250, 252–254, 258, 259, 270, 274, 275, 277, 288, 289, 294, 295, 296, 299
Lomonosov, 285
Longhi, Pietro, 108, 109
Lopokova, Lydia, 104, 108, 109, 111–117, 121, 126, 129–131, 134, 136–143, 146, 149, 181, 184, 194, 201, 204, 208, 209, 216, 217, 219, 220, 247, 255, 264, 281
Louis XIV, King of France, 198
Louis XV, King of France, 198
Louis XVI, King of France, 233
Lucas, Mrs., 194

Madrazzo, F. de, 57
Maikerska, Mlle., 222
Manoel, King of Portugal, 231
Manual of Classical Theatrical Dancing, The, 168, 182n.
Margaret [dresser], 156
Markova, Alicia, 244
Martin, Jean Baptiste, 200, 228

Mary, Princess, 207
Mary, Queen, 207
Massine, Leonide, 55, 74, 84, 99, 100, 104, 107, 110, 112, 113, 117–119, 121–126, 129, 136–140, 141, 143, 145, 146, 149, 157, 159–162, 166–168, 172, 183, 215–217, 219, 220, 222n., 236, 248–251, 255, 261, 272, 277–280, 284, 285, 287, 292
Matisse, Henri, 172
May's, 266, 270
Mayo, Eileen, 288, 289
Merry Wives of Windsor, The, 262
Messel, Oliver, 251
Metamorphoses [Steinberg], 97
Meyer, Baron de, 68
    Marcelle, 261
Miassine, Leonide, see Massine, Leonide
Michelangelo, 236
Mikolaichik, 204
Milhaud, Darius, 223, 261
Miller, Doreen, see Pavlovska, Mlle.
Miomandre, François de, 66
Miro, Joan, 258
Mocchi, Walter, 167
Molière, 248
Monteclair, 225
Monteux, Pierre, 75
Mordkin, Michael, 4, 5, 6, 7, 15
Morena, Dyta, see Istomina, Mlle.
Moreton, Ursula, 193, 216
Munings, Hilda, see Sokolova, Lydia
Murger, Henri, 93, 216
My Lady's Toilet, 109

Nabokov, Nicholas, 285
Napoleon, 56, 143

INDEX

Nelidova, Lydia, 41
Nemchinova, Vera, 127, 128, 140, 159, 204, 209, 222, 247, 248, 250, 255, 265
New and Curious School of Theatrical Dancing, The, 236
Nijinska, Bronislava, 38, 78, 79, 84, 157, 192, 195, 198, 199, 204, 207, 208, 222, 223, 225, 245-248, 256, 258
Nijinsky, The Art of, 82
Nijinsky, Vaslav, 6, 15-17, 24, 27, 28, 30-32, 35, 37, 40, 43-45, 47, 48, 51, 54, 55, 59, 60, 66-68, 70-72, 74, 75, 77-84, 84*n*., 100, 107, 112, 129, 142*n*., 174
Nijinsky, Vaslav, Vingt Dessins sur, 66
Nikitina, Alice, 212, 223, 229, 252, 265, 272, 274, 275, 277, 292
Novikov, Laurent, 7

Ode: Meditation on the Majesty of God on the Occasion of an Apparition of the Aurora Borealis, 285
Œuvre de Léon Bakst pour la Belle au Bois Dormant, L', 200
Olkhina, Mlle., 105. *See also* Wilson, Laura
Olympia, 105
Orlov, 49

Pagliacci, 41
Patrikieff, *see* Dolin, Anton
Pavane [Fauré], 284
Pavlova, Anna, 4, 5, 5*n*., 6, 7, 40, 78, 82, 173, 174
Pavlovska, Mlle., 105, 124
Penny plain, twopence coloured, *see* Juvenile Drama

Pergolesi, Giovanni Battista, 159
Peter the Great, 231
Petipa, Marius, 30, 51, 61, 114, 191, 192, 198, 203, 214, 235
Mlle., 105
Petrova, Vera, 265, 268, 282, 292
Pettit, Joyce, *see* Petipa, Mlle.
Pevsner, 272, 274
Pheidias, 15
Philpot, Glyn, 10, 83, 142, 143
Picasso, Pablo, 132, 142-144, 149, 150, 159, 184, 185, 280
Piltz, Marie, 20, 74, 75, 104
Pisanelle, La, 70
Planché, J. R., 267
Playfair, Sir Nigel, 197
Poe, Edgar Allan, 205
Poeltzich, Mlle., 78
Polignac, Princesse Edmond de, 221
Pollock, Benjamin, 3, 264
Polunin, Vladimir, 244, 284
Portsmouth Point, 262
Poulenc, Francis, 245, 257
Preobrajenskaya, Olga, 4
Prokofiev, Serge, 188, 278, 292
Pruna, Pedro, 248, 259
Ptitsenko, Mlle., 78
Pushkin, Nicholas, 93, 237

Queen of Norway, 207

Radina, Felia, 104, 126
Rastrelli, 231
Ravel, Maurice, 78, 85, 86, 87
Reeve, John, 270
Rieti, Vittorio, 253, 257, 277, 296
Rimsky-Korsakov, Nicholas, 60, 93, 120, 121, 218, 280

INDEX

Roberts, William, 263
Robinson, W. Heath, 148
Roehrich, Nicholas, 72, 73
Romanov, Boris, 71
Roseingrave, Thomas, 262
Rosovska, Zoia, 122
Rossini, G. A., 134, 140
Rouault, Georges, 292, 293
Rowlandson, Thomas, 262
Russian Ballet, Impressions of the, 123, 141, 204
Russian Ballet, Studies from the, 70

Salomé, 41
Sargent, John S., 32, 83
    Dr. Malcolm, 280
Satie, Erik, 149, 150, 261, 280
Sauguet, Henri, 272
Savina, Vera, 127, 166, 167, 216, 217, 220, 222, 222*n*., 229. *See also* Clark, Vera
Savoy Hotel, 90, 116, 131, 234
Scarlatti, Domenico, 107, 255, 262
Schmitt, Florent, 71
Schollar, Ludmilla, 4, 193, 204, 222
Schumann, Robert, 20, 88
Schwabe, Prof. Randolph, 142, 181, 203, 206, 207, 210
Segreto di Susanna, Il, 41
Sérénade, La [Stravinsky], 261
Serenade in G [Mozart], 217
Sergeyev, Nicholas, 192, 194, 214
Schervachidze, Prince A., 284
Sert, J. M., 98, 161, 284
Sevier, Michel, 141, 142
Shah of Persia, 148
Shakespeare, 3
Shaw, G. Bernard, 192
Sheversheyeva, Thamar, 220, 222, 229, 282

Sinding, Christian, 78
Sitwell, Sacheverell, 233, 237, 261–263, 266, 267, 270
Slavinsky, Thadeus, 187, 188, 190, 216, 217, 219, 222, 229, 250, 265
Snegouroutchka, 121
Sobeka, *see* Kochno, Boris
Socrate, 126, 284
Soirées de Paris, 280
Sokolova, Lydia, 38, 104, 110, 125, 137, 162, 191, 204, 216, 217, 222–225, 246, 250, 261, 265, 266, 269, 282
Song of Lel, The, 122
Spessiva, Olga, 193, 201, 203, 204, 208
Spessivtzeva, Olga, *see* Spessiva, Olga
Star, The [quoted], 225
Stedman School, 105
Steinberg, Maximilien, 97
Stendhal, 63
Stoll, Sir Oswald, 103, 128, 191, 199, 199*n*., 212*n*., 213*n*., 215, 229
Strauss, Johan, 266
Strauss, Richard, 41*n*., 98
Stravinsky, Igor, 17, 42, 97, 159, 172, 192, 193, 216, 256, 261, 277, 281–283, 296
Studies from the Russian Ballet, 70
Sudeikine, Serge, 71
Sutcliffe, George, 209, 210
Svetlov, Valerien, 93
Svoboda, Veceslav, 146

Taglioni, Filippo, 90
Taneyev, A., 60
Tarassowa, Mlle., 78
Tchaikovsky, P. I., 32, 81, 82, 191, 192, 212

INDEX

Tchelichev, Pavel, 285, 286
Tcherepnine, Nicholas, 32, 37, 88
Tcherkas, 222, 223, 229, 252
Tchernicheva, Lubov, 104, 105, 110, 112, 113, 119, 126, 129, 146, 159, 204, 222, 223, 226, 268
Teniers, David, 254
Theatres:
  London:
    Alhambra, 3, 128, 130, 193, 210, 212*n.*, 213*n.*
    Coliseum, 4, 6, 103, 104, 114, 115, 128, 216, 220–223, 226, 229, 244, 250, 251
    Covent Garden, 6, 7, 8, 41, 55, 159, 216, 219, 292
    Drury Lane, 68, 84, 85, 86
    Empire, 3, 4, 145, 146, 148, 220, 221
    Hippodrome, 4
    His Majesty's, 217, 255, 282, 288
    Lyceum, 265
    Palace, 4, 5, 5*n.*, 6, 7, 55, 77, 78, 80
    Pavilion, 255
    Princes, 183, 272
    St. Martin's, 219
  Milan:
    Scala, 223
  Monte Carlo:
    Opera, 86, 221
  Paris:
    Arts, 71
    Champs-Elysées, 87
    Châtelet, 84*n.*, 87, 265
    Opera, 221, 228
  Rome:
    Constanza, 166

Theatres—*ctd.*
  St. Petersburg:
    Maryinsky, 103, 192

Times, The, 7*n.*, 77, 85, 86, 257, 296
Tofts, 264
Tommasini, Vincente, 107
Trefilova, Vera, 174, 208, 255, 264
Troubridge, Una, 83
Trouhanova, Mlle., 71

Unger, 222
Utrillo, Maurice, 253

Valois, Ninette de, 216, 217, 219, 222, 223, 229, 282
Vanloo, 201
Vaudoyer, J. L., 25
Velasquez, 285
Verne, Jules, 290
Veronese, Paolo, 98, 99
Victoria, Princess, 207
Vic-Wells Ballet, 214
Vilzak, Anatol, 193, 222, 244
Vingt Dessins sur Vaslav Nijinsky, 66
Vladimirov, Pierre, 183, 190, 191, 194, 197, 204, 244
Volny, Maurice, 80, 81
Vronska, Alice, 128

Wadsworth, Edward, 263
Walton, William, 262
Wandering Dog, The, 91
Wassilevska, Alexandra, 104
Watteau, Antoine, 57, 226, 290
Webb [designer], 264
  H. J., 264
Weber, Carl von, 25

INDEX

Wells, H. G., 257, 290
White, Ethelbert, 141, 142
Whitworth, Geoffrey, 82
Willoughby, Vera, 142
Wilson, Laura, 105. *See also* Olkhina, Mlle.
Woizikowsky, Leon, 29, 104, 122, 124, 125, 137, 145, 162, 183, 216, 217, 219, 222, 223, 229, 245, 250, 254, 261, 265
Wolheim, Eric, 222

Wood, Christopher, 258
Woodhouse, Mrs. Gordon, 262

You'd Be Surprised, 219

Zaleska, Marie, 104
Zenon, F., 102, 103, 148
Zuloaga, I., 185
Zverev, Nicholas, 129, 137, 191, 204, 222, 229, 244, 247

CPSIA information can be obtained
at www.ICGtesting.com
Printed in the USA
LVHW112227261222
735891LV00007B/502